THE CARTEL OFFENCE

This book deals with the cartel offence introduced into UK law by the Enterprise Act 2002. It is now, for the first time, a criminal offence to operate certain cartel arrangements in the UK, and those found guilty of the offence face the prospect of fines and/or imprisonment. This presents new challenges for competition lawyers, who may not have expertise in criminal law, and for criminal lawyers who are unlikely to have expertise in the complex substantive issues raised by competition law. This book addresses these issues, providing a guide to the workings of the provisions, explanations of the definitions set out in the Act, and an analysis of the relationship of the new offence with the existing UK and EC competition law. Human rights issues and practical considerations in the application of the relevant procedural law are also dealt with. Relevant OFT guidance and statutory provisions are published in the Appendix.

The Cartel Offence

MARK FURSE
Senior Lecturer in Commercial Law,
The University of Glasgow

SUSAN NASH
Professor of Law,
The University of Westminster

•HART•
PUBLISHING

OXFORD – PORTLAND, OREGON
2004

Hart Publishing
Oxford and Portland, Oregon

Published in North America (US and Canada) by
Hart Publishing c/o
International Specialized Book Services
5804 NE Hassalo Street
Portland, Oregon
97213-3644
USA

Distributed in the Netherlands, Belgium and Luxembourg by
Intersentia, Churchillaan 108
B2900 Schoten
Antwerpen
Belgium

Hart Publishing is a specialist legal publisher based in Oxford, England. To order further copies of this book or to request a list of other publications please write to:

Hart Publishing, Salter's Boatyard, Folly Bridge,
Abingdon Road, Oxford OX1 4LB
Telephone: +44 (0)1865 245533 or Fax: +44 (0)1865 794882
e-mail: mail@hartpub.co.uk
WEBSITE: http//www.hartpub.co.uk

British Library Cataloguing in Publication Data
Data Available
ISBN 1–84113–373–6 (paperback)

Typeset by Hope Services (Abingdon) Ltd
Printed and bound in Great Britain on acid-free paper by
MPG Books Ltd, Bodmin, Cornwall

Contents

Preface

At first sight it may seem presumptuous to base a book on just 15 sections of a relatively new Act before the relevant law has even been applied in 'the real world'. However, the cartel offence, established in ss 188–201 of the Enterprise Act 2002 marks a fundamental development in the application of competition law in the UK. For the first time in over 200 years those found guilty of engaging in certain specified commercial agreements—the entry into which would in a world without regulation be rational profit maximising behaviour—face the prospect of individual prosecution, fines, and in some cases imprisonment. These provisions, not part of the mainstream of competition law, and directed to individual persons rather than to the 'undertakings' which are the subject of the prohibitions of EC competition law and the domestic Competition Act 1998, call for competition lawyers to understand certain aspects of criminal law, and for criminal lawyers to understand certain aspects of competition law. It is in the intention of contributing to this understanding that we have written this book, which has been designed primarily for practitioners, but which we anticipate will be of interest also to academics and students studying or working with this area.

Our aim has been to explain as clearly as possible, in the light of the current legal development of the offence, its terms, its relationship to the pre-existing civil law of competition, those aspects of criminal procedure of most connection to the offence, and certain matters of jurisdiction and procedure. In doing this we have relied upon the text of the Act, the Explanatory Notes to the Act, OFT guidelines, debates in Hansard, the comments of those who have already written on this subject, and our own understanding of the relevant areas of law. While we have not dealt at length with the debate leading up to the introduction of the law, and its likely effect on the domestic economy, we have in Chapter One considered generally the background to the offence, and in particular to the increasing trend amongst OECD member states to take strong action against cartels. The approach of certain OFT staff during the period leading up to the introduction of the offence was to characterise cartel conduct as 'theft'. We are not convinced that this label may be accurately applied to transactions which are entered into voluntarily (a better analogy might be to fraud), and the fact remains that some agreed conduct between would-be competitors may be justified on the grounds that it is efficiency enhancing (this is the general lodestone for the evaluation of conduct which encompasses some competitive restrictions in the civil law of competition).

We begin with a general discussion of the offence, and the place it occupies in the competition law landscape in the UK. Of particular concern here is the interaction of the offence and the procedures for its invocation with the civil procedures of the EC regime and the Competition Act 1998. In Chapter Two we deal in more detail with the terms of the offence, considering the circumstances in which breaches might occur, and the meaning of 'dishonesty'—the chosen legal standard. In the world of commerce the use of this rubric may lead to some difficulties. For example, at the time of writing, a number of public schools are under investigation by the OFT in relation to a potential breach of the Chapter I Prohibition of the Competition Act 1998. In essence the OFT is concerned that the schools may have participated illegally in fee-setting discussions and agreements. At the same time the schools' representatives are vigorously denying that they engaged in any dishonest or illegal conduct (however, this has not stopped some seeking to rely on the leniency programme offered by the OFT). In Chapter Three we deal in detail with the investigative mechanisms that will be applied to the offence, and are again concerned to deal as clearly as possible with the connections between the civil and criminal procedures. In this context we are concerned that the OFT, which sits at the heart of the civil system of competition enforcement in the UK, is also the body with the central role in the pursuit of breaches of the criminal cartel offence. In Chapter Four we deal with the leniency procedures designed to facilitate the prosecution of the offence, and in Chapter Five we deal with prosecutions themselves. We also consider here civil liabilities that might flow from breaches to those harmed by the breach. In Chapter Six we examine the territorial reach of the offence, both in terms of the subject matter and the procedures to be applied, including extradition. It remains a matter of uncertainty at the present time as to whether extradition to and from the US will be possible under the dual criminality requirements which are explained in this Chapter. Finally we consider in brief the steps that should be taken by those engaged in commerce to seek to comply with the provisions of the Act. In this context a useful compliance checklist has been provided by Simmons and Simmons solicitors.

Mark would like to thank in particular Professor Fraser Davidson, Head of Department at the time of writing, and Professor Noreen Burrows for their support. Maria Fletcher and Dr Iain MacNeil have both been generous with their time in discussing various aspects of the cartel offence and sharing their insights. Susan would like to thank Professor Andrew L-T Choo at Brunel University. Collectively we owe thanks to a number of people, including, but not limited to, Dr John Paterson of the University of Westminster, Richard Hart and all of those at Hart Publishing who have encouraged us in the writing of this book, and have contributed to its efficient publication.

The law in this book is up to date as at 20 June 2004.

Mark Furse
University of Glasgow

Susan Nash
University of Westminster

June 2004

1

Introduction to the Cartel Offence

INTRODUCTION

THE FACT THAT the Enterprise Act 2002 (EA 02) introduced into UK law a new criminal offence—the cartel offence—has not gone unnoticed.[1] The Department of Trade and Industry heavily trailed this headline-grabbing provision, while the Opposition, along with the CBI, were vocal in expressing their concerns. Part 6 of the Act (ss 188–202) presents new challenges to the business community (where approaches to competition law compliance may have to be rethought), to professional competition advisers (who are likely to have little experience of working with criminal law), and to criminal lawyers (who may find themselves entangled in factual matters with which they are largely unfamiliar). If the legislation functions as was hoped by the Government the introduction of the cartel offence may see a shift in the approach to competition law compliance by corporations and individuals. Instead of conducting an amoral cost-benefit analysis relating to infringements of the civil competition law provisions which continue to be enshrined in European Community (EC) law and in the Competition Act 1998 (CA 98), the new approach may lead to the acceptance of a moral code of conduct, from which deviation may be both punished, and for moral reasons, avoided by potential infringers.[2]

The offence is a stand-alone provision, not part of the wider body of competition law, either domestic or EC, although it cannot be seen in complete isolation. In this chapter we set out the broad terms of the offence (the details of the terms are considered more fully in the following chapter), explore the relationship between the offence and the more general body of competition law, and consider too the background to the offence, and in particular the 'Penrose Report'.[3] In this context some mention will also be made of the experience in the United States, where the availability of the criminal sanction in relation to breaches *inter alia* of

[1] See, for example, M Cutting, 'Reforming Competition Law' (2001) *New Law Journal* 996, and A Finfer, 'That Early-Morning Knock may not be the Postman' (2002) *The Times*, 1 October, Supplement, p 9. For a more substantial comment see C Harding and J Joshua, 'Breaking up the Hard Core: The Prospects for the Proposed Cartel Offence' [2002] *Criminal Law Review* 933 and I MacNeil, 'Criminal Investigations in Competition Law', (2003) *European Competition Law Review* 151.

[2] Issues relating to compliance with the law are dealt with in Chapter 7.

[3] OFT, *The Proposed Criminalisation of Cartels in the UK—A report prepared for the Office of Fair Trading by Sir Anthony Hammond KCB QC and Roy Penrose OBE QPM* (November 2001) [2002] UKCLR 97 (hereinafter the Penrose Report).

sections 1 and 2 of the Sherman Act of 1890[4] is widely perceived to be influential in encouraging compliance with those legal standards.

The offence is created by way of s 188 of the Act, which provides, in s 188 (1) that:

> 'An individual is guilty of an offence if he dishonestly agrees with one or more other persons to make or implement, or to cause to be made or implemented, arrangements of the following kind relating to at least two undertakings (A and B).'

Section 188 (2) sets out six categories of arrangement the implementation of which will be deemed to fall within the terms of the offence. Thus it is provided that:

> 'The arrangements must be ones which, if operating as the parties to the agreement intend, would—
>
> (a) directly or indirectly fix a price for the supply by A in the United Kingdom (otherwise than to B) of a product or service,
> (b) limit or prevent supply by A in the United Kingdom of a product or service,
> (c) limit or prevent production by A in the United Kingdom of a product,
> (d) divide between A and B the supply in the United Kingdom of a product or service to a customer or customers,
> (e) divide between A and B customers for the supply in the United Kingdom of a product or service, or
> (f) be bid-rigging arrangements.'

Even before the offence entered into effect on 20 June 2003 the Serious Fraud Office (SFO) was using existing powers to investigate a cartel. On November 9, 2003 the *Sunday Times* reported that 'on the morning of April 10 last year, the senior executives of several British drug companies were awakened by the sound of police banging on their front doors'.[5] It was reported that 'Operation Holbein', an investigation into allegations of fraud and price-fixing in the supply of generic drugs to the NHS[6] was the SFO's 'largest and possibly most expensive inquiry ever'. The link was inevitably made to the new offence, with the report's authors claiming that if the head of the SFO, Robert Wardle, was successful, he could 'pave the way for his office to become inquisitor general of Britain's commercial cartels'.[7] It was anticipated in the Penrose Report that there might be some six to ten prosecutions a year brought under the new offence, and that these would 'probably be complex and the majority will be high profile'.[8]

[4] Section 1 therefore provides in part that: 'Every person who shall make any contract or engage in any combination or conspiracy hereby declared to be illegal shall be deemed guilty of a felony'. Similar language, in relation to 'monopolisation' is found in s 2.

[5] 'Strong Medicine', *Sunday Times*, 9 November, 2003, Business Section, p 5.

[6] The OFT had already made two decisions relating to the pharmaceuticals industry, *Napp Pharmaceutical Holdings Ltd and Subsidiaries* CA98/2/2001 [2001] UKCLR 597, *Exclusionary Behaviour by Genzyme Ltd* CA98/03/03 [2003] UKCLR 950. Both these cases dealt with conduct falling under the Chapter II Prohibition, not with illegal agreements under the Chapter I Prohibition.

[7] See also *R (on the application of Kent Pharmaceuticals Limited) v Director of the Serious Fraud Office* [2003] EWHC 3002 (Admin), [2003] All ER (D) 298, where the court dealt with the extent to which seizure of various documents in the course of the investigation was lawful.

[8] Penrose Report, paras 3.6, 3.7.

GENERAL UK COMPETITION LAW AND ITS LINK WITH THE OFFENCE

The cornerstone of the UK competition law regime is the CA 98, which was introduced largely to align domestic competition law with that of the EC (discussed below). The two core provisions of the Competition Act 1998 are the Chapter I and Chapter II Prohibitions,[9] found in ss 2 and 18 respectively. The Chapter I Prohibition is the domestic equivalent of article 81 EC, and thus governs conduct which is in some way co-ordinated between two or more undertakings. Section 2 is, in part, in the following terms:

> (1) Subject to section 3, agreements between undertakings, decisions by associations of undertakings or concerted practices which—
> (a) may affect trade within the United Kingdom, and
> (b) have as their object or effect the prevention, restriction or distortion of competition within the United Kingdom,
>
> are prohibited unless they are exempt in accordance with the provisions of this Part.
>
> (2) Subsection (1) applies, in particular, to agreements, decisions or practices which—
> (a) or indirectly fix purchase or selling prices or any other trading conditions;
> (b) limit or control production, markets, technical development or investment;
> (c) share markets or sources of supply;
> (d) apply dissimilar conditions to equivalent transactions with other trading parties, thereby placing them at a competitive disadvantage;
> (e) make the conclusion of contracts subject to acceptance by the other parties of supplementary obligations which, by their nature or according to commercial usage, have no connection with the subject of such contracts

The Chapter I Prohibition replaced a range of earlier domestic legislation, which was heavily administrative in character, and which was perceived by many, although not all, to be toothless and ineffective. The Chapter II Prohibition relates to abuses of a dominant position by undertakings, and would not normally extend to conduct falling under the terms of the cartel offence, which requires that there be an agreement or arrangement between two or more parties (the full terms of the offence are dealt with in Chapter 2 below).

It will be noted that reference is made in s 2 to the term 'undertaking'. In both domestic and EC competition law 'undertakings' are the sole subjects of the substantive provisions on co-ordinated behaviour, and abuses of dominant position. There is no statutory definition of 'undertaking', which has been defined in case law as encompassing 'every entity engaged in commercial activity, regardless of the legal status of the entity, and the way in which it is financed'.[10] An individual may in certain circumstances be an undertaking, but only if acting in a commercial

[9] The Chapter II Prohibition is not dealt with further in this book. It relates to conduct which is in abuse of a dominant position, ie unilateral conduct, and is thus not linked in any direct way with the cartel offence.

[10] Case C–41/90 *Hofner and Elser v Macrotron GmbH* [1993] 4 CMLR 306, at para 21.

capacity—for example as an unincorporated business.[11] While it is possible under the terms of the CA 98 to ask questions of individuals and natural persons during the course of an investigation under the Act, and for such persons to commit procedural offences (such as the destruction of documents, or the obstruction of an investigation) the penalties for substantive infringements go exclusively to undertakings. Another key aspect of the regime is that it is civil in nature. In these two respects the cartel offence is fundamentally different: it is expressly directed *not* at undertakings, which cannot be incarcerated, but to individuals, and it relies upon the full panoply of criminal law and procedure.

In addition to giving the key role in its enforcement to the OFT (see below) the Competition Act 1998 also makes remedies available to injured third parties, who may bring actions before the appropriate civil courts. In practice there have been few such cases, the most likely scenario to give rise to a civil action being one where the Chapter I Prohibition is relied upon as a defence to a contractual action to establish that there is, in fact, no legally binding obligation on the defendant. Third parties have the right to make complaints under the Act, and those with sufficient standing may appeal decisions taken by the OFT or other regulator to the CAT. The Enterprise Act specifically provides that private prosecutions of the cartel offence may not be brought, save with the permission of the OFT, which is unlikely to be forthcoming. Section 190(2) thus provides that proceedings in England, Wales, and Northern Ireland may be brought only by the Director of the SFO (see below), or by or with the consent of the OFT. In Scotland proceedings may be brought by the Procurator Fiscal.

Although the decision was taken to separate the cartel offence from the more general competition law regime—the reasons for which are discussed below—there remain links between the systems. In particular the OFT, charged with the enforcement of the Competition Act 1998, is also the body with primary responsibility for the policing of the cartel offence, although in the latter aspect of its work it will rely heavily on an arrangement entered into with the SFO. More significantly, perhaps, is the fact that every breach of the cartel offence would also be an infringement of the Chapter I Prohibition of the CA 98, albeit that the former would be an offence committed by a named individual, and the latter an infringement by an undertaking.

There are also key points at which the nature of the CA 98 regime, and that of the cartel offence are fundamentally different. One which has received little comment to date is that in the former system in the vast majority of cases the interests of the personnel of the undertaking subject to investigation, and of the undertaking itself, have been the same. However, this dynamic may be somewhat altered by the amendment of the Company Directors Disqualification Act 1986 with the insertion of new ss 9A–9E allowing for the disqualification of company directors whose companies have been involved in conduct breaching the Act, where certain

[11] For the approach taken to public bodies in the UK see the OFT *Policy Note 1: The Competition Act 1998 and Public Bodies.*

conditions are met.[12] The cartel offence may further exacerbate tension between the interests of the company, and those of the person charged, leading to the need to employ separate counsel and to adopt different defensive strategies.

The OFT and the SFO[13]

The OFT is the body with primary responsibility for the enforcement of the CA 98. Following amendments to the domestic competition law architecture by the EA 02 the OFT is a non-ministerial government department, whose staff are civil servants. The OFT consists of a Chairman and 'no fewer than four other members appointed by the Secretary of State'.[14] The Competition Act gives the OFT substantial powers of civil enforcement, including powers of investigation and the ability to impose financial penalties, of up to 10 per cent of turnover for the preceding financial year, on undertakings for breaches of the Act's two prohibitions. Appeals from decisions of the OFT may be made to the Competition Appeals Tribunal (CAT), and from there to the Court of Appeal, although the latter body has indicated that it regards the Tribunal as a specialist body, the substance of whose decisions it is unlikely to review.[15] In addition to the OFT other sector regulators have concurrent powers under the legislation, exercising most, but not all, of the same powers as the OFT. In particular the regulators have the power to make decisions and impose penalties.

[12] The OFT has published its guidance *Competition Disqualification Orders* [2003] UKCLR 745. At para 4.16 of the guidance it is provided that:

> 'The greater the degree of the Director's responsibility for or involvement in a breach, the greater the likelihood that the OFT or Regulator will consider that person to be unfit to be concerned in the management of a company and hence, of a CDO application being made against that person. The OFT or Regulator:
> —is likely to apply for a CDO against a director who has been directly involved in the breach
> —is quite likely to apply for a CDO against a director whom it considers improperly failed to take corrective action against the breach
> —does not rule out applying for a CDO against a director whom it considers, taking into account that director's role and responsibilities, to have failed to keep himself or herself sufficiently informed of the company's activities which constituted the breach of competition law—whether an application is made in these circumstances will depend upon the OFT or Regulator's priorities.'

[13] As a consequence of the recommendations in the report of the Fraud Trials Committee (the Roskill Committee), in December 9, 1985, the SFO was set up to investigate serious or complex fraud.

[14] EA 02, sch 1, para 1.

[15] In *Napp Pharmaceutical Holdings Ltd v The Director General of Fair Trading* [2002] EWCA Civ 796, [2002] UKCLR 726, the Court of Appeal held that: 'These findings do not and could not involve points of law ... They cannot therefore be reviewed in this court. But even if we did have authority to review such findings, as the conclusion of an expert and specialist tribunal, specifically constituted by Parliament to make judgments in an area in which judges have no expertise, they fall exactly into the category identified by Hale LJ in *Cooke v Secretary of State for Social Security* [2001] EWCA Civ 734, [2002] 3 All ER 279, as an area in which this court would be very slow indeed to enter.' (per Buxton LJ at para 34.

The Director of the SFO has the power to conduct an investigation and prosecution into serious or complex fraud and can also take over other cases involving serious or complex fraud.[16] Section 2 of the CJA 87 provides the SFO with the necessary powers to obtain search warrants, and to compel persons to answer questions, provide information and produce documents for the purposes of the criminal investigation. Search warrants can be obtained from either the High Court or a justice of the peace. The SFO can issue a written notice under s 2 to anyone who in the ordinary course of business has information or documents that might be relevant to their investigation. In appropriate circumstances, the SFO can demand immediate compliance with the notice. Failure to answer questions or provide information without a reasonable excuse is a criminal offence. The CJA 87 contains similar safeguards as those found in the EA 02 in respect of the disclosure of documents covered by legal professional privilege and confidential banking communications. In Scotland, the Criminal Law (Consolidation) (Scotland) 1995 provides that the Lord Advocate can nominate a person to exercise the same powers as the SFO in respect of an investigation into serious or complex fraud. The Lord Advocate's nominee is the Head of the International and Financial Crime Unit.

GENERAL EC COMPETITION LAW AND ITS LINK WITH THE OFFENCE

Competition law is one of the more vibrant areas of EC law, and the principles underlying the application of the two primary provisions, articles 81 and 82 EC are well developed, albeit that some change to procedures in general, and to the application of article 81 in particular, has been effected from 1 May 2004. Article 81, which is the key provision to consider when discussing the cartel offence, is in the following terms:

1. The following shall be prohibited as incompatible with the common market: all agreements between undertakings, decisions by associations of undertakings and concerted practices which may affect trade between member states and which have as their object or effect the prevention restriction or distortion of competition within the common market, and in particular those which:
   (a) directly or indirectly fix purchase or selling prices or any other trading conditions;
   (b) limit or control production, markets, technical development, or investment;
   (c) share markets or sources of supply;
   (d) apply dissimilar conditions to equivalent transactions with other trading parties, thereby placing them at a competitive disadvantage;

[16] The factors to be taken into account when deciding to investigate include the value of the alleged fraud, which should exceed £1 million; whether the case is likely to give rise to national publicity and public concern; whether the case requires specialist knowledge; whether legal, accountancy and investigative skills will be used; whether there is a significant international dimension and whether there is a need to use the SFO's special investigative powers.

(e) make the conclusion of contracts subject to acceptance by the other parties of supplementary obligations which, by their nature or according to commercial usage, have no connection with the subject of such contracts.

2. Any agreements or decisions prohibited pursuant to this Article shall be automatically void.
3. The provisions of paragraph 1 may, however, be declared inapplicable in the case of:
   — any agreement or category of agreements between undertakings;
   — any decision or category of decisions by associations of undertakings;
   — any concerted practice or category of concerted practices;

which contributes to improving the production or distribution of goods or to promoting technical or economic progress, while allowing consumers a fair share of the resulting benefit, and which does not:

(a) impose on the undertakings concerned restrictions which are not indispensable to the attainment of these objectives;
(b) afford such undertakings the possibility of eliminating competition in respect of a substantial part of the products in question.

By virtue of Council Regulation 1/2003[17] article 81 is deemed to have direct applicability and direct effect in its entirety, such that the entire article, including the exemption in the third paragraph, may be relied on before national courts and national authorities in the appropriate circumstances. Prior to the reforms brought forward by Regulation 1/2003, the third paragraph of article 81 did *not* have direct effect, leading to the unsatisfactory position where the EC Commission had exclusive competence to grant exemptions, such that courts or national authorities faced with a dispute falling within the article were constrained from dealing with all the relevant issues and law.

It is clear that article 81 is intended to extend to the prohibition of cartels where the necessary jurisdictional factors are in place, and there have been a significant number of decisions taken by the EC Commission condemning the operation of cartels, and in some cases imposing substantial penalties. More recent decisions for example, have dealt with cartels operating in relation to graphite electrodes,[18] citric acid,[19] brewers in Luxembourg,[20] industrial and medical gases,[21] and vitamins[22] (the latter being part of a chain of actions whose ripples have been felt around the world arising from the prising open by the US authorities of the lysine

[17] Council Regulation (EC) No 1/2003 of 16 December 2002 on the implementation of the rules on competition laid down in articles 81 and 82 of the Treaty (2003) OJ L1/1, which replaced Council Regulation 17/62, First Regulation implementing articles 85 and 86 of the Treaty (OJ Sp Ed [1959–62] p 87).

[18] Commission Decision 2002/271/EC *Graphite Electrodes* (2002) OJ L 100/1.

[19] Commission Decision 2002/742/EC *The Citric Acid Cartel* (2002) OJ L 239/18.

[20] Commission Decision 2002/759/EC *Luxembourg Brewers* (2002) OJ L 253/21.

[21] Commission Decision 2003/355/EC (amending and consolidating Commission Decision 2003/207/EC) *Industrial and Medical Gases* (2003) OJ L 123/49.

[22] Commission Decision 2003/2/EC *Vitamins* (2003) OJ L 6/1. Penalties in this case were large indeed, with Hoffmann-La Roche alone paying a total of €426m.

cartel lead by Archer Daniels Midland[23]). In December 2003 the EC Commission took action against a cartel which had been operating for 29 years, the longest-lasting cartel uncovered by the Commission.[24] In all, in 2003, the Commission took action against five hard-core cartels. In the three years ending in 2003 the Commission adopted 25 cartel decisions, and imposed fines totalling €3.2 billion.[25]

A good example of the extent to which cartel conduct—even in a climate of civil illegality and heavy administrative penalties—may be organised, can be found in the case of the insulated pipe cartel, condemned by the EC Commission in 1998,[26] and dealt with on appeal by the Court of First Instance (CFI) in 2001.[27] According to the facts set out in the decision, which was upheld on appeal by the CFI, at the end of 1990 four Danish producers reached an agreement relating to district heating pipes. One of their first moves was to co-ordinate a price increase applied on both the Danish and export markets. Quotas were agreed on for the sharing of the Danish market, and a 'contact group' was created consisting of the sales managers of the undertakings concerned. From then on, in respect of each tender assigned to any particular member of the group, the other members were informed of the proposed bid offer, and then would submit bids that were higher in order to protect the designated supplier. Two German producers joined in the meetings of the Danish producers from the autumn of 1991, and an agreement was reached on the sharing of the German market in August 1993. In 1994 the producers agreed to fix quotas for the entire European market, and developed a wider-ranging cartel with a two-tier structure. At the top of the hierarchy was the 'directors' club', which consisted of the chairmen or managing directors of the relevant undertakings, and which allocated quotas to each undertaking in the market, and in each of the national markets. By this time the relevant markets extended in addition to those of Austria, Finland, Italy, the Netherlands and Sweden. Within certain national markets 'contact groups' consisting of local sales managers were set up and were given the task of administering the agreements by assigning individual projects and co-ordinating bids for these. The Commission began its investigation, following a complaint, in June 1995, carrying out simultaneous unannounced investigations at ten undertakings or associations of undertakings. Even following the launch of the investigation the German contract group continued to meet, although it switched the place of its meetings to Zurich, outside the jurisdiction of the EC. These meetings continued until March 1996. There was only major competitor in the industry which did not join the cartel—Powerpipe AB, and steps were taken to eliminate this undertaking as a competitive threat to the cartel. Some

[23] For a gripping history of the uncovering of this cartel, and the development of the consequent investigation, see K Eichenwald, *The Informant* (New York, Broadway Books, 2000)

[24] Commission press release IP/03/1700, 10 December 2003, 'Commission fines members of organic peroxides cartel'.

[25] See Commission press release IP/03/1706, 16 December 2003, 'Commission fines three companies in industrial copper tubes cartel'.

[26] Commission Decision 1999/60, *Pre-Insulated Pipe Cartel* (1999) OJ L 24/1.

[27] *Re Pre-Insulated Pipe Cartel: LR AF 1998 A/S v EC Commission* case T–23/99 [2002] 5 CMLR 10.

cartel members recruited key Powerpipe employees. Subsequently a collective boycott of Powerpipe's customers and suppliers was organised by the cartel. In its decision the Commission imposed heavy fines on those members of the cartel who did not benefit to some degree from the operation of the leniency regime which was then in place.

The nature of the relationship between EC and domestic competition law has changed somewhat over the years, although the underlying, and immutable principle has remained that in the event of any conflict between Community and national law, the former takes precedence.[28] Some uncertainties however remained in the details relating to the application of national law where there was no direct conflict between the two regimes, and these were largely addressed by Regulation 1/2003. The main thrust of this Regulation has been to decentralise the Community competition law regime by creating a network of national competition authorities (NCAs) each constituent of which will be fully authorised, and indeed required, to apply the substantive rules of the Treaty relating to competition in their entirety, and, crucially, to the exclusion of national laws in the event of conflict arising between the two. The nature of this new relationship is clearly spelt out in recital 8 of the Regulation, which makes specific reference to the maintenance of national criminal sanctions, and which is set out here in full:

> In order to ensure the effective enforcement of the Community competition rules and the proper functioning of the co-operation mechanisms contained in this Regulation, it is necessary to oblige the competition authorities and courts of the Member States to also apply Articles 81 and 82 of the Treaty where they apply national competition law to agreements and practices which may affect trade between Member States. In order to create a level playing field for agreements, decisions by associations of undertakings and concerted practices within the internal market, it is also necessary to determine pursuant to Article 83(2)(e) of the Treaty the relationship between national laws and Community competition law. To that effect it is necessary to provide that the application of national competition laws to agreements, decisions or concerted practices within the meaning of Article 81(1) of the Treaty may not lead to the prohibition of such agreements, decisions or concerted practices if they are not also prohibited under Community competition law. The notions of agreements, decisions and concerted practices are autonomous concepts of Community competition law covering the co-ordination of behaviour of undertakings on the market as interpreted by the Community Courts. Member States should not under this Regulation be precluded from adopting and applying on their territory stricter national competition laws which prohibit or impose sanctions on unilateral conduct engaged in by undertakings. These stricter national laws may include provisions which prohibit or impose sanctions on abusive behaviour toward economically dependent undertakings. *Furthermore this Regulation does not apply to national laws which impose criminal sanctions on natural persons except to the extent that such sanctions are the means whereby competition rules applying to undertakings are enforced.* [emphasis added]

This recital is given legal effect in article 3 of the new Regulation. It must immediately be noted that the cartel offence is aimed at *individuals*, not at undertakings,

[28] See, for example, *Costa v ENEL* case 6/64 [1964] CMLR 425.

and hence falls within the final sentence of the recital. A more general caveat can be made in relation to national competition law generally, which is that to the extent that it is concerned with conduct which has no impact on trade between member states it remains a matter of strictly national competence. However, it would clearly be unsatisfactory to have in place regimes that were substantially different depending on whether there was, or was not, an effect on trade between member states. It is clear that the cartel offence may apply to situations where there is an effect on trade between member states. Indeed, one prospect that concerned critics of the legislation was that the UK authorities could act against a cartel active in more than one state, imposing heavier sanctions on those in the UK than on those outside the UK. The territorial aspects of the offence are discussed in more detail in Chapter 6, below, but it can be noted at this stage that the Government intended when the legislation was brought forward to target individuals in respect of global or EC cartels in which the undertakings participating were targeted under existing cartel powers.[29]

A further consequence of the approach set out in Regulation 1/2003 is that where an undertaking benefits from the benefit of the legal exception provided for in the third paragraph of article 81, member states are precluded from prohibiting the agreement. This is expressly provided for in article 3(2). The changes brought about by the modernisation programme have not, as was feared by some commentators prior to the programme becoming clear, undermined the relationship between the cartel offence and EC law. During the debates on the passage of the Bill reference was made to an ongoing dialogue with the EC Commission in this respect, which, it was suggested, showed that 'the Commission therefore has no concerns on this front'.[30]

In passing it is worthy of note that the Draft Treaty establishing a Constitution for Europe[31] provides at article 12 that 'The Union shall have exclusive competence to establish the competition rules necessary for the functioning of the internal market'. The Constitution is unlikely to be fully ratified for a number of years, and it is unlikely that this provision would jeopardise the operation of the cartel offence.

In the White Paper, *Productivity and Enterprise*[32] published before the final text of Regulation 1/2003 was made public, the relationship between the proposed offence and the EC regime was discussed, albeit not in great detail. It was clear that at that time the Government did not consider that there would be any significant tension between the obligations flowing from the operation of the EC regime and the prosecution of the cartel offence. The interplay between the two systems was discussed in the following terms:

[29] See, eg, the Under Secretary of State, Standing Committee B, col 174.
[30] Under Secretary of State, Standing Committee B, col 171.
[31] Submitted to the European Council Meeting in Thessaloniki, 20 June, 2003.
[32] DTI, Cm 5233, July 2001.

7.43 The European Commission's modernisation proposals would decentralise powers to enforce Article 81. In most cases where cartels are suspected in the UK, the OFT will investigate. Under modernisation, the imposition of penalties would be a matter for Member States' law rather than Community law. The OFT would therefore be able to act against those agreements it believes breach article 81. This should help to simplify court proceedings.

7.44 Some—mainly global cartels—will be investigated by the European Commission. In such cases, the Government intends that the new criminal offence will allow the UK authorities to take action separately against individuals involved in the cartel. *The agreement will be caught by the new offence where it was implemented or intended to be implemented in the UK.*

7.45 EC procedures are conducted under the civil standards of evidence. So where the OFT wished to bring a case against individuals involved in the cartel, it would need to ensure that evidence was gathered to criminal standards. Where evidence had been used in a prior case by the Commission, the OFT investigators might have to secure fresh evidence for a criminal trial to proceed. The Government proposes, however, that *a prior finding EC proceedings should be admissible in a subsequent criminal trial.*[33]

THE BACKGROUND TO THE OFFENCE[34]

The economic arguments against cartels

The fact that a number of OECD members have taken or are in the process of taking such strong steps against cartels reflects in part, but may not necessarily be caused by, a consensus as to the economic damage caused by cartel activity. In industries where the appropriate circumstances exist firms have an incentive to engage in cartel activity. By doing so they raise prices, restrict output, and are able to act collectively as if they were a single monopolist. Thus profits increase, surplus income moves from the consumer to the producer, and there is a 'deadweight welfare loss' to society as a result. Whether the producer is more deserving of the income transferred from the consumer to the producer is a socio-political judgment that lies outside the ambit of positive industrial economics.

The features that are necessary for a price-setting cartel to exist are as follows. (1) The cartel must be able to raise a price. Whether it can do this will depend in part on the response of consumers to price increases in that product. (2) The cartel must be able to agree on a price. (3) The cartel should be profitable in the face of legal intervention. This is to say that the anticipated profits should be greater than penalties discounted by the risk of detection. For this to hold the assumption is that the members of the cartel are amoral, rational economic actors. (4) It must

[33] Emphases in original.

[34] See generally, Swedish Competition Authority, *Fighting Cartels—Why and How? (The 3rd Nordic Competition Policy Conference in Stockholm, September 2000)* (Stockholm, 2001).

be profitable to operate the cartel in light of the costs of doing so.[35] A number of market characteristics will affect the likelihood of co-ordination arising: (1) the number of firms in the market; (2) market concentration; (3) the extent to which products are varied or homogenous; and (4) the existence or otherwise of some co-ordinating mechanism among the participants.[36] The position is summarised by Bishop and Walker:

> In many industries, firms have an incentive to form cartels. The success of a cartel depends largely on the elasticity of demand facing the cartel members. The less elastic the demand curve, the greater the increase in price that can be achieved. For this to be the case, the ability of fringe firms outside the cartel to expand output or the scope for new entry must be limited.
>
> However, firms also have a natural incentive to deviate from such cartel agreements once they are formed. Cartels can only be sustained over time if cartel members are able to detect and adequately punish firms which deviate from the cartel agreement. For this reason, cartels often introduce a number of measures designed to prevent cheating. These include agreeing to fix more than just price levels, *eg* dividing the market, fixing market shares or establishing trigger prices.[37]

While the so-called 'hard core' cartels are generally presumed to be axiomatically harmful, and are subject to per se restrictions in the US, and are generally condemned under article 81(1) EC, and the Chapter I Prohibition, there are some circumstances in which some justification for cartel activity may be made.[38] This is most obviously the case in 'crisis cartels'.[39] Where a downturn in sales across an industry is so severe and long lasting that fixed assets have to be dismantled an argument may be made that short to medium term agreements on prices and output may stabilise the industry, and minimise the damage. In both the EC and the US such arrangements have been permitted.[40] Although the offence was framed so as to minimise the scope for economic debate, it will presumably be possible to argue that a crisis cartel is *not* dishonest (the meaning of dishonesty generally, and more specifically in the context of the cartel offence, is dealt with in the following chapter).

[35] These factors are discussed in more detail in S Bishop and M Walker, *Economics of EC Competition Law: Concepts, Application and Measurement* (London, Sweet & Maxwell, 1999), at 4.10–4.11.

[36] This may be either a 'legitimate' organisation, such as a trade association, subverted to an illegitimate purpose, or a mechanism put in place for the express purpose of overseeing cartel operations. In the latter case there must first have been some form of contact between the undertakings involved which leads to the formation of the cartel and the need for a controlling mechanism.

[37] See N 35 above at 4.23.

[38] See N 34 above.

[39] See M Neumann, *Competition Policy: History, Theory and Practice* (Cheltenham, Edward Elgar, 2001), p 103.

[40] Particularly in the context of the restructuring of the coal and steel industry under the ECSC Treaty.

Investigating, detecting, and deterring cartel conduct

It has long been recognised that attacking co-ordinated anti-competitive conduct raises particular problems for competition law enforcers. The prohibitions of the Competition Act took effect on 1 March 2000, since which time there have been few decisions taken in which infringement decisions have been made in respect of cartel conduct. Although infringements of the Competition Act are deemed to be civil, rather than criminal, the standard of proof that has been set by the Competition Appeals Tribunal (CAT) is somewhat high. In the case of *Napp*,[41] a case dealing with the abuse of a dominant position, the Competition Commission Appeals Tribunal (CCAT, as it then was) considered in some detail the standard of proof to which an infringement must be established by the Director General of Fair Trading (DGFT) under the Act. The CCAT started from the point that infringements of the Act 'are not classified as criminal offences in domestic law' (para 105), while recognising that article 6 of the European Convention on Human Rights and Fundamental Freedoms applies to the proceedings.[42] Further the CCAT found that:

> 'the standard of proof which me must apply in deciding whether infringements of the Chapter I or Chapter II prohibitions are proved is the civil standard, commonly known as the preponderance or balance of probabilities, notwithstanding that the civil penalties imposed may be intended by the Director to have a deterrent effect' (para 105).

While there are only two standards of proof in English law,[43] the criminal and the civil, within the civil standard, 'the more serious the allegation, the more cogent should be the evidence before the court concludes that the allegation is established on the preponderance of probability' (*Napp*, para 107). At the key passage in *Napp* the CCAT held that:

> Since cases under the Act involving penalties are serious matters, it follows . . . that strong and convincing evidence will be required before infringements of the Chapter I and Chapter II prohibitions can be found to be proved, even to the civil standard. Indeed, whether we are, in technical terms, applying a civil standard on the basis of strong and convincing evidence, or a criminal standard of beyond reasonable doubt, we think in practice the result is likely to be the same. We find it difficult to imagine, for example, this Tribunal upholding a penalty if there were a reasonable doubt in our minds, or if we were anything less than sure that the Decision was soundly based. . . . formally speaking, the standard of proof in proceedings under the Act involving penalties is the civil standard of proof, but that standard is to be applied bearing in mind that infringements of the Act are serious matters attracting severe financial penalties. It is for the Director to satisfy us in each case, on the basis of strong and compelling evidence, taking into

[41] *Napp Pharmaceutical Holdings Ltd and Subsidiaries v The Director General of Fair Trading* [2002] CAT 1, [2002] CompAR 13.

[42] One implication of this was that the CCAT held 'that the burden of proof rests throughout on the Director to prove the infringements alleged' (at para 100).

[43] See *In re H and Others (Minors) (Sexual Abuse: Standard of Proof)* [1996] AC 563, per Lord Nicholls at 586–87. The same is true of Scotland.

> account the seriousness of what is alleged, that the infringement is duly proved, the undertaking being entitled to the presumption of innocence, and to any reasonable doubt there may be. (paras 108–9)

In *Claymore Dairies Ltd and Express Dairies plc v The Office of Fair Trading*[44] the CAT felt compelled to make some observations in the course of a wider dispute about the approach to the burden of proof specific to Chapter I cases (and in particular to a procedural stage falling short of the making of a final decision). This followed the raising of concerns to the effect that the *Napp* standard should not be read so as to deter the OFT making infringement decisions in respect of the Chapter I Prohibition. In a number of speeches, and policy documents, it had already been made clear that the OFT was finding it difficult to successfully take enforcement action against cartels, and questions had been raised as to the extent to which it might rely on oral evidence rather than more concrete documentary evidence. The CAT commented on the *Napp* standard in the following terms:

> In our view, there is no rule of law that, in order to establish a Chapter I infringement, the OFT has to rely on written or documentary evidence. The oral evidence of a credible witness, if believed, may in itself be sufficient to prove an infringement, depending on the circumstances of a particular case. Of course, if the OFT is relying primarily on a witness rather than on documents, it will no doubt look for support in the surrounding circumstances, for example, the dates and timing of price increases. It will no doubt ask itself whether there is reason to believe that the witness may be untruthful or mistaken but, as at present advised, we do not think there is any technical rule which precludes the OFT from accepting an oral statement of a witness at face value if it thinks it right to do so.
>
> Similarly, there is no rule of law that evidence must emanate from a participant to the cartel. Although evidence at one remove, as it were, may be less compelling than direct evidence of what was said or done by a person present at a particular meeting, indirect evidence and circumstantial evidence generally, may well have a powerful role to play in the factual matrix of a case.
>
> In addition . . . the OFT may well be entitled to draw inferences or presumptions from a given set of circumstances, for example, that the undertakings were present at a meeting with a manifestly anti-competitive purpose, as part of its decision-making process. (paras 8–10)

While this discussion lies within the framework of the civil regime, it demonstrates the difficulties facing the OFT and concurrent regulators in the enforcement of the Chapter I Prohibition, and may be seen as supporting the extension of investigatory powers available in relation to the cartel offence.

The DTI raised the prospect of criminalising cartels, along with the Treasury, in *The UK's Competition Regime.* Here the authors of the report noted that:

> 'Although the Competition Act 1998 strengthens the deterrent effect against anti-competitive behaviour, the project team is concerned that it may not go far enough. In particular, the penalties for engaging in cartels may not be enough to deter such action.

[44] [2003] CAT 18 [2004] CompAR 177.

> The Project team concludes that American, and other experience suggests that there is a strong case for introducing criminal penalties, including custodial sentences, for those who engage in cartels alongside a new civil sanction of director's disqualification'.[45]

These proposals were developed further in the White Paper *A World Class Competition Regime.*[46] It was in response to these moves that the Director General of Fair Trading established a review conducted by Sir Anthony Hammond and Roy Penrose to examine the relevant issues and to make recommendations. The review focussed on six main issues: (a) the definition of the criminal offence; (b) prosecutions; (c) investigations; (d) leniency and immunity from prosecution; (e) the interplay between civil and criminal proceedings; and (f) penalties and the mode of trial. While the conclusions reached in the review are not in every instance mirrored in the final legislation they merit further consideration here.

The Penrose Report

The Penrose report was commissioned by the OFT and published in November 2001.[47] The authors were asked to 'review on behalf of [the OFT] what options would provide an effective system to implement a decision to introduce criminal penalties for individuals perpetrating cartels', taking into account in particular the need for a system to be compatible with the ECHR, to be efficient, and to deliver results.

In relation to the first of the matters set out above, the definition of the criminal offence, the report recommended that this should *not* be directly linked to either article 81 EC, or to the Chapter I Prohibition, and that it should be more limited. The key recommendation in this respect was that the offence should cover 'hard-core' cartels: price fixing agreements, market-sharing agreements, bid-rigging agreements and agreements to restrict output or set quotas. Such a restrictive approach would, the report suggested, exclude 'cartels which might attract exemption under either domestic or EC law' (para 2.4). As noted above it would be incompatible with Community legal obligations to condemn a cartel whose operation was authorised by a legal exception under article 81(3). The second key recommendation was that the offence should include a requirement of dishonesty. The conclusions in this respect, which were heavily debated in the progress of the Bill through Parliament, are set out here in full:

> The advantage of this approach is (a) it signals that the offence is serious and should attract a substantial penalty and (b) it would go a long way to preclude a defence argument that the activity being prosecuted is not reprehensible or that it might have

[45] At para 1.1. The provisions of the Enterprise Act relating to Director's Disqualification are found at s 204 of the Act.

[46] DTI, Cm 5233, July 2001.

[47] 'Proposed Criminalisation of Cartels in the UK: A Report Prepared for the Office of Fair Trading by Sir Anthony Hammond KCB QC and Roy Penrose OBE QPM', OFT 365 [2002] UKCLR 97.

> economic benefits or is an activity which might have attracted exemption domestically or under EC law. The possible disadvantage is that some might argue that an offence which depends on an approach of 'dishonesty' may be difficult for juries to understand. However, given the context in which hard core cartels take place, we believe that, in most cases, the facts will demonstrate that the parties realised what they were doing was dishonest and was contrary to the law. (para 2.5).

The report's authors were clearly concerned about removing any potential linkage between the offence and the exemption/exception procedure provided for in article 81(3) EC and in respect of the Chapter I Prohibition. While it was not considered to be 'possible entirely to preclude the risk of such a defence succeeding however the offence is formulated' the authors shared 'the views of the DTI and others that the alternative route of requiring the proof of dishonesty is less likely to run that risk' than was an approach which would have linked the offence with the definition of anti-competitive conduct in the existing legislation (para 2.6). The meaning of 'dishonesty' in this context is discussed further in Chapter 2. The final issue considered in relation to the definition of the offence was whether it should be capably of applying to companies as well as to individuals. As we have already seen, a saving grace from the EC point of view is that the offence is applicable to individuals only, and not to undertakings. This point is also relevant in relation to the application of the *non bis in idem* rule, discussed in Chapter 5, below. The report concluded that:

> There seems to be general agreement that it should apply only to individuals and we are also of that view. There is a superficially attractive argument to the effect that there would be an advantage in being able to bring criminal proceedings against both at the same time, so that separate civil proceedings under the Competition Act 1998 against the company would not be necessary. On the other hand, it would be consistent with EC law and practice for undertakings to be dealt with under civil procedures and contacts with EC officials suggest that they favour that approach. (para 2.11)

Another question that taxed the report's writers was that of which body was to be responsible for carrying out prosecutions. In the White Paper the Government had suggested that there were good reasons for the OFT to be the lead prosecutor, but recognised too that this would entail the OFT developing new expertise. The Report concluded that the OFT would *not* be the most appropriate body to prosecute the new offence in light of the underlying principles of criminal procedure set out in the Phillips Report[48] of fairness, openness, accountability and efficiency. Concerns focussed around the small number of cases anticipated each year, and the fact that these would be likely to be both complex and high profile. The lawyers needed to handle such cases would:

> need to be highly experienced prosecutors, well versed in handling disclosure issues and, where informants and covert surveillance techniques have been used, in dealing with highly sensitive evidence, where public immunity issues are likely to arise.[49]

[48] Royal Commission on Criminal Procedure, January 1981, para 6.8.
[49] Penrose Report, para 3.7.

Recruitment of such staff onto a small team would, it was suggested, be difficult. Further concerns were raised relating to the inevitable tendency of prosecutors operating in such small teams 'to become isolated from general developments in criminal law and practice'.[50] Again, it was suggested that in such small teams, where a close relationship existed between the organisation and the team, that the prosecutors could develop a solicitor/client relationship, serving the policy goals of the organisation, rather than that of a 'relationship of a prosecuting lawyer exercising an independent judgment'.[51] There was no perceived benefit to be gained in contracting the work out to independent private firms, and the conclusion that flowed from a consideration of the relevant public authorities was that the SFO was the obvious option. The benefits of assigning this task to the SFO were spelt out at paras 3.14–3.16:

> To some extent, the arguments in favour of this option are the obverse of the arguments against creating an in-house prosecuting capability in the OFT. The SFO has a substantial team (about 36) of prosecutors with experience of conducting major criminal trials, who are well versed in handling sensitive disclosure and abuse of process issues. . . . This option would serve the criteria of fairness, openness and accountability . . .
>
> There are other arguments in favour of the SFO. Its responsibilities for prosecuting serious fraud cases are close to and would sit comfortably with the new cartels offences and it regards them as already coming within its existing criteria . . . It is used to managing multi-disciplinary teams of lawyers, accountants and police officers and this expertise could be invaluable in handling cartel cases where lawyers, accountants, investigators and economists would be likely to be involved. In discussions, the SFO indicated that it would envisage that the OFT investigators working on a case would, if it was decided to pursue a criminal investigation, be integrated into a team working under the direction of an SFO case controller. If necessary, the OFT lawyers with competition law expertise could be seconded for periods to the SFO . . . the OFT investigators would liaise with the SFO, ensuring that arrangements operated smoothly and in a way which did not prejudice the success of any criminal prosecution.
>
> A further advantage in the SFO being the prosecuting authority is that it has powers to compel answers to be given to questions which it puts in the course of its investigations. Under section 2 of the Criminal Justice Act 1987 these answers are available as evidence except for the purpose of criminal proceedings against the person questioned (emphasis in original).

A further question was that of which body was to *investigate* the alleged offence. The OFT had, by the time of the Penrose report, built up a body of expertise in relation to investigations under cartels carried out under the Competition Act, but not all of the staff of the Cartels Investigation Branch had experience of conducting criminal investigations.[52] Again the conclusions drawn were influenced by an expectation of a relatively light workload. The report recommended that:

[50] Para 3.8.
[51] *Ibid.*
[52] See paras 4.9–4.10 of the Penrose Report.

> the current investigative resource within the Cartel Investigations Branch should, following appropriate additional training, undertake criminal investigations into 'hard core' cartel activity as well as continuing to pursue those complains where the civil process under CA98 is deemed to be more appropriate.[53]

Not all the powers available to the police would necessarily need be made available to the OFT. For example the report did not suggest that the OFT personnel would need to have the power of arrest, or to stop and search persons or vehicles. In the unlikely scenario that the need for such activity arose it was argued that the assistance of the police should be called upon. However, it was recognised throughout the report that the OFT would need to comply with the relevant codes of practice when questioning persons reasonably suspected of having committed an offence, when entering and searching premises, seizing property, and interviewing suspects. These issues are discussed in more detail in Chapter 3, below, and the approach of the Penrose report to leniency issues is discussed in Chapter 4, below.

A particularly vexatious issue is that of the link between the Chapter I Prohibition and article 81 EC and the cartel offence. It is a matter of some concern that the same body may be involved in the investigation of all three matters, but that different legal safeguards and procedures may apply to these different investigations. Although we have seen already that the CAT requires a very high standard of proof, approaching the criminal standard, in the establishment of an infringement of the Chapter I Prohibition the fact remains that that standard is sought via procedures that are not subject to the protections afforded to a person subject to a criminal prosecution. Part 6 of the Penrose reported focussed on the thorny issue of the relationship between the proposed criminal offence and the existing civil infringements, and paid special attention to the separation of proceedings, and the order in which actions might be taken. The suggestion that civil proceedings should precede criminal prosecutions was largely dismissed on the grounds that not

> a great deal of benefit would be derived since any finding of an infringement by the undertaking under civil law would probably have to be re-proved to criminal law standards in order to be sufficient to convict individuals.[54]

The key considerations advanced in this respect in the Penrose report are to be found in paras 6.9–6.10, which are reproduced here in full:

> 6.9 (J) *We recommend that, wherever possible, criminal proceedings against individuals should precede any related civil proceedings against undertakings.* This should preclude arguments by the defence in criminal proceedings that their case had been prejudiced. A lesser disadvantage of civil proceedings being conducted in advance of criminal proceedings is that this would allow individuals to 'rehearse' their defence arguments prior to facing cross-examination in the criminal court.

[53] Para 4.12.
[54] Para 6.8.

6.10. Difficulties may arise in respect of decisions issued by the EC against undertakings found to have infringed article 81 as a result of their participation in cartel agreements. It is our understanding that the EC, with its wider public interest responsibility to the citizens of all EC member states, would be unlikely to stay its own civil proceedings pending the completion in the UK of any related criminal proceedings against individuals. We would suggest that this issue will need to be treated on a case by case basis, acting on guidance from the SFO as to whether publicity arising from the EC's civil case might prejudice later criminal proceedings under circumstances in which the EC Decision precedes the conclusion of criminal proceedings in the UK.

In the latter respect there are clearly constraints on the ability of a formal solution to be sought. The supremacy of EC law requires that it be given full effect in the member states, and as part of the network of national competition authorities the OFT is required to adhere to this principle. At the same time there may well be public policy considerations which favour bringing a prosecution under the cartel offence as a priority over the making of an infringement decision in respect of a breach of article 81 EC. No formal arrangements have been made in this respect. However, in 2002 Margaret Bloom, discussed this problem in the following terms:

> We have worked closely with the European Commission to ensure that the interface between Community and national law is carefully worked out. . . . The OFT will discuss with the Commission the handling of individual EC cartel cases where the UK may wish to mount a criminal prosecution. These will be considered on a case by case basis.[55]

The experience in the United States

That the experience of the US with criminal enforcement of s 1 of the Sherman Act has influenced UK policy is beyond doubt. The comments in the Treasury/DTI report into UK productivity and competition relating to the US model have already been quoted above.

It is interesting therefore that at the same time as noting the efficacy of the US approach (and see below for a list of other OECD states operating a criminal regime in this respect) in the White Paper the US experience in cartel detection was cited as demonstrating the longevity of (detected) cartel conduct:

> '. . . if fines are to deter firms and their executives effectively, they need to be set at a level which is greater than the expected gains from participating in a cartel.
>
> US evidence shows that cartels often raise prices by around 10 per cent. Increasing prices will have some dampening effect on demand, so a cartelist might increase its profits by a smaller proportion. Conservatively they might do so by around 5 per cent. *If the cartel operates for six years (as the average US cartel is thought to do)*, then the total benefit might be 30 per cent of annual turnover.

[55] Bloom, M 'Key Challenges in Public Enforcement: A Speech to the British Institute of International and Comparative Law', 17 May 2002, OFT website (www.oft.gov.uk).

> The Competition Act 1998 allows fines to be imposed at this level . . . But not all cartels will be caught. *In the US, estimates suggest that only a sixth of cartels are detected*'.[56]

During the passage of the Bill through Parliament an unnamed representative of the US Attorney General was quoted with approval as saying: 'I have had numerous lawyers pleading with me to avoid a gaol term for their client and offering to pay any sum imaginable. I have never had anyone offering to spend another week in gaol in return for a lower fine'.[57] It is worthwhile then, exploring the US approach and experience.

Section 1 of the Sherman Act is in more general terms than is the UK cartel offence. It provides, in part, that:

> Every contract, combination in the form of trust or otherwise, in restraint of trade or commerce among the several States, or with foreign nations, is declared to be illegal. Every person who shall make any contract or engage in any combination or conspiracy hereby declared to be illegal shall be deemed guilty of a felony, and, on conviction thereof, shall be punished by a fine not exceeding $10,000,000 if a corporation, or, if any other person, $350,000 or by imprisonment not exceeding three years, or by both said punishments, in the discretion of the court.[58]

Thus criminal liability extends to both corporations, as well as to individuals. Although the provision is wide reaching the reality is that the Department of Justice, Antitrust Division (hereinafter, DOJ) prosecutes hard core behaviour: price fixing, market division and bid rigging, but does not prosecute vertical agreements. Until the early 1990s criminal prosecutions were relatively rare, although there had been some high profile examples with long lasting effects. Thus, for example, the indictment filed on June 22, 1960, against a number of defendants, including the blue-chip Westinghouse Electric Corporation, and four other corporations, as well as 12 named individuals, sent ripples through US industry that had a long term effect.[59] In 1993 the policy of the DOJ switched to one of aggressive prosecution of cartel conduct, and a carrot—an effective leniency policy—was introduced, alongside a big stick—the credible threat of very high corporate fines, and individual imprisonment, for those convicted. This policy has clearly borne fruit, and in some respects has since been mirrored by the EC, as well as by the UK. Notwithstanding the perceived efficacy of these penalties, on October 29, 2003 the Antitrust Criminal Penalty Enhancement and Reform Act was introduced as a Bill by the Senate Committee's Antitrust, Competition Policy, and Consumer Rights Subcommittee. If enacted this Bill will further strengthen the penalties for criminal violations of the Sherman Act. The draft legislation increases the maximum gaol term from three years to ten years, raises the fine for individuals to $1m, and for corporations to in excess of $100m.

[56] Box 7.3 (emphasis added).
[57] *Hansard*, 2 July 2002, col 157.
[58] 15 USC 1.
[59] See generally Walton, *Corporations on Trial: The Electric Cases* (Belmont, Wadsworth Publishing Company, 1964).

As of January 2003 there were nearly 40 sitting grand jury investigations into cartels operating at the international, as opposed to purely domestic, level, and international investigations accounted for close to half of the DOJ's criminal investigations. The DOJ had uncovered evidence of meetings of international cartels in over 100 cities in more than 35 countries, including most of the Far East, and nearly every country in Western Europe.[60] A particular feature of the recent enforcement activity has been a marked increase in prosecutions against individuals, and a corresponding increase in the imposition of sentences of imprisonment. In 2002 the average gaol sentence imposed on an antitrust defendant was in excess of 18 months, and in all over 10,000 days' sentences were handed down. Between 1997 and 2002 more than 30 defendants received gaol terms in excess of one year. In the fiscal year 2003 a total of 23 individuals were given gaol sentences, amounting to some 6,791 days. While the majority of these sentences were against American nationals, a number were imposed in respect of foreigners. Defendants from a number of countries, including those in the EC—Germany, Sweden and France, have served prison sentences in the US. In the sorbates cartel seven top Japanese executives were indicted, and as at autumn 2003 were fugitives. The increased reliance on criminal law sanctions by other states also makes extradition easier to achieve, given the requirement of dual criminality (discussed in detail in Chapter 6). Thus the DOJ is prepared to use the INTERPOL 'red list' in respect of indicted fugitives, and will pursue extradition where these suspects are detained. It has been noted therefore that:

> With the stiffening resolve that foreign governments are taking toward punishing cartel activity and their increased willingness to assist the United States in prosecuting cartel activity, the safe harbours for antitrust offenders are rapidly shrinking.[61]

The policy of imposing criminal fines on corporations, while not being reflected in the UK cartel offence, has also been lucrative for the public coffers in the US. Since the beginning of the fiscal year 1997 the DOJ had, by January 2003, recovered over $2 billion in criminal fines. Of particular note is the $500 million paid by Hoffmann-La Roche for its participation in the vitamins cartel. BASF AG paid a further $225 million in respect of the same cartel. It will be noted that the former defendant also paid some €426 million to the EC Commission (see above). In addition to the fines two Swiss executives of Hoffmann were gaoled, as were executives from BASF.

Perhaps a key breakthrough in demonstrating the efficacy of a criminal investigation came in the lysine cartel case, which saw the prosecution, with the aid of a—somewhat unreliable—whistle-blower within the Archer Daniels Midland Company (ADM). With the assistance of the FBI a covert surveillance operation was mounted which implicated senior executives of ADM and a number of other

[60] S D Hammond, 'A Summary Overview of the Antitrust Division's Criminal Enforcement Program', Presented in New York on January 23, 2003.

[61] *Ibid.*

high-profile companies. The uncovering of the lysine cartel led on to the exposure of cartels in citric acid, sodium gluconate, sodium erythobate, and maltol.

A clear contrast between the US and UK approaches could be seen in the attacks mounted on the Sotheby's/Christies cartel which set commission rates for sellers throughout the late 1990s. The prosecution of this cartel by the DOJ led to a gaol term being handed down for the owner of Sothebys, Mr Taubman. The cartel was operated, and terminated, before the Chapter I Prohibition came into effect. However, comparisons with the US regime have not been to everyone's taste. During the passage of the Act one acerbic MP commented that:

> I am sure that part of the justification for the Government's wish to bring criminal sanctions, including imprisonment for up to five years, into the cartels regime, is a comparison with the American system, where such sanctions have been in place for some time—hence Mr Taubman's fate. I suspect that there will be an attempt to draw a parallel between our debate and that case, in which Mr Taubman, sadly, is about to go to some rather upmarket 'Club Fed'. According to The Times he has the choice of a variety of places. One in Louisiana 'has weight rooms, computer terminals, bingo nights and sunbathing area.' All in all it does not sound like a particularly arduous regime for Mr Taubman and other white-collar criminals.
>
> . . .
>
> The Government wish to bring that regime into our system so that a 78-year-old diabetic with a number of other medical conditions would go to prison for a year. I am not quite sure what purpose that would serve. I suppose that the argument is that it would be a deterrent to others. Again, we say that is another affection for the American system.[62]

As indicated above the US approach to leniency is seen as having been central to the success of the enforcement activity. In essence the approach is that it is better for one guilty party to go free as long as the cartel is destroyed/punished than it is for an entire cartel to remain undetected. This policy is given expression in the DOJ Corporate Leniency Policy, announced on August 10, 1993, and the Leniency Policy for Individuals, announced exactly one year later. These policies are certain in their operation, and allow an individual or corporation contemplating the schemes to make an informed assessment of the likelihood of their application. In the case of an individual three conditions are set for leniency to be granted. These are: (1) that at the time the individual comes forward to report the illegal activity, the DOJ has not received information about the illegal activity from any other source; (2) the individual 'reports the wrongdoing with candor and completeness' and provides full and continuing cooperation throughout; (3) the individual was not involved in coercing any other party to participate in the cartel, and was neither the ringleader nor the coordinator of the cartel.[63] The approach taken by the OFT is considered more fully in Chapter 4, below.

[62] Mr Waterson, Standing Committee B, 23 April 2002, coll 146–47.

[63] For a general discussion of the DOJ's policy see G R Spratling, 'Making Companies an Offer they Shouldn't Refuse', (February 1999, DOJ website).

The prosecution of cartels—OECD recommendations

The UK approach to taking a more severe approach in relation to cartel conduct is consistent with recommendations of the Organisation for Economic Cooperation and Development, which, whilst not being heavily engaged in the promotion of competition law initiatives, does take an interest in the area. At the Council session in March 1998 the OECD adopted a 'Recommendation of the Council Concerning Effective Action Against Hard Core Cartels'.[64] This was based on the principles enshrined in article 5b of the Convention, and in recognition of the fact that 'hard core cartels are the most egregious violations of competition law and . . . injure consumers in many countries by raising prices and restricting supply'.[65] The ensuing recommendation was, in part, in the following terms:

> A. CONVERGENCE AND EFFECTIVENESS OF LAWS PROHIBITING HARD CORE CARTELS
>
> 1. Member countries should ensure that their competition laws effectively halt and deter hard core cartels. In particular, their laws should provide for:
>   (a) effective sanctions, of a kind and at a level adequate to deter firms and individuals from participating in such cartels; and
>   (b) enforcement procedures and institutions with powers adequate to detect and remedy hard core cartels, including powers to obtain documents and information and to impose penalties for non-compliance.
> 2. For purposes of this Recommendation:
>   (a) a 'hard core cartel' is an anti-competitive agreement, anti-competitive concerted practice,[66] or anti-competitive arrangement by competitors to fix prices, make rigged bids (collusive tenders), establish output restrictions or quotas, or share or divide markets by allocating customers, suppliers, territories, or lines of commerce;
>   (b) the hard core cartel category does not include agreements, concerted practices or arrangements that i) are reasonably related to the lawful realisation of cost-reducing or output-enhancing efficiencies; ii) are excluded directly or indirectly from the coverage of a member country's own laws, or iii) are authorised in accordance with those laws. However, all exclusions and authorisations of what would otherwise be hard core cartels should be transparent and should be reviewed periodically to assess whether they are both necessary and no broader than necessary to achieve their overriding policy objectives. After the issuance of this Recommendation, members should provide the Organisation annual notice of any new or extended exclusion or category of authorisation.

[64] 25 March 1998, [C/M(98)7/PROV].

[65] Recommendation, preamble.

[66] It is unlikely that the OECD intended 'concerted practice' to carry the same meaning as it does in the EC, where the phrase has been interpreted to relate to a situation where 'without having been taken to the stage where an agreement properly so-called has been concluded knowingly substitutes for the risks of competition co-operation in practice between them . . .' (cases 40–48/73 etc *Cooperative Vereniging 'Suiker Unie' UA v Commission* [1976] 1 CMLR 295, para 26).

The above definition of a hard-core cartel was relied on by the Government in its White Paper (discussed below). At the time of the OECD Recommendation a number of member countries had in place criminal sanctions in relation to hard-core cartel conduct: Austria (although subsequently this law has been amended, with the criminal sanction being removed); Canada (fine up to C$10m, jail term of up to five years for individual officers, or both); France (fines only); Germany (for collusive tendering, up to five years imprisonment, or a fine); Ireland (fine for an undertaking on criminal conviction, or for an individual, plus imprisonment for up to two years); Japan (criminal fine up to Yen 100m in the case of an entrepreneur, imprisonment up to three years or a fine up to Yen 5m in the case of a person); Korea (imprisonment up to three years, or fine up to KRW 200m); Norway (fines and imprisonment up to six years); Switzerland (fines up to CHF 100,000); and, of course, the United States (fine up to the larger of (a) US$10m (corporations) and US$350,000 (others) or (b) twice the amount gained from the violation or lost by the victim, and imprisonment up to three years).[67] It will be noticed therefore that the UK has joined three of the four largest EC economies in imposing criminal sanctions, although it is in a minority in encompassing imprisonment among these.

The White Paper, responses, and debates in Parliament

In the White Paper, *Productivity and Enterprise: A World Class Competition Regime*, published in July 2001,[68] the Government was clear in its intention of bringing forward a new criminal offence. In the introduction to the paper the proposed measures were introduced in the following manner:

> A Strong Deterrent Effect
> Hard-core cartels are highly damaging to consumers and to the economy in general. The Government believes that the current level of fines against those who engage in cartels does not provide an adequate deterrent.
> There is a strong case for introducing criminal sanctions against individuals who engage in hard-core cartels:
> - The new criminal offence would need to catch price-fixing, market-sharing and bid-rigging cartels.
> - It should target individuals who set up and maintain cartels, and also senior executives or directors who either condone or encourage the arrangement.
> - There would be real advantages for the main prosecuting authority to be the OFT.
> - The Government intends that the OFT should be able to bring a criminal case against an individual whenever a cartel is implemented or intended to be implemented in the UK—this would include cases where the case against the firm is pursued by the European Commission.[69]

[67] OECD Recommendation Annex A.
[68] DTI, Cm 5233, July 2001.
[69] White Paper, executive summary.

In emphasising the need to target the offence against individuals, rather than against the companies making the profit from the cartel, the Government relied in part upon perceived failings in the then present system of civil sanctions. Noting that one option was to increase fines significantly, with a possibility of them rising to six to ten times the present level the Government suggested that this level of penalty would not be proportionate to the offence. In part this was because research undertaken in the United States suggested that were firms required to pay the optimal fine on conviction of a cartel offence more than half would have gone into liquidation. In particular it was argued that in practice a cartel may have extended to only one aspect of the company's business, would have involved only a few executives with possibly other senior management being completely unaware of the cartel's existence, and that to punish the company as a whole would be to unfairly 'damage innocent employees, shareholders and creditors who have done nothing to harm consumers or break the law'.[70] The emphasis of the policy was then set out at paras 7.16–7.18:

> 7.16 Therefore, the Government believes that for cartels, the level of fines against firms should remain at the same level as at present—but that there should be specific sanctions against individuals engaging in the cartel. The threat of a criminal conviction and the possibility of a prison sentence means that individuals are more likely to think very carefully before engaging in cartels. Or, if they are directed to do so by their managers, they may be far more willing to inform the authorities.
>
> 7.17 Some countries impose criminal fines against individuals involved in serious competition breaches. The Government believes that this would improve the deterrent effect of our regime, but is unlikely to provide adequate protection against cartels. In practice firms could find ways to cover the costs for individuals fined. The New Zealand Government is currently seeking to outlaw exactly this behaviour.
>
> 7.18 The Government's recent peer review of competition policy asked competition experts for their views on the increased deterrence of criminal penalties. In the UK, 83 per cent of those questioned believed that the introduction of criminal penalties against individuals who engage in cartels would improve our regime.

While the thrust of the policy set out here is clear, there are some apparent contradictions underlying it, and the issue of decision making, particularly in relation to illegal decisions, and compliance frameworks, is glossed over here. The issue of compliance with competition law, as well as the design of compliance programmes, is considered in the final chapter of this book, but note should be made here of the fact that the interrelationship between decisions made by and on behalf of individuals, and those made by and on behalf of complex organisations, such as large corporations, is highly complex. For example, if decisions relating to cartel participation are made only be a few executives, and in the interests of only a part of the company, why would the company subsequently take the decision to subsequently indemnify those individuals on detection and the imposition of a fine? Presumably any such move would be subject to review by the company's owners and shareholders, who would need to be persuaded of the benefits to the company as a whole in adopting such a

[70] Para 7.15.

policy. Elsewhere in the White Paper it is explicitly recognised that employers 'are the main beneficiaries of the cartel',[71] and the position was contrasted with that in relation to insider dealing, where the employer would only rarely be the beneficiary.

Two main options were set out in relation to the definition of the offence itself. The first would have pinned the offence to the existing competition law of either article 81 EC, or the Chapter I Prohibition. The Penrose report had already identified what would likely be the core problem with this approach, and this was reiterated in the White Paper, where the dangers of requiring 'a lay jury with no competition expertise to consider potentially complex economic arguments'[72] was recognised. The preferred option, and the one adopted in the Bill, was to separate the offence from wider competition law enforcement. Instead, 'the offence would be defined as the dishonest participation in an agreement which has, as a purpose, one or more of the specified hard-core cartel activities'.[73] The terms of the offence are considered more fully in the following chapter.

Reaction to the proposal for the cartel offence was, predictably, mixed. The Consumers' Association (CA) welcomed the move, and agreed that the current civil penalties under the Competition Act 1998 were inadequate. In its briefing paper *Criminalisation of Cartels: What is all the fuss about?* the CA made clear its view that the proposals were a necessary addition to the OFT's arsenal, and that they would change significantly the risk analysis for companies carrying out a cost-benefit analysis into breaching competition law. It further pointed out that 'cartel activities are already prohibited. It is difficult to conceive of another area in which significant harm is done to the public without there being criminal penalties'.

While the CBI generally welcomed the plans for the Enterprise Bill, it was fiercely critical of the inclusion of the proposed cartel offence. Thus its Deputy Director General, argued that 'plans to criminalise cartels were premature and had not yet been fully thought through. The current system encourages companies to cooperate with the authorities but criminalisation could undermine this'.[74] Referring to the fact that the UK would be in a minority of EC member states to operate a criminal law regime in respect of anti-competitive conduct he further argued that the plans would 'put UK companies at a competitive disadvantage to rivals in Europe'.[75] The terms of the offence itself were criticised as being 'vague and uncertain'.[76] In a *Parliamentary Brief* published on 10 April 2002 the CBI attacked the proposals for the cartel offence, arguing that there would be a number of adverse unintended consequences. First, it argued that the proposals would undermine the EC Commission's attempt to introduce a single competition law for the EC single market. Second it was suggested that the operation of the offence would jeopardise the leniency programme operated by the EC

[71] Para 7.36.
[72] Para 7.30.
[73] Para 7.31.
[74] CBI news release, 31 July 2001.
[75] CBI *Media Focus*, 1 August 2001.
[76] CBI issue statement, 21 October 2002.

Commission (this issue is considered further in chapter 4). Third it argued that criminalisation 'could also undermine the relationship between the OFT and business by making companies far less willing in future to provide sensitive business information on a voluntary basis'. At the least, the CBI suggested, the 'Government should delay introducing the proposal for the time being, at least until the existing civil fines have been shown to be insufficient'.

The progress of the Bill

The Enterprise Bill was brought before Parliament on 26 March 2002, and received Royal Assent on 7 November 2002, almost two years to the day on which the Competition Act received Royal Assent. Analysis of the passage of the Bill would suggest that there were a number of problems in the text as first presented. In all nearly 750 amendments were made, and a large number of these emanated from the Government itself. In this text we have dealt, as appropriate, with the discussions relating to the cartel offence, but have not considered debates on other parts of the Act. The full references to cartel offence discussions, both in Committee, and on the floor of both Houses, is as follows (all dates are 2002): Standing Committee B, 18 April, coll 133–42; 23 April, coll 145–78; coll 181–216; second reading Hansard (HL) 2 July, coll 138–90; House of Lords Committee, Hansard (HL) 18 July, coll 1536–44; 22 July, coll 132–54; Third Reading, Hansard (HL) 28 October, coll 34–86; House of Commons, consideration of Lords' amendments, Hansard 30 October, coll 899–971 (but see particularly col 942).

AFTERWORD

It remains to be seen whether breaches of the cartel offence will be vigorously pursued, although the OFT, naturally, insists that the provisions will constitute a vital plank in acting against hard-core anti-competitive conduct. For example, in a speech delivered in May 2002, Margaret Bloom dealt in part with the new offence:

> Are these new powers necessary? Will they be used? The short answer is 'Yes'. We are uncovering around one cartel a month. We are now uncovering more serious ones. This activity is equivalent to theft.[77] It has no redeeming features. Effective deterrence is very important. However, we will select carefully the cartels for criminal prosecutions, concentrating on the serious ones. We expect that there will be a relatively small number of prosecutions—but they will have a significant deterrent effect. The first prosecutions will reach the courts in a few years'.[78]

[77] It need hardly be pointed out that cartel activity is somewhat different from theft. The latter may be characterised as a coerced transaction; the customer of, or supplier to, a cartel, enters into the transaction voluntarily, but receives false information about the transaction mechanisms. However, the analogy appears to have taken root, and was frequently made in the parliamentary debates; see for example, the Under Secretary of State, Standing Committee B, col 169.

[78] See above n 55.

2

The Offence

INTRODUCTION—PROHIBITED CONDUCT

IN THE WHITE Paper, discussed in the previous chapter, it was expressly recognised that:

> To be effective, it is critical that the offence is defined in a way which is both clear and easy for business and the courts to understand. It must also be actively applied so that its deterrent effect is genuinely felt. The Government recognises that defining the offence is a complex task . . .'[1]

It was always going to be the case that the offence would extend only to hard-core cartel conduct. Some explanation of this was given in the White Paper:

> 7.19 The new criminal offence will cover hard-core cartels only—widely recognised as the most serious form of competition breach. The most common form of hard-core cartel involves illegal price-fixing—where a number of firms agree what price should be charged for a particular product. In most cases, this will be above what the competitive market price would be.
>
> 7.20 However, cartels can also involve conduct which achieves the same economic result by different means. This includes agreeing not to compete for each other's customers—which leaves each firm free to set higher prices (market sharing). Or firms could agree to reduce levels of output—which also increases the price that they can charge.
>
> 7.21 In some cases, firms will agree to inflate the price charged in a tender-bidding process and enter bids which ensure that one company in the cartel will win, but on better terms than would otherwise by the case (collusive tendering). The OFT believes that public sector contracts are particularly vulnerable to these practices. As such, they could hit taxpayers hard—because Local Authorities or Government departments have to pay more for public services.
>
> 7.22 In all these cases, the effect is the same—prices rise and consumers pay more than they should. The Government intends that the new criminal offence will cover each of these different types of cartel. . . .

This followed the approach recommended in the Penrose report, which considered in part whether the offence might extend to vertical, as well as to horizontal, conduct:

> We understand the view of those who are experts in the field of competition law is that the criminal offence should only be applicable to horizontal agreements between

[1] DTI, Cm 5233, July 2001, para 7.33.

> individuals representing 'competing' undertakings operating at the same level of the supply-chain for the purposes of the agreement in question. It should not apply to vertical agreements, many of which are considered to have pro-competitive or other beneficial effects . . .[2]

Price fixing at the horizontal level is prohibited whether it be direct, or indirect. While the most obvious form of price fixing would be that which set a single price, or set of prices, for a single customer or customers, it is also possible to envisage situations in which there might be co-ordination on discounts, quantity rebates and so on. Any such arrangement that would have the same effect as a direct agreement to set selling prices may fall foul of the provision.[3]

Accordingly s 188 of the Act therefore relates to dishonest agreements of the kinds specified in s 188(2) relating to at least two undertakings. Because the offence is defined as making such arrangements, it is not necessary that they be implemented. However, where arrangements are entered into outside the UK it is a requirement that the arrangement is implemented in the UK (territorial aspects of the offence are considered in more detail in Chapter 6, below). The four categories of arrangement that are condemned are: price-fixing; limitation of production or supply; the sharing of markets; and bid-rigging. As noted in the *Explanatory notes*, these forms of conduct 'comprise the most serious forms of anti-competitive activity and as such are a sub-set of the practices for which undertakings may be pursued under the civil provisions of the CA 98'.[4] The details of the arrangements specified in s 188(2) are as follows:

> 'The arrangements must be ones which, if operating as the parties to the agreement intend, would—
> (a) directly or indirectly fix a price for the supply by A in the United Kingdom (otherwise than to B) of a product or service,
> (b) limit or prevent supply by A in the United Kingdom of a product or service,
> (c) limit or prevent production by A in the United Kingdom of a product,
> (d) divide between A and B the supply in the United Kingdom of a product or service to a customer or customers,
> (e) divide between A and B customers for the supply in the United Kingdom of a product or service, or
> (f) be bid-rigging arrangements.'

It is provided in addition in s 188(3) that in the case of s 188(2)(a), (b) and (c), that B—as defined above—must be engaged in the practice in addition to A, such that its price, supply or production must also be fixed. This requirement is set out clearly in the *Explanatory notes* at para 408 in the following terms:

> Subsection (3) requires, in the case of price-fixing or limitation of production or supply, that for the offence to be committed the other party must reciprocally have intended that the agreement, if implemented according to the intentions of the parties, should result

[2] Penrose report, para 1.12.
[3] See, for example, the Under Secretary of State, Standing Committee B, col 165.
[4] *Explanatory notes*, Para 406.

in one of these activities. This means that agreements are not criminal where the agreement only requires one party to fix prices or limit production or supply as defined. This further requirement does not apply in the case of market-sharing and bid-rigging where the activities are by definition reciprocal.

Further conditions relating to the horizontal nature of the arrangements are set out in s 189. In each of the instances set out in s 188, it is necessary, as an additional element of the offence, that the supply of the product or service by A would be 'at a level in the supply chain at which the product or service would at the same time be supplied by B in the United Kingdom' (s 189(1)).

Section 188(2)(a)—price fixing arrangements

Section 188(2)(a) relates to horizontal price fixing arrangements, perhaps the most generally recognised form of a cartel. For this section to apply the relevant arrangements must be such as to constitute a direct, or indirect, reciprocal fixing of a price by both A and B for a product or service in the UK to a third party or parties. Although s 188(2)(a) makes reference only to A, s 188(3) provides that B must also be an active party to the arrangement. There is no requirement for the product or service to be identical, or indeed even substitutable (ie in the same relevant market for the purposes of article 81 EC or the Chapter I Prohibition of the CA 98) but, by virtue of s 189(1) it is necessary for the prosecution to demonstrate that 'A's supply of the product or service would be at a level in the supply chain at which the product or service would at the same time be supplied by B' in the UK. In practice there would in most cases be little benefit to be gained from fixing the prices of non-substitute products as there would be no power to do so in the face of competition from others. Note that A and B may both operate at various levels of the supply chain, and may be fully vertically integrated companies, or may have very different structures. What matters in each case is that *the products or services in question*, are supplied at the same level in the chain. This may be to final consumers, to intermediaries, or may relate to raw materials or other inputs. There is no requirement that the supply be to domestic consumers—those in industry may be as much a victim of a cartel as individual shoppers. The arrangement as to price would not necessarily have to be one which lead to an increase in prices by both parties. In fact even an arrangement which led to the parties lowering their prices (for example to provide a joint response to the threat of entry into the market affected) would be caught if it could be shown to have been entered into dishonestly. Equally, an arrangement under which B would maintain its price at a constant level while A increased its price would be caught. Setting a range within which either A or B would set its price would also constitute an infringement, as any range must have an upper and lower bound. Further, the question is not whether A and B would have reached the same position without co-ordination, but whether they have co-ordinated. However, the fact that the parties would have reached the same position without co-ordination may go some way to challenge a finding of 'dishonesty'.

Section 188(2)(b) and (2)(c)—limitations of supply or production

Sections 188(2)(b) and (c) relate to the limiting of production or supply. As these are equivalent, if not identical, they are dealt with here together. To limit supply or production ultimately has the same effect as an increase in prices, all other things being equal. For the arrangements to fall within the offence both A *and* B must limit the production or supply of goods or services which would be supplied at the same level in the supply chain. It would appear to follow that an agreement between A and B to refuse to supply C could be caught by this subsection as well as a more generic agreement to reduce supplies overall. This could give rise to difficulties given the fact that the test of dishonesty presumably allows some consideration of relevant economic and industrial circumstances. For example, it might not be dishonest for A and B to refuse to supply C where A and B could more profitably supply D. On the other hand, the question may legitimately be asked why A and B have entered into agreements in relation to the supply of C, when such decisions would more normally be taken unilaterally.

There is a territorial nicety in relation to a limit on production in that the only requirement is that the production be in the UK. In other words, there is no requirement that the goods or services being produced be supplied in the UK. Unlike the case with the Chapter I Prohibition of the CA 98 there is no requirement here to show that there would be an effect on trade within the UK or a part of it for the offence to bite.

A difficulty could arise in respect of both of these elements of the offence (as well as with bid-rigging) if parties were not to act simultaneously. Suppose for example, A were to cut its production or supply of a product in 2005, and B were to do so in 2006. It might be somewhat difficult to demonstrate—particularly in the absence of supporting documentation setting out communication between the parties—that there had been an arrangement to do so. It is doubtful that the offence could be sustained by way of a pure economic analysis. Such an approach, while not rejected by the ECJ in the *Wood Pulp* case, was at least not enthusiastically embraced, and that was in the context of a civil proceeding. In that case the EC Commission had acted against an alleged cartel and, because of jurisdictional issues, had found it difficult to obtain documentary evidence. Instead the Commission relied largely on the fact that the observed market behaviour did not match that which would be expected in the absence of collusion.[5] Rebutting such an approach in this case the ECJ held that:

> In determining the probative value of those different factors, it must be noted that parallel conduct cannot be regarded as furnishing proof of concertation unless concertation constitutes the only plausible explanation for such conduct. It is necessary to bear in mind that, although article [81 EC] prohibits any form of collusion which distorts competition, it does not deprive economic operators of the right to adapt themselves intelligently to the existing and anticipated conduct of their competitors . . .

[5] *Wood Pulp* Commission Decision 85/202 (1985) OJ L85/1.

Accordingly it is necessary in this case to ascertain whether the parallel conduct alleged by the Commission cannot, taking account of the nature of the products, the size and number of the undertakings and the volume of the market in question, be explained otherwise than by concertation.[6]

Given the difficulties of establishing such an offence by way of pure economic evidence in a civil context it is inconceivable that such an approach could be taken in relation to a criminal action, particularly when one considers the necessity of establishing the appropriate level of dishonesty. It is then, incumbent on the prosecuting authority to bring forward some documentary or testamentary evidence to establish the existence of the ingredients of the offence.

Section 188(2)(d) and (2)(e)—market sharing arrangements

For an arrangement to infringe either of sub-sections (2)(d) and (e) it must be one which would lead to a division of the market or customers between A and B in the UK. Any such division need not necessarily be on the basis of a geographical allocation, but could be by any means whereby individual customers were denied the choice of supplier of the product or service in question.

Section 188(2)(f)—bid-rigging

Bid-rigging arrangements are defined in s 188(5) as being

> . . . arrangements under which, in response to a request for bids for the supply of a product or service in the United Kingdom, or for the production of a product in the United Kingdom—
> (a) A but not B may make a bid, or
> (b) A and B may each make a bid but, in one case or both, only a bid arrived at in accordance with the arrangements.

It is further provided in s 188(6) that bid-rigging arrangements are excluded from the scope of this provision where the person requesting the bids was notified of the arrangements at or before the time of the making of the bid. This would presumably in any event have flowed from the definition of the offence, as it would be hard to sustain a case based on dishonesty, where the supposed 'victim' of the offence knew that the arrangements were in place through the direct communication of the parties (this argument is considered further below). It is interesting therefore that in the *Explanatory notes* the position is taken that '[b]id-rigging is the only one of the prohibited activities where for all practical purposes the

[6] *Re Wood Pulp Cartel: A Ahlstrom Oy v Commission* joined cases C 89/85 etc [193] 4 CMLR 407, paras 71–72.

carrying out of the activity described in this section will in itself invariably indicate a dishonest intention'.[7]

Frazer et al note that the terms of the offence in this respect 'cover the classic bid-rigging scenarios, where there is an agreement that only one member of the ring will enter the bid, or where the members of the ring agree who will make the winning bid'.[8] In the case of the *Pre-Insulated Pipe Cartel*[9] for example a bid-rigging scheme was in place. This was described by the EC Commission in the following terms:

> A retired business executive with close personal connections to ABB who had formerly been on the board of IC Møller was engaged as a consultant to act as the 'co-ordinator' of the cartel.
>
> The Contact Group, which allocated the business amongst the cartel members, maintained a data-base of projects and customers on a lap-top computer. It was decided in advance who was going to 'win' the contract in question. For each project, the 'favourite' (that is, the firm to which the contract was assigned) informed the other participants of the price it intended to quote and they then submitted tenders at a higher price in order to 'protect' the supplier designated by the cartel.[10]

Although it has been argued by a number of parties that bid-rigging arrangements are to be regarded as *per se* dishonest, even in this case it would be possible to construct scenarios where the element of dishonesty was open to doubt. Suppose, for example, that A could agree with B to bid exclusively for contract Y, with B subsequently being left free to bid for tender Z, where there was limited capacity in the relevant industry, such that each firm could only undertake to fulfil one of the contracts. Such an arrangement might have the benefit of reducing uncertainty for the firms involved, although it would likely result in higher prices being offered by the bidder in respect of each contract than would otherwise be the case at least with respect to the first of the contracts, but not of the second by which time, if the scenario set out here held true, there would be only one bidder left.

JURISDICTION AND PROSECUTING AUTHORITY

The lead prosecutor in most cases will be the SFO, although the OFT also has the power to prosecute offences. Prosecutions may only be brought with the consent of the OFT, and private prosecutions are unlikely to be countenanced. In Scotland prosecutions will be brought by the Lord Advocate. In the case of cross-jurisdictional cases, according to OFT guidance, 'the jurisdiction in which a case

[7] At para 409.

[8] T Frazer, S Hinchcliffe and K George, *Enterprise Act 2002: The new law of mergers, monopolies and cartels* (London, The Law Society, 2003), at para 4.14.

[9] Commission Decision 1999/60, *Pre-Insulated Pipe Cartel* (1999) OJ L 24/1, on appeal *Re Pre-Insulated Pipe Cartel: LR AF 1998 A/S v EC Commission* case T–23/99 [2002] 5 CMLR 10, discussed in Chapter 1.

[10] Commission Decision 1999/60, at para 33.

will be brought will depend on the outcome of discussions between the OFT, the SFO and the Lord Advocate's office, and will follow the well-established principles that govern other criminal prosecutions'.[11] The structure and roles of the OFT and SFO are considered in more detail in Chapter One.

THE MEANING OF DISHONESTY

Section 188 provides, therefore, that a person is guilty of a cartel offence if he or she 'dishonestly agrees with one or more other persons to make or implement, or cause to be made or implemented, arrangements of the following kind relating to at least two undertakings'.[12] The test for dishonesty in England and Wales, which is a question of fact to be determined by the jury, was established in the case of *R v Ghosh*.[13] The appellant, a consultant surgeon convicted of dishonestly obtaining money by deception, contrary to the Theft Act 1968, s 15, submitted that the trial judge had misdirected the jury as to the meaning of dishonesty. Lord Lane CJ observed that establishing a satisfactory test required consideration of whether the dishonesty in question related to a course of conduct or described a state of mind. If the former, then it could be 'established independently of the knowledge or belief of the accused. But if, as we think, it is the latter, then the knowledge and belief of the accused are at the root of the problem'.[14] In a judgment which has stood the test of time, the Court of Appeal settled on a double test for dishonesty which involves both objective and subjective considerations. Thus the *Ghosh* direction requires that:

> In determining whether the prosecution has proved that the defendant was acting dishonestly, a jury must first of all decide whether according to the ordinary standards of reasonable and honest people what was done was dishonest. If it was not dishonest by those standards, that is the end of the matter and the prosecution fails.
>
> If it was dishonest by those standards, then the jury must consider whether the defendant himself must have realised that what he was doing was by those standards dishonest. In most cases, where the actions are obviously dishonest by ordinary standards, there will be no doubt about it. It will be obvious that the defendant himself knew that he was acting dishonestly. It is dishonest for a defendant to act in a way which he knows ordinary people consider to be dishonest, even if he asserts or genuinely believes that he is morally justified in acting as he did.[15]

[11] OFT Guidance, *The Cartel Offence: Guidance on the issue of no-action letters for individuals*, para 2.7.

[12] Section 188(1). The *actus reus* of the offence has been described as 'absurdly complex, taking two pages and 14 subsections of dense text to sort out' (G Peretz, and J Lewis, 'Go directly to jail: Losing badly in "Monopoly"' (2003) *New Law Journal* 99). In fact the provisions are not unduly tortuous, and represent an attempt to define the offence with a reasonable degree of precision.

[13] [1982] QB 1053, [1982] 2 All ER 689, (1982) CR App R 154, CA. It remains unclear whether dishonesty is a feature of the Scots law of theft, the *mens rea* of which is an intention to deprive. However, there are indications that in some cases the defendant's dishonesty may be relevant. See for example, *Mackenzie and Maclean* 1981 SLT (Sheriffs Court) 40 and *Kane v Frail* 1997 SLT 1274.

[14] [1982] 2 All ER 689 at 696.

[15] *Ibid.*

Thus, in all cases in which honesty is an issue the jury is required to determine whether the act done would, according to the standards of reasonable people, be considered to be dishonest, and then to consider whether the defendant would have realised that this was the view of reasonable people. If the answer to both questions is in the affirmative, then dishonesty is established.

The purpose of basing the offence on the standard of 'dishonest' conduct was to define it tightly, although it was suggested in the debates on the passage of the Act that the definition was anything but tight.[16] However, it was pointed out in Committee that an opposition amendment to replace 'dishonestly' with 'knowingly or recklessly' would have significantly *expanded* the scope of the offence. According to the Under-Secretary of State, the:

> 'sort of evidence that would point to dishonesty is likely to include a failure to seek legal advice, combined with attempts to disguise or hide activity. For example, holding secret meetings and the absence or destruction of records, and other such practices, would be instances of such evidence.'[17]

Peretz and Lewis have recognised that the standard of 'dishonesty' is one that will be familiar to criminal lawyers, although not to the competition bar.[18] They are probably correct when they write that in the context of the cartel offence

> 'the question of whether individuals acted dishonestly is likely to be determined by the extent to which they were open about what they were doing. If, for example, the agreement operated by covert meetings held under a soubriquet, with all records being destroyed, it will probably not be hard to establish dishonesty, the badges of fraud being present'.[19]

In one recent civil case, for example, the OFT made an infringement decision in respect of an arrangement entered into by an auctioneers' association in Northern Ireland, but did not impose a penalty in part on the grounds that the arrangement

[16] It has been suggested that the persons drafting this legislation failed to understand fully the role of dishonesty in the criminal law and used it to 'bridge a perceived weakness in the objective definition of the prohibited conduct'. See C Harding, and J Joshua, 'Breaking Up the Hard Core: the Prospects for the Proposed Cartel Offence' [2002] *Criminal Law Review* 933–44 at 939.

[17] *Hansard*, Standing Committee B, col 136.

[18] Interestingly, in *R v Saunders and others* [1996] 1 Cr App R 463, the defendant argued unsuccessfully that the test for dishonesty involved consideration of the common standards of honesty employed in the City. The main issue in the trial was whether the appellants were proved to have acted dishonestly. MacCulloch has expressed concerns about the application of the test in the context of the cartel offence in the following terms:

> 'This leads to the question, would the ordinary person serving on a jury in a complex cartel case be able to utilise the test with any degree of surety? While the average jury member will be fully aware of dishonesty within theft and the moral view of ordinary people, it is questionable whether they have adequate experience of the morality of company directors while negotiating arrangements between multi-national companies' (MacCulloch, A 'The Cartel Offence and the Criminalisation of UK Competition Law' [2003] *Journal of Business Law* 616.)

[19] See above n 12.

was made public.[20] It might also be the case that those on the periphery of cartels, who have not played a leading role in either their formulation or enforcement, may be acting in a less dishonest way than others. However, in the civil context

> It is settled case law that where an undertaking participates, even if not actively, in meetings between undertakings with an anti-competitive object and does not publicly distance itself from what occurred at them, thus giving the impression to the other participants that it subscribes to the results of the meetings and will act in conformity with them, it may be concluded that it is participating in a cartel resulting from those meetings.[21]

It will be noted that it is an offence to 'make' any of the arrangements subsequently referred to. It is not necessary, therefore, for the arrangement to be implemented. However, in relation to arrangements entered into outside the UK, it is necessary that the arrangement be implemented in the UK. It should be noted further that the inchoate offences of conspiracy and attempt apply to the cartel offence.[22]

ATTEMPTS AT CARTELISATION

The meaning of the phrase 'the arrangements must be ones which, if operating as the parties to the agreement intend, would—' was explained by the Under Secretary of State as reflecting the intention to 'criminalise dishonest agreements between individuals and to do so independently of whether their agreement is actually implemented as they intend—or at all—by their respective companies'.[23] This is to say that the activity of formulating an unsuccessful cartel, or even one which has no prospect of success, is illegal. This is consistent with the position under the general law of Article 81 EC and the Chapter I Prohibition in which it has been established that those in a failed cartel are liable for breaches of the appropriate law.[24] In a subsequent explanatory letter to the Committee the Under Secretary of State referred to the Criminal Attempts Act 1981 (which does not apply to the law in Scotland, where attempts remains a matter of common law).

While the arguments in favour of the adoption of a test of dishonesty are strong, there are some difficulties with such a definition, although it is not likely that these will be important in practice, in part because of the operation of the civil regime

[20] Decision CA98/1/2003, *Decision of the Northern Ireland Livestock And Auctioneers' Association of Undertakings to Recommend that its Members Introduce a Buyer's Commission in Northern Ireland Cattle Markets* [2003] UKCLR 433.

[21] See above n 9.

[22] The principle feature of these offences is that they are committed although the substantive offence has not been completed, and arguably before any harm has been done. In England and Wales attempt is defined in the Criminal Attempts Act 1981 and the offence of conspiracy is set out in Part I of the Criminal Law Act 1977 as amended by the Criminal Attempts Act 1981.

[23] Standing Committee B, col 138.

[24] See, for example, *Ferry Operators—Currency Surcharge* Commission Decision 97/84 (1997) OJ L26/23; and *Polypropylene* Commission Decision 86/398 (1986) OJ L230/1 in which a number of cartel initiatives collapsed, although others were successful.

alongside the criminal law regime. We have seen above that in relation to bid-rigging arrangements it is expressly provided that where the person requesting the submission of the bid(s) is notified in due time that an arrangement is in place, there will be no offence. This, presumably, reflects the fact that the person requesting the bids may then take this into account in the purchasing process. It is also evidence which is suggestive of a lack of dishonesty. If A and B enter into a price-fixing arrangement and then notify the world that they have done so, would such an arrangement be dishonest? It will be noted that the Under Secretary of State suggested a number of elements that might point to dishonesty, such as the failure to seek legal advice, or to take it if offered, or to conceal the arrangements. Suppose however, that legal advice *was* sought, or that the parties well knew that the arrangements would infringe civil prohibitions, and that there was no concealment. What then is the position where the offence is predicated on dishonesty? It seems somewhat of a curiosity that in the case of bid-rigging it is not an offence where the requestor is told of the rigging. It is not inevitably going to be the case that the requestor will have an alternative. If, for example, there are only two potential suppliers of the products or services in question the requestor may have no choice but to pay a monopoly price, such that a transfer of income from the purchaser to the supplier takes place that would not have taken place in a more properly competitive market. The justification for such a policy might be that in this case the purchaser would be able to initiate a civil action for damages based on a breach of the Chapter I Prohibition of the CA 98, or on article 81 EC, depending on the jurisdictional factors.[25] It is perhaps no more than an anomaly that those who operated a naked, publicised cartel, could not be successfully prosecuted. If there is a rationale for such a result it must lie in the fact that in such a case an action under either article 81 EC or s 2 of the CA 98 would be certain of success—there being no need to prove dishonesty in such a case.

APPRECIABILITY

One of the things achieved in the definition of the offence is the sundering of this part of the law from the Chapter I Prohibition of the CA 98, although as we have seen in Chapter One, and throughout this work, there are practical links between the two. One benefit of withdrawing the link is that it eliminates any consideration of the concept of appreciability of agreements, or *de minimis* provisions. Under EC law the EC Commission has codified the approach taken to small agreements in its *de minimis* notice.[26] Under this notice the relevant thresholds for the application of article 81(1) are different depending on whether the agreement is a horizontal

[25] It has also been noted too that such conduct 'may also amount to the exercise by the undertakings of joint dominance under Part II of [the CA 98]', See above n 8, at para 4.14. For damages and private claims see further Chapter 5, below.

[26] (2001) OJ C368/13, and see also press release IP/02/13, 7 January 2002.

or a vertical agreement. In the case of a horizontal agreement, the combined market share of the parties is set at 10 per cent.

At the same time however, agreements containing hard-core restrictions and which fix market prices, or which share markets, or impose minimum resale prices may have an appreciable effect even where the parties combined market shares are below those set out in the guideline. If it was needed this is further evidence of a general policy intention not to overlook hard core horizontal restrictions, whatever the level of market share at which they are imposed.[27]

Following the modernisation programme the same approach is taken by the OFT in respect of the Chapter I Prohibition.

[27] Note however, that s 39 of the CA 98 excludes undertakings involved in 'small agreements' from paying penalties in respect of infringements. By virtue of the Competition Act 1998 (Small Agreements and Conduct of Minor Significance) Regulations 2000, SI 2000/262 the relevant threshold is set at £20 m.

3

Investigation

INTRODUCTION

IT WAS CLEAR to the authors of the Penrose Report (see Chapter 1, above) that the OFT would need access to extensive powers of investigation in order to effectively combat illicit cartel activity:

> We have learned from the OFT investigators that agreements to enter into 'hard core' cartel activities are often made in clandestine meetings by relevant employees of the undertakings concerned. Those meetings are often held on neutral territory such as hotels. It seems to us that the opportunity to obtain evidence of the discussions that led to such agreements would have a powerful effect on any future criminal proceedings and we therefore consider that the OFT investigators should be authorised to carry out intrusive surveillance within the provisions of s 32 [of the Regulation of Investigatory Powers Act 2000 (discussed below)] and property interference within the provisions of s 92 of the Police Act 1997. We are also of the opinion that the OFT should have access to intelligence from the interception of communications in appropriate case.[1]

Despite some concerns being raised during its passage through Parliament, the EA 02 does equip the OFT with considerable coercive powers to conduct an investigation into suspected criminal cartels, including the use of covert surveillance measures. In addition to discussing the ambit of these powers, we also briefly outline the powers of investigation available to the OFT and other concurrent regulators under the CA 98. This is because it is possible that an investigation may start out under these powers, and then subsequently trigger a criminal investigation under the EA 02. Although in making its initial enquiries into suspected cartel activity, the OFT has indicated that it will act in accordance with the Police and Criminal Evidence Act 1984 (PACE) and follow all the relevant criminal codes of practice, having two sets of investigatory powers and procedures may cause some confusion.[2] Further, issues could arise with regard as to the use to which any evidence obtained during the course of the CA 98 investigation may be used by the OFT in criminal investigations. In Chapter 7 we also consider the position in

[1] Penrose Report, para 4.21.

[2] OFT Guidance Note Powers for investigating criminal cartels, para 4.1. PACE introduced several procedural safeguards to provide suspects with protection from unlawful and unfair treatment. It represented an attempt by Parliament to balance countervailing public interests, and is by necessity a detailed and complex piece of legislation. Since its inception it has undergone some significant revision, but its basic structure has remained intact. Revised codes of practice came into force in April 2003. PACE has no legal status in Scotland. However, when conducting an investigation in Scotland there is nothing to prevent OFT officers from following the codes.

respect of information obtained during the operation of the leniency programmes operated in respect of the CA 98 and articles 81 and 82 EC.

INFORMATION GATHERING IN THE CONTEXT OF CIVIL PROCEEDINGS

Information gathering and investigations under the Competition Act 1998

The OFT has substantial powers to gather information and conduct investigations under the CA 98, and in respect of investigations under EC law. Indeed, the CCAT described the powers of the OFT as being 'wide ranging and draconian', noting that they may 'substantially affect the civil rights and obligations of those concerned'.[3]

The OFT, or other appropriate regulator, is given the power by way of s 25 of the CA 98 to conduct any investigation where it has 'reasonable grounds for suspecting' that there has been an infringement of either of the two prohibitions set out in the CA 98. Upon presentation of a written notice to that effect the OFT may require 'any person to produce to it a specified document, or to provide it with specified information which it considers relates to any matter relevant to the investigation' (s 26(1)). According to the policy of the OFT, as spelt out in its guideline *Powers of Investigation*, this is the procedure that will be most often used in relation to investigations under the CA 98. The OFT has the express power to take copies of documents, or extracts from them. In justifying these extensive powers the Government argued that 'the statutory investigatory powers must be able to cater for the very worst case of unscrupulous concealment of evidence of a cartel or other anti-competitive behaviour', although it accepted too that 'full use of the powers provided in the [CA 98] should . . . be unnecessary'.[4]

Investigations at the premises of undertakings may be undertaken either with, or without, notice being given to the undertaking concerned. Section 27, CA 98, gives the OFT the power to 'enter any business premises'. The power to enter domestic premises under a warrant is given in s 28A in the case where documents to which s 26 applies may be held on them. This power can, in effect, be used only when the domestic premises are also being used as business premises. In relation to many of the investigations that will be carried out under this part of the CA 98 the investigating officer is required to give two working days' notice before the power of entry is enforced (s 27(2)). Section 27(3) however, gives the OFT the power, where there is a 'reasonable suspicion' that the premises are being occupied by a party to an agreement under investigation, to waive the two-day notice period. This period may also be set aside where 'the investigating officer has taken all such steps as are reasonably practicable to give notice but has not been able to

[3] *Institute of Independent Insurance Brokers v The Director General of Fair Trading* [2002] Comp AR 141, para 57.

[4] Hansard (HL) 17 November 1997, col 388 and 391.

do so' (s 27(3)(b)). Under these provisions the OFT has the power to take any necessary equipment with it, and any person on the premises may be required 'to produce any document which [the OFT] considers relates to any matter relevant to the investigation', and to 'provide an explanation of it' (s 27(5)(b)). Any person on the premises may further be required to 'state to the best of his knowledge and belief, where any such document is to be found (s 27(5)(c)).

While investigations conducted under s 27 of the Act require two days' notice, save in the circumstances outlined above, s 28 permits the OFT to conduct an investigation without a warning following the issuing of a warrant to that effect by a judge. A warrant may be sought either where documents required to be produced under ss 26 or 27 have not been produced, or where there is a reasonable ground for believing that if the notice required by s 27 was given the documents would be destroyed, removed, or concealed (s 28(b)). A warrant may also be requested where an investigating officer acting under the powers in s 27 has been unable to gain access to the relevant premises. The sensitive matter of the issuing of such warrants was considered in the case of *Office of Fair Trading v X*.[5] Here the OFT applied for a warrant without notice, following a suspicion held by the OFT that the unnamed defendants had been engaged in price fixing. Morrison J was 'satisfied that what is summarised in . . . skeleton argument, justifies me in concluding that there are presently reasonable grounds for suspecting that the defendants have been engaged in unlawful conduct'.[6] The practical dynamics underlying such investigations are nicely dealt with by the judge at para 5:

> On the basis of . . . the first affidavit of Edward Francis Lennon, a principal investigation officer in the Cartel Investigations Branch of the Competition Enforcement Division of the OFT, I am satisfied that there are reasonable grounds for suspecting that there are, on the premises named in the warrants, documents which the OFT are entitled to see in the course of their investigation. As to the second requirement, the evidence shows that a 'warning shot across the defendants' bows' has already been fired by the Director General of Fair Trading. The target companies, if they have been doing what the OFT suspect, are likely to have taken steps to make detection difficult and to be continuing so to act. The stakes are high, since the penalties if guilt is established are likely to be high. The entities being investigated include one of a substantial size, and whose reputation, apart from its financial position, may be damaged if incriminating material is found. There is, therefore, a strong inducement or motive for hiding the truth. The material which the OFT are most interested to see is relatively easy to conceal, given advance notice. For these reasons, I am satisfied that there are reasonable grounds for suspecting that the written material would be concealed or destroyed. It is in the public interest that if there has been wrongdoing it is uncovered and revealed.

[5] *Application for a warrant under the Competition Act 1998* [2003] EWHC 1042 (Comm), [2003] UKCLR 765.

[6] At para 3.

All of the above would presumably hold true in the course of any criminal investigation into the cartel offence, save that it is to be hoped that the OFT would not have fired a 'warning shot across the defendants' bows'.

The court then dealt with the question of whether the procedures applied by the OFT infringed the human rights of the defendants, in the light of the application of article 6 of the Convention. The court noted first that such questions had already been dealt with by the CFI and ECJ in relation to the similar powers held by the EC Commission under what was then Regulation 17. In essence the approach of the ECJ was that the EC Commission was performing a legitimate role under the Treaty, and that there was a legal right to challenge the lawfulness of the decision of the Commission to hold an investigation, as well as any final decision made by the Commission. In the case of the UK, Morrison J held, at paras 9–10 that there were strong parallels to the EC approach:

> All of these matters apply with similar force under the domestic legislation. The OFT is the guardian of free competition in this member state, and the statutory provisions are designed to ensure that it can fulfil that role: the powers to carry out an investigation are an essential feature of its functions. Its powers to enter premises, search and ask questions about documents are not more extensive than are available to the Commission.[7] And the exercise of these powers are subject to extensive 'guarantees'. IN the first place, the OFT is required by the Act to come to a High Court judge to obtain a warrant. It must satisfy the court that there are reasonable grounds for the OFT's suspicion that competition is being unlawfully distorted and that there are likely to be found relevant documents (my words [ie those of Morrison J]), and that a warrant is necessary to avoid the suppression of documents. The OFT must comply with the formalities specified in the relevant Practice Direction. . . .
>
> Here, the rights of the defendants are protected: their rights under Community law have been fully respected. The defendants may apply to the court for relief; they have a right to legal representation and are encouraged to seek legal advice; the privilege in client-lawyer communications is protected . . .
>
> The same reasoning applies to the second aspect of article 6. It seems to me perfectly reasonable that the OFT should, just as the Commission does, have power to ask questions about the material which they turn up during their search. There may well be codes or technical notes which require elucidation so that the investigation may properly proceed.

The judge found similarly that article 8 of the Convention was not being breached by the powers given to the OFT and their subsequent exercise. In this respect the judge again pointed to the need to curb price cartels, which was, he said, the aim of the legislation. 'For this purpose', Morrison J held, 'the OFT must carry out an investigation where that is justified, as here'.[8]

Once any such warrant has been issued, the powers are the same as for s 27, with the key exception that force may be used in making entry into the premises, and

[7] Strictly speaking this is incorrect. There are some matters in which the OFT has stronger powers under the CA 98 than the EC Commission had under Regulation 17, or has under Regulation 1/2003. However, a full discussion of these powers lies outside the remit of this book.

[8] At para 13.

in carrying out investigations after that point (s 28(2)(a)). While this right to use force, something not guaranteed to the EC Commission, was criticised by the Opposition, the Government clung to it, with Lord Simon being 'thoroughly of the view that the right to entry using reasonable force is a necessary part of ensuring that the process of investigation goes forward'.[9] Later it was suggested that these powers were to be exercised only at 'the very limits of investigation [in] exceptional cases 'in which we know that the rogues have thus far repelled all boarders'.[10] The first time that s 28 powers appear to have been used was in the case of the investigation leading to the infringement decision *Market Sharing by Arriva plc and FirstGroup plc.*[11] In this case the OFT applied to the High Court and to the Court of Session in Scotland for warrants to enter premises, and to exercise powers under s 28 of the Act. Warrants were issued on the 4 and 6 October 2000, and unannounced visits to the premises concerned took place just under a week later.[12]

Undertakings are entitled to have access to legal advice during the course of an investigation, although this is not unfettered. In the *Powers of Investigation* guideline the OFT says only that 'the investigating officer will grant an a request to wait a short time for legal advisers to arrive at the premises before the investigation continues if he considers that it is reasonable to do so in the circumstances'.[13]

Any person who does not comply with a requirement imposed under ss 26, 27 or 28 is guilty of an offence, and may be liable to a fine. Penalties, including imprisonment, may be opposed where an authorised investigating officer is obstructed (s 42), or where documents are destroyed (s 45), or where evidence is given which is materially false or misleading, and the person giving the evidence knows it to be so or is reckless (s 44).

Information gathering and investigations under Regulation 1/2003

The increasingly close cooperation required between member states and the EC Commission in the enforcement of EC competition law, and the provisions applicable to the exchange of information between members of the network of competition authorities further complicates the landscape when considering cartel investigations, whether civil or criminal. As from 1 May 2004 the applicable framework rules, and the specific rules relating to the role and power of the EC Commission are to be found in Regulation 1/2003.[14]

[9] Hansard (HL) 17 November 1997, col 406.

[10] *Ibid*, col 409.

[11] CA 98/9/2002, [2002] UKCLR 322.

[12] See para 7 of the Decision.

[13] Para 4.11. This provision was also set out in The Competition Act 1998 (Director's Rules) Order, SI 2000/293, at para 13.

[14] Council Regulation 1/2003 on the implementation of the rules of competition laid down in articles 81 and 82 (2003) OJ L1/1.

The Commission is empowered to make four types of substantive decisions under the Regulation. These are: the finding of an infringement, and the requirement that this be terminated if it is continuing (article 7); decisions imposing interim measures in cases where there is the 'risk of serious or irreparable damage to competition' (article 8); commitment decisions (article 9);[15] and findings of inapplicability (article 10). The powers of investigation that the Commission has at its disposal are set out in Chapter V of the Regulation. Where national authorities carry out investigations on behalf of the Commission, a scenario envisaged in article 22, they shall 'exercise their powers in accordance with their national law' (article 22(2)). In other words, in the course of an investigation into a possible breach of article 81 EC requested by the EC Commission, the OFT would rely on its powers under the CA 98. It is not spelt out in the Regulation that the OFT would not be able to use its powers under the EA 02 in relation to the cartel offence, but this flows from the general stance taken in the Regulation towards the equivalence of powers and protections in the member states in relation to the enforcement of EC competition law.

Article 18 empowers the Commission to request or require—by way of a decision—that undertakings 'provide all necessary information'. Necessary information is that which is needed by the Commission in order for it to 'carry out the duties assigned to it'. The CFI has, in the past, given a wide meaning to 'necessary information' and it is unlikely that this approach will change.[16] Article 23 permits the Commission to impose financial penalties on undertakings who supply incorrect or misleading information in response to either a request or a decision, or who fail to comply with a decision requiring that information be given. The penalty may be up to 1 per cent of the total turnover of the undertaking in the preceding business year. Article 24 further provides for periodic penalty payments of up to 5 per cent of the average daily turnover of the undertaking in the preceding business year to be paid in the event of non-compliance with a formal decision. The Commission is obliged to forward to the relevant national authorities copies of the request or decision. National authorities, and governments, are required to provide the Commission with all necessary information gathered by them necessary to allow the Commission to carry out its duties. Although the Regulation deals expressly with the transfer of information gained by it, or by other national authorities, to another national authority, and in particular with the use that may be made of this in criminal proceedings, it does not deal with the flow in reverse. Consider, for example, the position where the OFT, successfully or not, used its powers under the cartel offence in the investigation and prosecution of those individuals running a cartel. Might the EC Commission be able to require that this information be given to it to support an action under article 81? The better answer must be that it is. While evidence gained in a civil investigation may not be used in

[15] A commitment decision may be taken where the Commission would proceed to an infringement decision, but the undertaking offers commitments which would terminate the infringement.

[16] See, eg, *SEP v Commission* case T–39/90, [1992] 5 CMLR 33.

a criminal prosecution where protections are higher than in civil procedures,[17] on the face of it there seems no reason why information gained in the course of a criminal procedure which is subject to the safeguards provided by PACE and its codes of practice, should not then be used in a civil procedure.[18]

Article 19 of Regulation 1/2003 allows the Commission to 'interview any natural or legal person *who consents to be interviewed* for the purpose of collecting information relating to the subject-matter of an investigation' (emphasis added). This power is not a substantial one, as coercion is not an option, and no penalties may be imposed on those natural or legal persons who do *not* consent to be interviewed. Indeed this power is weaker than hinted at in recital 25, where it is noted that

> The detection of infringements of the competition rules is growing ever more difficult, and, in order to protect competition effectively, the Commission's powers of investigation need to be supplemented. The Commission should in particular be empowered to interview any persons who may be in possession of useful information and to record the statements made.

The Commission's powers of inspection are set out in article 20. These powers are extensive, but are not as potent as are those of the OFT under the CA 98. The Commission may, in order to fulfil its duties under the Regulation, conduct all necessary inspections of undertakings, and to this end its officials and other duly authorised persons are empowered:

(a) to enter any premises, land and means of transport of undertakings and associations of undertakings;
(b) to examine the books and other records related to the business, irrespective of the medium on which they are stored;
(c) to take or obtain in any form copies of or extracts from such books or records;
(d) to seal any business premises and books or records for the period and to the extent necessary for the inspection;
(e) to ask any representative or member of staff of the undertaking or associations of undertakings for explanations on facts or documents relating to the subject-matter and purpose of the inspection and to record the answers.

As with article 18 the Commission may proceed either with or without a formal decision to that effect. In the event that a decision is taken the undertaking is

[17] EA 02, s 198 provides

In the 1998 Act, after section 30 there is inserted—
"30A Use of statements in prosecution
A statement made by a person in response to a requirement imposed by virtue of any of sections 26 to 28 may not be used in evidence against him on a prosecution for an offence under section 188 of the EA 02 unless, in the proceedings—
(a) in giving evidence, he makes a statement inconsistent with it, and
(b) evidence relating to it is adduced, or a question relating to it asked, by him or on his behalf."

[18] The Police and Criminal Evidence Act 1984 and its codes of practice have no application in Scotland. However, the OFT Guidance Note Powers for investigating criminal cartels, para 3.17 indicates that OFT officers operating in Scotland will follow these procedures when exercising their search and seizure powers under the Act.

obliged to cooperate with the inspection, and if it does not so faces the same penalties as apply for non-compliance with the obligations imposed in relation to article 18 by way of articles 23 and 24. Where the Commission does encounter obstruction there is an obligation on the part of the national authorities to assist it in the performance of its duties, and, if necessary, by 'requesting where appropriate the assistance of the police or an equivalent enforcement authority, so as to enable them to conduct their inspection' (article 20(6)). Where national procedures would require that authorisation from a judicial authority be required before such action this shall be applied for, and it is presumed that such authorisation would not be withheld were the Commission to be acting properly within the terms of the Regulation. The role of the court in this procedure is circumscribed by article 20 (8) which provides, inter alia, that the national court may not 'call into question the necessity for the inspection nor demand that it be provided with the information in the Commission's file' Only the ECJ has the power to review the legality of the Commission decision.

Article 21 of the Regulation provides the Commission with a power which was not present in the earlier Regulation 17, under which it may inspect 'other premises'. Somewhat ambiguously these powers of inspection may be invoked only where necessary to establish that there is a 'serious breach' of articles 81 or 82 (article 21(1)). Any decision taken in this respect can only be executed where there has also been prior authorisation from the appropriate national judicial authority (article 21(3)), although the same limitations in this respect apply as with article 20.

Some limitations on the use to which information obtained by the Commission and national authorities may be used, and protections regarding the publication of such information, are provided in article 28, which deals with professional secrecy. Subject to the rules of articles 12 and 15, discussed below, 'information collected . . . shall be used only for the purpose for which it was acquired'. In addition,

> without prejudice to the exchange and to the use of information foreseen [elsewhere in the Regulation] the Commission and the competition authorities of the member states, their officials, servants and other persons working under the supervision of these authorities as well as officials and civil servants of other authorities of the member states shall not disclose information acquired or exchanged by them pursuant to this Regulation and of the kind covered by the obligation of professional secrecy (article 28(2)).

The exchange of information between members of the network, and with the Commission, is governed by articles 11 and 12 of the Regulation. The position is summarised in recital 16, which is in the following terms:

> Notwithstanding any national provision to the contrary, the exchange of information and the use of such information in evidence should be allowed between the members of the network even where the information is confidential. This information may be used for the application of articles 81 and 82 of the Treaty as well as for the parallel application of national competition law, provided that the latter application relates to the same case and does not lead to a different outcome. Where the information exchanged is used

by the receiving authority to impose sanctions on undertakings there should be no other limit to the use of the information other than the obligation to use it for the purpose for which it was collected given the fact that the sanctions imposed on undertakings are of the same type in all systems. The rights of defence enjoyed by undertakings in the various systems can be considered as sufficiently equivalent. However, as regards natural persons, they may be subject to substantially different types of sanctions across the various systems. Where that is the case, it is necessary to ensure that information can only be used if it has been collected in a way which respects the same level of protection of the rights of the defence of natural persons as provided for under the national rules of the receiving authority.

INFORMATION GATHERING AND INVESTIGATIONS UNDER THE ENTERPRISE ACT 2002

Before commencing a criminal investigation into an offence under s 188 of the Act, the OFT must establish reasonable grounds for suspecting that a cartel offence has been or is about to be committed.[19] In order to obtain sufficient evidence to prosecute, the OFT has been given extensive coercive powers to investigate the affairs of suspects. These include the power to compel persons to answer questions or provide other information, including handing over documents which may be relevant to the investigation, to obtain warrants to enter and search premises, to retain material relevant to the inquiry or to conduct intrusive surveillance operations. In order to provide some procedural protection for suspects, these powers will be exercised in accordance with PACE and all the relevant codes of practice applicable to criminal investigations. The OFT's criminal powers are similar to those available to the SFO under s 2 of the Criminal Justice Act 1987 (CJA 1987) to investigate serious fraud.[20] Indeed, it is anticipated that OFT staff engaged in an investigation into cartel activity will be working closely with the SFO who may also make use of their powers under the CJA 1987.[21] However, it has been agreed that

> Where the SFO and the OFT are exercising their formal powers of investigation under either the CJA 1987 or the Enterprise Act to compel documents and/or information, the SFO or the OFT will make it clear in writing to the persons concerned the specific power that is being used.[22]

Failure to comply with OFT requests for information without reasonable excuse could result in a criminal prosecution and the imposition of a fine or imprisonment. The exercise of these powers will often result in an invasion of privacy and

[19] EA 02, s 192(1).

[20] The SFO was set up initially to facilitate the investigation and prosecution of complex fraud. Section 2(2) of the Criminal Justice Act 1987 gives the Director of the Serious Fraud Office a range of essentially inquisitorial powers to obtain evidence in relation to serious fraud.

[21] The basis on which these two bodies will co-operate to investigate and prosecute in respect to a cartel offence where serious fraud is suspected is set out in a Memorandum of Understanding which is discussed in Chapter 5.

[22] OFT Guidance note, *Powers for investigating criminal cartels*, para 3.23.

the confiscation of property. Accordingly, the Act places limits on the OFT's powers of investigation to ensure an investigation does not result in undue interference with the rights and liberties of the individual. These powers can only be used for an investigation into criminal cartel activity

> . . . where it appears to the OFT that there is good reason to exercise them for the purpose of investigating the affairs, or any aspect of the affairs, of any person.[23]

It has been questioned whether the decision to commence a formal investigation should be left to the OFT.[24] Sufficient information to commence proceedings may also come to light through more informal means such as telephone calls or correspondence with individuals or in a voluntary interview. Further, information gathered during an OFT investigation into company infringements under the CA 98, which may run parallel to a criminal investigation might also give rise to reasonable suspicion. The source of the information that provides sufficient grounds to suspect that individuals are engaging in anti-competitive behaviour could be a whistle-blowing employee or ex-employee, and individuals or undertakings making use of the OFT's leniency programme.

Compulsory interviews and requests for information

Section 193 provides the OFT with the power to conduct compulsory interviews. A written notice must be sent requesting persons under investigation to attend at a given time and place to answer questions, or produce other information including specific documents.[25] A written request can also be sent to others if the OFT reasonable believes they may have information relevant to the investigation. The written notice must give an indication of the subject matter and purpose of the investigation and the time and place where the interview will be held or where and when the documents should be produced.[26] Original documents can be retained or copies made, and the person producing the documents can be asked questions relating to them.[27] Failure to produce documents will require an explanation and the OFT can ask questions as to their whereabouts. Under this provision access can be gained to information recorded in any form, which includes material stored electronically.[28] The time given to produce information or documents will depend upon the complexity of the case and the amount of information to be produced. In some circumstances, the OFT can demand that material is handed over immediately.[29] A notice issued under s 193 must also explain that failure to comply with

[23] EA 02, s 192(2).

[24] House of Commons Standing Committee Debates: Enterprise Bill, Standing Committee B, Tuesday 23 April 2002.

[25] EA 02, s 193(1).

[26] *Ibid* s 193(2).

[27] *Ibid* s 193(3).

[28] *Ibid* s 202.

[29] See above n 22 para 3.4

a request for information without a reasonable excuse is a criminal offence under s 201 of the Act.[30] A person attending a compulsory interview under powers provided by s 193(1) must be cautioned in accordance with PACE code C and informed of their right to legal advice and the evidential significance of any answers given.[31] Code C, para 10.1 requires that a caution be issued once there are reasonable, objective grounds for suspecting that a person has committed an offence

> . . . before any questions about an offence, or further questions if the answers provide the grounds for suspicion, are put to them if either the suspect's answers or silence (i.e. failure or refusal to answer satisfactorily) may be given in evidence to a court in a prosecution.

However, a person can be interviewed without the need to issue the standard caution if questions are necessary for other purposes such as establishing identity or obtaining consent.[32] While evidence gathered under the Act is subject to the usual evidentiary considerations, the Act places specific restrictions on the use of statements obtained under compulsion.[33] Accordingly, statements made in response to questions asked by the OFT using its criminal investigation powers may only be used as evidence in criminal proceedings against the maker of the statement in two situations.[34] Firstly, if he or she is prosecuted for knowingly or recklessly making a false or misleading statement in interview, which is contrary to s 201(2), and secondly if the person is prosecuted for some other offence and introduces evidence that is inconsistent with the statement.[35] However, this restriction does not prevent statements being used in evidence against other people in a prosecution for an offence under s 188.

Voluntary interviews

In addition to the formal procedures available under the Act, the OFT can obtain information about cartel activity from individuals or on behalf of an undertaking at any time. This information may be in the form of written correspondence, telephone conversations or informal interviews. However, where a person decides to provide information on a voluntary basis, they must be cautioned and informed of their right to legal advice. If the person volunteering information chooses to seek legal advice, the interview will not begin until their legal representative

[30] EA 02, s 193(5).

[31] See above n 22 para 4.2.

[32] PACE, code C para 10.1 a–e.

[33] EA 02, s 197.

[34] Similar restrictions apply to answers to questions required under s 2 of the CJA 1987.

[35] Changes to the hearsay rule introduced by the Criminal Justice Act 2003 have recently upgraded the evidential value of inconsistent statements in criminal proceedings. Thus statements obtained under compulsion, which are inconsistent with evidence tendered at trial, can now be used as evidence of fact rather than being used as evidence that relates to the credibility of the maker of the statement.

arrives. A major distinction between voluntary and compulsory interviews is that the person volunteering information can refuse to answer questions without committing an offence. This must be made explicit to the interviewee. During the interview the person will be reminded from time to time that the interview is voluntary, that he or she is not under arrest and may leave at any time. Attention must also be drawn to the fact that answers given during a voluntary interview under caution may be used against undertakings in a civil investigation under the CA 98.[36] Furthermore, subject to the usual rules of evidence in criminal proceedings, statements made during voluntary interview can be used as evidence in prosecutions for the cartel offence.

Search warrants

Sections 194–5 make provision for the OFT to conduct on-site investigations and to confiscate relevant documents. An application for a warrant to enter and search premises is made by the OFT to the High Court in England and Wales, and by the procurator fiscal to a sheriff in Scotland.[37] Section 194(1) provides that a judge or sheriff can issue a warrant provided that he or she is satisfied that there are reasonable grounds for believing

(a) that there are relevant documents on the premises which the OFT has power under s 193 to require to be produced for the purposes of an investigation; and
(b) that—
    (i) a person has failed to comply with a requirement under that section to produce the documents;
    (ii) it is not practicable to serve a notice under that section in relation to them; or
    (iii) the service of such a notice in relation to them might seriously prejudice the investigation.

The warrant permits a named OFT officer, and other OFT employees who have written authorisation, to enter premises using such reasonable force as is necessary and to search for material which appears relevant to the criminal investigation. Generally, the execution of search warrants and the seizure of property will be conducted in accordance with the revised PACE code B which provides some procedural safeguards and should ensure compliance with article 8 of the European Convention on Human Rights. The timing of a search is dependent upon the circumstances of the case. Thus, dawn raids are permissible if searching premises at a reasonable time would frustrate the purpose of the search.[38] The OFT has indicated that officers do not intend to wait for legal advisers to arrive before beginning a search. However, if documents or other material are to be removed

[36] See above n 22 para 4.2.
[37] An application to a High Court judge will rule out the opportunity to seek judicial review of a decision to grant a warrant.
[38] PACE code B, para 6.2.

under 'seize and sift' powers officers may be prepared to wait a reasonable time for lawyers to arrive.[39] Officers entering premises under a warrant should carry evidence of identity and the warrant, which specifies the subject matter and the purpose of the investigation must be produced. The occupier will, wherever possible, be given a copy of the warrant and a copy of the notice that summarises the extent of the powers being used and explains the rights of the occupier.[40] Before entering premises an attempt should be made to communicate with the occupier and obtain their consent to enter unless the premises are unoccupied or there are reasonable grounds for believing that this would frustrate the object of the search or endanger officers or other people.[41] If the occupier is not present, a copy of the warrant endorsed with the time and date of the search must be left in a prominent place.[42] If force has been needed to gain entry, the premises must be left secure.[43] Documents can be retained and any necessary steps taken to preserve or prevent interference with them. During the search, questions can be asked as to where missing documents might be found.[44] In appropriate circumstances, people not employed by the OFT but who have specific skills can attend on-site investigations.[45] Thus for example, IT experts can be authorised to assist OFT officers retrieve information from a computer database. Provided relevant information is accessible from a computer found on premises named in the warrant, it can be downloaded, printed and retained.

Seize and sift powers

Section 194 amends Part 1 of Schedule 1 of the Criminal Justice and Police Act 2001 (CJPA), which has the effect of incorporating into the Act the 'seize and sift' powers introduced by s 50 of the CJPA 2001.[46] Thus, if it is not practicable to examine documents on the premises to determine whether they can be retained, they can be removed and examined elsewhere. This power will permit the OFT to remove original documents and other material in order to examine them properly. Further, the OFT can retain other material which is 'inextricably linked' to documents which they do have grounds to remove. This is described in Code B, Note 7H as

> . . . material it is not reasonably practicable to separate from other linked material without prejudicing the use of that other material in any investigation or proceedings. For example, it may not be possible to separate items of data held on computer disc without

[39] See above n 22 para 3.15.
[40] PACE Code B paras 6.7 and 6.8.
[41] Code B para 6.4.
[42] Code B para 6.8.
[43] Code B para 6.13.
[44] EA 02 s 194(2)
[45] *Ibid* s 195.
[46] *Ibid* s 194(5). It should be noted that the OFT's civil powers of seizure under s 28(2) CA 98 are set out in Part 1 of schedule 1 of the CJPA 2001.

damaging their evidential integrity. Inextricably linked material must not be examined, imaged, copied or used for any purpose other than for proving the source and/or integrity of the linked material.

Thus, where there is a reasonable suspicion that electronically stored data is relevant to an investigation, the computer on which the information is stored can be seized. In order to provide some procedural safeguards, there is a requirement to provide a written notice[47] and a duty to return legally privileged material.[48] Further, PACE code B sets out specific procedures for the exercise of the seize and sift powers. Code B, para 7.7 states that

> Officers must be careful they only exercise these powers when it is essential and they do not remove any more material than necessary. The removal of large volumes of material, much of which may not ultimately be retainable, may have serious implications for the owners, particularly when they are involved in business or activities such as journalism or the provision of medical services. Officers must carefully consider if removing copies or images of relevant material or data would be a satisfactory alternative to removing originals.

Confiscated material that is subsequently found to be not sufficiently relevant to the investigation should be returned as soon as is reasonably practical.[49] Where possible, persons from whom the material is seized or their representative should be present during the sifting process.[50] Material retained under these powers must be kept separate from material seized under any other power.[51] While relevant material can be retained for use as evidence at trial or 'to facilitate the use in any investigation or proceedings of anything to which it is inextricably linked',[52] if it becomes apparent that legally privileged, excluded or special procedure material has been seized which cannot be retained, it must be returned as soon as is reasonably practicable without waiting for other material to be sifted.[53] In deciding whether to exercise the search and sift procedure several factors must be taken into account including

> . . . the length of time and the number of persons required to carry out the determination or separation on the premises; whether the determination or separation would (or would if carried out on the premises) involve damage to property; the need for any special apparatus or equipment to carry out the determination or separation; and whether the separation (either in itself or if carried out on the premises by the only practicable means) would be likely to prejudice the use of some or all of the material to be taken.[54]

[47] CJPA 2001 s 52.
[48] *Ibid* s 55.
[49] Code B para 7.8.
[50] Code B para 7.8.
[51] Code B, para 7.8. This may involve placing material in sealed bags or containers, a process known as 'bagging up'.
[52] Code B, para 7.14(ii).
[53] Code B, para 7.9B.
[54] CJPA s, 50(3).

Although the seize and sift procedure is subject to safeguards against abuse,[55] it can be anticipated that incorporating this power into the Act will give rise to issues relating to article 8 of the European Convention on Human Rights.

Seizure of real evidence[56]

Under its criminal powers of investigation, the OFT can seize and retain original documents. Copies should be provided as soon as is reasonably practicable. The requirement that confiscated property should be returned as soon as possible applies to copies, images or other material created because of seizure of original material.[57] However, where necessary evidence seized during a search may be retained for use at trial. This accords with the usual practice in criminal investigations. The procedures used in respect to the handling, storage and management of documents and other material, which may become exhibits at trial, must conform to the standards of a criminal investigation. Documents seized in civil investigations under the CA 98 may be admissible in subsequent criminal prosecutions under the EA 02. Accordingly, the OFT has indicated that it intends to adopt the criminal standard in respect to the storage and management of material seized under the CA 98.[58] Further, the OFT may use its criminal powers provided by the EA 02 to obtain original versions of documents obtained under its civil powers. Any documents or other material covered by legal professional privilege that has been taken in error must be returned immediately.

Legally privileged material and confidential banking information

Confidentiality between a lawyer and his or her client is considered to be one of the basic requirements of the right to a fair trial.[59] Provisions in the EA 02 which permit the OFT to obtain access to documents and other material do not extend to communications between legal advisors and their clients. Section 196 provides that

> A person may not under section 193 or 194 be required to disclose any information or produce any document which he would be entitled to refuse to disclose or produce on grounds of legal professional privilege in proceedings in the High Court, except that a lawyer may be required to provide the name and address of his client.

[55] See Home Office Circular 19/2003 issued 1 April 2003.

[56] Real evidence is 'evidence possessing physical characteristics which speak for themselves in an objective fashion'. Dawson J in *Cleland v R* (1982) 151 CLR 1. Thus real evidence will include documents and other material found during the search of premises.

[57] PACE Code B, Note 7E.

[58] See above n 22 para 4.9.

[59] *S v Switzerland* (1992) 14 EHRR 202.

However, this protection does not apply to documents or communications made in the furtherance of a crime on the ground that these communications form an exception to the general rule relating to legal professional privilege. Hence, communications between a legal advisor and a client that assist the client to implement a cartel agreement will not be protected regardless of whether the lawyer was acting knowingly or unwittingly. In accordance with the usual evidentiary rules, the privilege is the privilege of the client and can only be waived by the client. On occasion, the client may choose to disclose privileged documents in order to benefit from the OFT's leniency programme. The Act also provides the same safeguards for confidential banking communications as provided by s2(10) of the CJA 1987. Thus s 196(2) provides that a person may not be required to disclose information or produce documents if

> . . . he owes an obligation of confidence by virtue of carrying on any banking business unless—
> (a) the person to whom the obligation of confidence is owed consents to the disclosure or production; or
> (b) the OFT has authorised the making of the requirement.

Documents subject to legal professional privilege may be removed under the 'seize and sift' powers contained in s 50 of the CJPA 2001 and examined elsewhere. As soon as it becomes apparent that legally privileged documents have been seized, they must be returned as soon as is reasonably practicable.[60] An application for their return can be made to the 'appropriate judicial authority' under s 59 of the CJPA 2001. Although the person from whom they were taken will usually make the application, anyone who can establish a sufficient interest in them can apply for their return.

Access to legal advice

A person required to attend a compulsory interview must be informed of their right to legal advice. Similarly, anyone suspected of involvement in a criminal cartel offence must be cautioned and informed that they may seek legal advice before being interviewed.[61] By contrast, there is no obligation to provide access to legal advise before beginning a search of premises where delay could hinder the search and seizure of real evidence. Para 3.15 of the OFT Guidance Note, *Powers for investigating criminal cartels* says

> When executing a warrant obtained under the Enterprise Act in respect of a suspected criminal offence the OFT officers will not wait for an individual's legal advisers to arrive before commencing the search. However, a friend, neighbour or other person will be allowed to witness the search unless the named officer in charge of the search has reasonable grounds for believing that the presence of the person would seriously hinder the

60 PACE code B, para 7.9B.
61 The standard criminal caution is set out in PACE code C para 10.5.

> investigation or endanger officers or other people. During the course of a search under a warrant, the OFT officers may be prepared to wait a reasonable amount of time for an undertaking's or an individual's legal advisers to arrive if it is the OFT's intention to remove material from the premises where it is not reasonably practicable to examine it properly on the premises, although the rest of the search will proceed without delay.

While formal interviews will generally wait until after the OFT has finished searching premises, it is anticipated that during a search people may volunteer information. Although under no obligation to answer questions, people offering information must be cautioned and advised of their right to legal advice. The guidance note indicates that, in accordance with PACE code B 6.12, no caution is considered necessary if persons are asked questions relating solely 'for the purpose of furthering the proper and effective conduct of a search'. These questions could be requests to provide computer passwords or the combination to a safe.[62]

Surveillance powers

In the Penrose Report (see Chapter 1, above) it had been suggested that the OFT be added to the list of organisations referred to in Schedule 1, part 1 of Regulation of Investigatory Powers Act 2000 (RIPA 2000) which would enable OFT investigators to undertake directed surveillance, and to use covert human intelligence sources. It was also recommended that the OFT should be designated under s 25(1)(g) of RIPA 2000 such that communications data could be obtained and in appropriate circumstances disclosed.[63] Section 199 and Schedule 26 of the Act amends the RIPA 2000 and adds the OFT to the list of agencies who can apply for authorisation to conduct intrusive surveillance operations in the UK. Section 200 amends Part III of the Police Act 1997 to provide the OFT with the authority to interfere with private property in order to gain access to premises to install surveillance devices. Before the OFT can deploy the use of intrusive surveillance, it must be established that it is necessary to prevent or detect the cartel offence and that the surveillance activity is proportionate to what is to be achieved by it. These powers can only be used for the sole purpose of investigating or preventing cartel activity under the EA 02, and cannot be used in a civil investigation under the CA 98.

The use of intrusive surveillance techniques by law enforcement agencies represents a potential threat to individual privacy and, in a liberal democracy, requires regulation by clear, precise legal rules. The lack of regulation of covert surveillance techniques in the UK has been the subject of academic criticism for many years.[64] Responding to mounting criticism from the European Court of Human Rights,

[62] See above n 22 para 3.16.

[63] See paras 4.18–4.20 of the Penrose Report.

[64] See for example, K Ewing and C Gearty, *Freedom under Thatcher: Civil Liberties in Modern Britain* (Oxford, OUP, 1990), L Lustgarten and I Leigh *In from the Cold: National Security and Parliamentary Democracy* (Oxford, OUP, 1994), A Tomkins, 'Intercepted Evidence: Now you hear me, now you don't' [1994] 57 *Modern Law Review* 941.

the government introduced the RIPA 2000 in an attempt to balance the needs of law enforcement with the right to privacy. This legislation was introduced to regulate the interception of communications and other forms of covert evidence gathering techniques to ensure compliance with the Human Rights Act 1998. It provides some procedural safeguards against abuse including a requirement that all applications for authorisations must be scrutinised and approved by the Surveillance Commissioners. However, despite the European Court of Human Rights expressing a preference for entrusting supervisory control to a judicial body, the RIPA 2000 does not make provision for judicial authorisation of intrusive surveillance operations in the UK.[65]

Under the RIPA 2000, authorisation can be sought for three types of covert surveillance operations. These are defined in s 26 as 'directed surveillance' which are non-intrusive investigations undertaken for the purposes of a specific investigation; 'intrusive surveillance' which is covert surveillance carried out in relation to anything taking place on residential premises[66] or in any private vehicle; and the conduct and use of covert human intelligence sources, which involves the use of informants and undercover agents. Thus, authority may be obtained to monitor the movement of people and vehicles or to place listening devices in private homes, hotel rooms or in office premises. The grounds on which intrusive surveillance will be authorised is that the activity is proportionate to what is to be achieved by it, and that it is necessary for the purpose of preventing or detecting serious crime. An additional factor to be taken into account is whether the information could reasonable be obtained by other means. Under s 32 of the RIPA 2000, the power to authorise intrusive surveillance lies with the Secretary of State and listed senior authorising officers. Except in urgent cases, authorisations to conduct intrusive surveillance will not take effect until approved by a Surveillance Commissioner and a written notice of the Commissioner's decision is given to the person who granted the authorisation.[67] Applications for authorisations are regulated by a code of practice. Where surveillance is likely to result in any person acquiring knowledge of matters covered by legal professional privilege, confidential personal information, or confidential journalistic material, authorisation must be obtained from a Surveillance Commissioner, who must be a serving or former High Court judge. Evidence obtained by the use of these surveillance practices is admissible in criminal proceedings subject to the normal rules of evidence.

Intrusive surveillance activities under the EA 02 will generally involve placing either a person or a device inside residential premises or in a private vehicle to hear or observe activities. In the *Explanatory notes* to the Act it is envisaged that following information obtained from an informant 'the OFT could, for example, use

[65] See *Klass v Federal Republic of Germany* (1978) 2 EHRR 214; *Huvig v France* (1990) 12 EHRR 528; *Kopp v Switzerland* (1998) 27 EHRR 91.

[66] 'Residential' is defined in s 48(1) of the RIPA 2000 as premises used as living accommodation. 'Premises' will include moveable structures.

[67] RIPA 2000 s 36.

these powers to record a meeting of cartelists in a hotel room.'[68] Authorisation to conduct intrusive surveillance operations during a criminal investigation into cartel activity will normally be granted by the Chairman of the OFT, and will require prior approval by the Surveillance Commissioner before the operation commences. Authorisation will be granted only where the intrusive surveillance operation is considered to be necessary to prevent or detect an offence under s 188 of the Act, and any measures taken must be in proportion to what is to be achieved. While it is clearly the intention of the cartel offence that all the categories of hard-core cartels set out in the legislation are to be condemned with equal weight, it might in practice be possible to draw some distinction between price and market allocation cartels with industry wide coverage in vital sectors, and smaller, less effective cartels in less important areas. The possibility remains that some distinction may be drawn from case to case as to the powers to be used. In cases of urgency, authorisation may be obtained from either the Chairman or a designated officer who will give notice to the Surveillance Commissioners as soon as is reasonably practical, explaining the reasons for using the urgency procedure. The OFT's guidance note sets out the procedure to be followed in urgent cases

> . . . if prior approval from a Surveillance Commissioner cannot be sought and granted in time, the Chairman of the OFT (or a designated officer of the OFT) will authorise the deployment of intrusive surveillance and give notice to a Surveillance Commissioner as soon as is reasonably practicable, explaining why it was necessary to use the urgency provisions. If the Surveillance Commissioner is at any time satisfied that there were no reasonable grounds for believing the case was urgent, he may quash the authorisation and surveillance must cease immediately.[69]

Thus the surveillance operation must cease immediately if it appears that there are no reasonable grounds for believing the operation was urgent. This procedure is in line with the existing procedural safeguards in the RIPA 2000. The OFT anticipates that the urgency procedure will only be used in exceptional circumstances.

Installing surveillance equipment on private property may amount to trespass. However, for the purpose of covert surveillance operations under the Act, interference with property by an officer of the OFT is authorised under s 200 which amends ss 93–94 of the Police Act 1997. This legislation, which provides a statutory basis for the authorisation of police surveillance operations involving interference with property has been amended to authorise officers of the OFT to install surveillance equipment. However, in the *Explanatory notes* to the Act it states that when authorisation for the planting of surveillance devises is granted

> . . . the OFT intends to outsource the technical deployment of the intrusive surveillance activity to other public authorities which already have access to these powers and practical experience of exercising them.[70]

[68] Explanatory note, para 430.
[69] See above n 22 para 5.3.
[70] Explanatory note para 431.

In addition to the powers provided by the Act in respect of cartel investigations, the OFT applied to the Home Office for an order to grant authorised officers access to other surveillance methods provided by ss 28 and 29 of RIPA 2000.[71] Consequently, the OFT can now authorise the use of directed surveillance and covert human intelligence sources in both civil and criminal cartel investigations. This provides for the monitoring of people and vehicles and the use of informants. Further, the OFT is authorised for the purposes of a criminal investigation, to obtain access to communications data, which involves obtaining details of postal and telephone records.[72] Codes of practice relating to the procedures for conducting intrusive surveillance operations will be issued in due course.

Parallel investigations

The OFT has indicated that when conducting its initial enquiry into cartel activity it intends to use its criminal powers under the EA 02 rather than rely on the civil powers provided by the CA 98. Acknowledging the problem, the OFT accepts that frequently it will

> . . . not be in a position to know whether to investigate using its formal powers under the Enterprise Act or the CA 98. In making its enquiries however, the possibility that the criminal cartel offence may have been committed will be borne in mind by the OFT. This means that, where appropriate, OFT officers will act in accordance with PACE, all the relevant Codes of Practice and the Criminal Procedure and Investigations Act 1996, or in Scotland, the applicable Scottish criminal law and procedure.[73]

This approach will have the benefit of reducing the potential for challenges to the admissibility of evidence in any subsequent criminal or civil proceedings. It also indicates that the 'reasonable grounds' and 'good reason' requirements provided by s 192 of the Act are likely to be interpreted liberally.

Documents seized during a search under the OFT's criminal powers, and documents obtained by the SFO under the CJA 1987 can be used during civil proceedings under the CA 98.[74] Documents obtained under the CA 98 will be admissible in a criminal prosecution under the EA 02.[75] Statements obtained under compulsory powers provided by the CA 98 will only be used in a criminal prosecution in limited circumstances.[76] Voluntary statements made in a civil investigation must be obtained under caution before they can be used in evidence.[77] While the possibility of instituting civil proceedings against undertakings will be borne in mind during the criminal investigation, at any stage the decision

71 SI/2003/3171.
72 SI/2003/3172.
73 OFT Guidance Note, *Powers for investigating criminal cartels*, para 4.1.
74 *Ibid*, para 4.4 and 4.5.
75 *Ibid*, para 4.9.
76 *Ibid*, para 4.8.
77 *Ibid*, para 4.8.

can be taken to abandon the criminal action and proceed only with the CA 98 investigation. The individuals under investigation will be informed of the decision.[78] If during a civil investigation under the CA 98 information comes to light which gives reasonable grounds for suspecting that a cartel offence has been committed

> . . . the OFT will consult with the SFO as to the merits of commencing a criminal investigation. In certain cases, the OFT will progress an investigation using its CA 98 powers (which may or may not have commenced prior to any SFO involvement), while an SFO led criminal investigation is being progressed. Suitable procedures will be adopted to ensure that the two investigation teams maintain an on-going dialogue and to ensure that the CA 98 investigation does not prejudice the parallel criminal investigation.[79]

The OFT has stated that it will 'co-operate to co-ordinate the progress' of investigations in European Commission cartel investigations which could involve the commission of a s188 offence.[80]

THE RIGHTS OF THE DEFENCE

The Act introduces safeguards to protect confidentiality and to prevent undue interference with privacy rights. It also provides safeguards in respect of legally privileged communications and restricts the use of information obtained under compulsory powers. In addition to the specific safeguards contained within the Act, there exist a range of procedural mechanisms within the criminal justice system that are designed to safeguard the rights of suspects and defendants. These procedures provide protection from unlawful and unfair treatment during the investigation process and guarantee the right to a fair trial. Fair trial guarantees derived from article 6 of the European Convention on Human Rights include the right to remain silent and the privilege against self-incrimination, rights closely linked to the presumption of innocence, which should not be restricted without significant justification. Legislative provisions found to effectively 'extinguish the very essence' of these rights will be contrary to the European Convention on Human Rights.[81]

[78] *Ibid*, para 4.6.

[79] *Ibid*, para 4.6.

[80] *Ibid*, para 4.10.

[81] The Human Rights Act 1998 requires courts in the United Kingdom to take account of decisions of the European Court of Human Rights when determining a question arising in connection with a Convention right. Furthermore, domestic legislation must now be read and given effect in a way which is compatible with Convention rights.

The privilege against self-incrimination

Two questions arise here for consideration with respect to the EA 02. First, would using compelled statements obtained under the powers provided by s 193 and s 194 as evidence in a criminal prosecution of the interviewee constitute a violation of article 6? Secondly, would a prosecution under s 201 for failure to provide information in a compulsory interview breach article 6? In order to avoid self-incrimination problems, restrictions have been placed on the use of statements obtained by the OFT using its compulsory powers provided by the Act. While statements obtained under compulsion may be used in evidence against others, they cannot be tendered as evidence against the maker in a prosecution for the cartel offence. These statements also cannot be used against an individual's employer in an investigation under the CA 98. Statements obtained under compulsory powers provided by the CA 98 cannot be used in evidence in a criminal prosecution unless the defendant makes reference to them, or tenders evidence which is inconsistent with the statement. Although these provisions appear to be Convention compliant, Strasbourg jurisprudence is less than clear on this matter.

Using compelled statements as evidence

In *Saunders* v *UK*,[82] the Court held that regardless of whether transcripts obtained by the SFO under compulsory powers were directly self-incriminating, the fact that the authorities made use of them in subsequent criminal proceedings was a violation of article 6. The public interest in the prosecution of complex and serious cases was insufficient to justify the admission of the evidence.[83] The privilege against self-incrimination

> presupposes that the prosecution in a criminal case seek to prove their case against the accused without resort to evidence obtained through methods of coercion or oppression in defiance of the will of the accused.[84]

As a consequence of the *Saunders* decision, legislation was introduced in the UK that restricted the use of compelled statements in criminal proceedings.[85] Similarly, in order to provide some safeguard against a breach of the privilege against self-incrimination, provisions of the EA 02 limit the use of statements

[82] (1996) 23 EHRR 313.
[83] (1996) 23 EHRR 313, para 74.
[84] *Ibid*, para 68.
[85] The Youth Justice and Criminal Evidence Act 1999, through s 59 and Schedule 3, makes amendments to the following legislation: Insurance Companies Act 1982; Companies Act 1985; Insolvency Act 1986; Company Directors Disqualification Act 1986; Building Societies Act 1986; Financial Services Act 1986; Companies (Northern Ireland) Order 1986; Banking Act 1987; Criminal Justice Act 1987; Companies Act 1989; Companies (Northern Ireland) Order 1989; Insolvency (Northern Ireland) Order 1989; Friendly Societies Act 1992; Criminal Law (Consolidation) (Scotland) Act 1995; Proceeds of Crime (Northern Ireland) Order 1996.

obtained under the OFT's compulsory powers of investigation. Section 197 provides

(1) A statement by a person in response to a requirement imposed by virtue of section 193 or 194 may only be used in evidence against him—
  (a) on a prosecution for an offence under section 201(2); or
  (b) on a prosecution for some other offence where in giving evidence he makes a statement inconsistent with it.

(2) However, the statement may not be used against that person by virtue of paragraph (b) of subsection (1) unless evidence relating to it is asked, by or on behalf of that person in the proceedings arising out of the prosecution.

Accordingly, statements made in compulsory interview can only be tendered as evidence in criminal proceedings against the maker in two situations.[86] Firstly in a prosecution under s 201(2), which provides that it is an offence to knowingly or recklessly makes a false or misleading statement in compulsory interview. Secondly, where a person is prosecuted for another offence and gives evidence that is inconsistent with a statement made in compulsory interview. Similar restrictions will apply to the use in evidence of answers provided in response to questioning under s 28 of the Criminal Law (Consolidation)(Scotland) Act 1995, which provides powers in respect to the investigation of serious fraud.[87] The Act introduces similar restrictions as to the use that can be made of statements obtained from an individual or on behalf of an undertaking under ss 26–28 of the CA 98 as part of a civil investigation. Thus s 198 amends CA 98 to provide some protection against self-incrimination in respect to statements obtained under compulsion. These statements may not be used in evidence against the maker in a prosecution for cartel activity unless, he or she gives evidence in the proceedings which is inconsistent with this statement and evidence relating to the statement is adduced or questions asked relating to it by the maker or on his or her behalf.[88]

Some doubt remains in Convention jurisprudence as to whether the privilege against self-incrimination applies to documentary evidence.[89] While in *Funke* this right attached to bank documents and chequebooks in the applicant's possession, in *Saunders* a distinction was drawn between compelled statements and real evidence.[90] The Court considered that the right against self-incrimination did not to apply to material having

[86] Answers to questions required by the SFO under s 2 of the CJA 1987 may only be used in evidence in criminal proceedings under the same circumstances set out here. See OFT Guidance Note January 2004, para 6.5.

[87] See OFT Guidance Note, January 2004, para 6.5. For further discussion see CHW Gane and CN Stoddart *Criminal Procedure in Scotland: Cases and Materials*, (Edinburgh, W Green, Sweet and Maxwell, 1994).

[88] Section 30A CA 98.

[89] The term 'documents' in ss 192–201 of the EA 02 includes electronically stored data.

[90] In *Funke v France* (1993) 16 EHRR 297 the European Court of Human Rights held that attempts by French customs authorities to compel the applicant to produce bank statements violated article 6. See generally A S Butler, '*Funke v France* and the Right against Self-Incrimination: A Critical Analysis' (2000) 11 *Criminal Law Forum* 461.

> an existence independent of the will of the suspect such as, inter alia, documents acquired pursuant to a warrant, breath, blood and urine samples and bodily tissue for the purpose of DNA testing.[91]

Preferring *Funke* to *Saunders* on this point, the Court in *JB* v *Switzerland*[92] found that a prosecution for failing to produce possibly incriminatory documents breached article 6(1). Where the penalty for failing to provide a statement was 'essentially punitive and deterrent in nature,[93] it was immaterial that the provision was contained within non-criminal legislation. The quality of the Court's reasoning in this case has been subjected to some criticism.[94] The Court of Appeal has been prepared to draw a distinction between compelled statements on the one hand, and the production of a pre-existing document or real evidence on the other. In *R v Hundal*[95] for example, the court was satisfied that the use as evidence of documents obtained under compulsory search powers under Schedule 7 of the Terrorism Act 2000 did not contravene article 6. Thus while it would be objectionable to use evidence which the accused was forced to create by the use of compulsory powers, using compulsory powers to oblige the defendant to deliver up evidence which was already in existence and had an existence independent of the will of the accused would not be contrary to the fair trial guarantees provided by article 6.[96]

Prosecution for a failure to comply with a request under s 193 or s 194

Failure to comply with requests for information in compulsory interview conducted under s 193 or s 194 without a reasonable excuse will result in a criminal prosecution under s 201. Although prosecutions for failure to provide information in criminal investigations clearly have the potential to engage article 6, there is authority to suggest that the demand for information made in the course of an extra-judicial procedure where there is no suggestion that compelled statements would be used in subsequent criminal proceedings will not violate article 6. In *IJL* v *UK*[97] the Strasbourg court was prepared to draw a distinction between criminal investigations and administrative inquiries and found that a requirement for an individual to give information demanded by an administrative body would not, of itself, infringe article 6. In this case the nature and purpose of investigations conducted by DTI inspectors suggested that

> the functions performed by the inspectors appointed under section 432(2) of the Companies Act 1985 were essentially investigative in nature and that they did not

[91] (1996) 23 EHRR 313, para 69.
[92] Application no 31827/96, 3 May 2001.
[93] *Ibid*, para 48.
[94] A Ashworth, 'The Self-Incrimination Saga', *Archbold News*, 27 June 2001, 5; IH Dennis, *The Law of Evidence* 2nd edn, Sweet and Maxwell (2002) p 141.
[95] 2004 All ER (D) 35 Feb
[96] *A-G's Reference (No 7 of 2000)* [2001] EWCA Crim 888; [2001] 2 Cr App R 286.
[97] (2000) 33 EHRR 225.

> adjudicate either in form or in substance. Their purpose was to ascertain and record facts which might subsequently be used as the basis for action by other competent authorities—prosecuting, regulatory, disciplinary or even legislative. . . . a requirement that such a preparatory investigation should be subject to the guarantees of a judicial procedure as set forth in article 6(1) would in practice unduly hamper the effective regulation in the public interest of complex financial and commercial activities.[98]

Similarly, in *R* v *Hertfordshire County Council, ex p Green Industries Ltd*,[99] the House of Lords found that using compulsory powers to take statements in the course of an administrative investigation is not in conflict with article 6. This case concerned s 71(2) of the Environmental Protection Act 1990, which impliedly excluded self-incrimination as a reasonable excuse for refusing to answer questions. While noting obscurities in the Strasbourg court's reasoning in *Funke*,[100] Lord Hoffmann was satisfied that the *Saunders* judgment was clear on the issue of the use of compulsory powers in preparatory investigations:

> . . . European jurisprudence under article 6(1) is firmly anchored to the fairness of the trial and is not concerned with extrajudicial inquiries. Such impact as article 6(1) may have is upon the use of such evidence at a criminal trial. Although it is true that the council unlike the DTI inspectors, had power to prosecute in criminal proceedings, I do not think that the request for information under section 71(2) could be described as an adjudication, 'either in form or in substance.' The Saunders case is therefore no authority for allowing the appellants to refuse to answer.[101]

The Court of Appeal in *R* v *Kearns*[102] found that the demand for information by the Official Receiver under section 354(3)(a) of the Insolvency Act 1986 was a proportionate legislative response to the problem of administering and investigating bankrupt estates:

> The relevant part of the Insolvency Act 1986 is designed to deal with the social and economic problem of bankrupts. It is in the public interest that the affairs of bankrupts should be investigated, that the assets are traced and got in, and that the assets are then distributed to creditors. . . . The bankrupt is frequently the only person who can provide the necessary information about the bankrupt estate. There is, in our view, an obvious need for a statutory regime that imposes a duty on a bankrupt to co-operate in providing full and accurate information . . . Equally clearly that duty should be backed up by appropriate statutory sanctions to ensure that the duty is carried out properly.[103]

[98] *Ibid*, para 100 (italics added).

[99] [2000] 2 WLR 373. See generally H Davies and B Hopkins, 'Environmental Crime and the Privilege against Self-Incrimination' (2000) 4 *International Journal of Evidence and Proof* 177; J Fisher and E Schulster, 'Finding the Right Balance' (2000) 150 *New Law Journal* 988; M Scanlan and R Monnick, 'Investigatory Powers and the Right to a Fair Trial' (2000) 144 *Solicitors Journal* 652; M Stallworthy, 'The Regulation and Investigation of Commercial Activities in the United Kingdom and the Privilege against Self-Incrimination' [2000] *International Company and Commercial Law Review* 167.

[100] [2000] 2 WLR 373, 382.

[101] Ibid, 381–2.

[102] [2002] EWCA Crim 748; [2002] 1 WLR 2815. See generally A Henderson, 'Defining the Limits of Silence (2)' (2002) 146 *Solicitors Journal* 508.

[103] [2002] EWCA Crim 748; [2002] 1 WLR 2815, para 55.

The statutory regime created by s 201(1) of the Act, which imposes a similar duty on individuals to provide information is likely in the current climate to be found Convention compliant.

Disclosure of confidential information

To protect confidentiality the Act imposes some general restrictions and conditions for the disclosure of specified information obtained by the OFT during its investigation into criminal cartels.[104] Failure to comply with these restrictions, or the improper use of information disclosed under these provisions will amount to an offence.[105] If this information relates to the affairs of an individual or any business of an undertaking, it must not be disclosed during the lifetime of that individual or while any undertaking is in existence. However, disclosure is permitted if the information is already legitimately in the public domain,[106] if there are other powers or duties to disclose which exist apart from the Act,[107] if consent to disclose is obtained from the relevant parties[108] and if disclosure is required for the purposes of a Community obligation.[109] Provided disclosure is considered proportionate, and provided information is used only for the purpose for which it is disclosed, a public authority can disclose information in connection with a criminal investigation or prosecution in the United Kingdom, or to assist in the decision whether to begin or end a prosecution.

In appropriate circumstances, the OFT can also disclose information to an overseas public authority for the purpose of facilitating a criminal investigation.[110] However, the Secretary of State can intervene and prohibit disclosure if it appears more appropriate that the investigation for which the information was requested should be conducted either in the UK or in another country. The OFT has indicated that requests for disclosure which raise issues of extraterritoriality will be forwarded to the Secretary of State.[111]

[104] EA 02, s 237.

[105] EA 02, s 245.

[106] Section 237(3).

[107] Section 237(6). For example, from May 2004 article 12 of Regulation 1/2003 on the implementation of the rules on competition laid down in article 81 and 82 will provide the Commission and the designated national competition authorities the power to exchange information to apply articles 81 and 82. Thus there will be no need for the authorities to rely on section 243 of the Act.

[108] Section 239.

[109] Section 240.

[110] The EA 02 s 234.

[111] Consultation paper on Part 9 of the Act—*The overseas disclosure of information*, para 3.5, fn 9. For further discussion of disclosure of information see chapter 6.

The right to privacy

Intrusive surveillance operations are likely to amount to an invasion of privacy and will not be Convention compliant unless adequate safeguards are in place to ensure protection against misuse.[112] Problems which have arisen from the lack of a statutory scheme to ensure surveillance operations were in 'accordance with the law', as required by article 8, have largely been addressed by the Police Act 1997 and the RIPA 2000.[113] Whether the scheme for granting authorisations to the OFT to engage in a wide range of covert surveillance activities is entirely Convention compliant remains to be seen. However, Convention jurisprudence indicates that information obtained in breach of privacy rights may still be adduced as evidence without necessarily infringing fair trial rights.[114] Similar privacy considerations will arise in respect of the disclosure of information.

[112] *Klass v FRG* (1978) 2 EHRR 214.
[113] See for example *Murray v United Kingdom* (1994) 19 EHRR 193.
[114] *Khan v United Kingdom* (2001) 31 EHRR 45.

4

Leniency

INTRODUCTION

ONE OF THE central tenets underlying the new robust approach to cartels is that the threat of serious consequences for participation is to be balanced by leniency in favour of those who come forward to provide details of cartel activity from within the cartel. It was recognised in the Penrose Report that the leniency policy operated under the CA 98 was widely publicised, and that 'the interests of customers and consumers in ensuring that such practices are detected . . . outweigh the interests in imposing financial penalties on those undertakings which co-operate'.[1] In this respect 'whistle-blowing' is to be distinguished from complaints made by those outside the cartel. The EC Commission adopts a similar approach, recognising in its leniency notice that

> 'certain undertakings involved in this type of illegal activity are willing to put an end to their participation, and inform it of the existence of such agreements, but are dissuaded from doing so by the high fines to which they are potentially exposed. . . . it is in the Community interest to grant favourable treatment to undertakings which co-operate with it. The interests of consumers and citizens in ensuring that secret cartels are detected and punished outweigh the interest in fining those undertakings that enable the Commission to detect and prohibit such practices'.[2]

Some concern has been expressed that the EC leniency programme may be undermined if immunity granted by the EC Commission did not protect those who might face criminal prosecution in one or more of the member states.[3] The issues relating to the interaction of the EC programme with the UK offence are dealt with below.

The leniency programme operated by the DOJ (discussed in chapter 1) has been widely viewed as a success, and this perception led to changes in the EC leniency programme, and influenced the programme adopted by the OFT to apply in relation to the CA 98 (both of these programmes are discussed below). However, the White Paper recognised some of the limitations involved in simply copying over the approach taken in the US. In the latter regime the prosecuting authority has

[1] Penrose Report, para 5.1. Almost identical language is used in the OFT's guidance *The Cartel Offence: Guidance on the issue of no-action letters for individuals* at para 3.1.

[2] Commission notice on immunity from fines and reduction of fines in cartel cases (2002) OJ C45/3, [2002] 4 CMLR 26, paras 3–4.

[3] See J Arp and C Swaak, 'Immunity from Fines for Cartel Conduct Under the European Commission's New Leniency Notice, *Antitrust*, Summer 2002, pp 59–66.

the power to 'plea-bargain' with informants in a selective and case-sensitive manner. It was noted in the White Paper, at para 7.50, that 'the UK does not have a formal mechanism akin to plea-bargaining'.

One of the concerns expressed vociferously by those concerned about the introduction of the cartel offence was that the threat of criminal penalties would in fact undermine the approach to leniency. The Penrose Report identified the features that an effective leniency policy would need (but did not make recommendations as to the details of that policy):

> 5.9 The difficulty faced by the OFT is how to provide sufficient comfort against criminal prosecution and the imposition of custodial sentences for potential whistleblowers who inform on other cartel participants. In particular, the OFT would need a policy which would:
> —provide sufficient 'certainty' to whistleblowers that they would not personally face criminal prosecution, and
> —be consistent with the existing leniency policies operated under civil procedures in both the UK and the EC in respect of undertakings whilst
> —maintaining the integrity of the SFO as the prosecuting authority and the criminal justice system in the UK as a whole.

In Committee the Under Secretary of State explained that:

> It is most important to have a transparent leniency programme, which is an essential element in successfully cracking and prosecuting cartels. . . . Informants often provide vital evidence, which can be used in prosecution and punishment of a ringleader and others. Leniency is cost-effective; it provides for prosecution without a long and expensive investigation. The US experience shows a good combination of the stick of criminal sanctions and the carrot of leniency which can be used together to defeat cartels.
>
> The OFT no-action letters are subject to a set of conditions; for example, not being a ringleader, admitting guilt, co-operating fully and so forth. They certainly do not give carte blanche to those who are guilty to get away with it. If the conditions of the letter are broken—for example, if the holder of the letter turns out to have been a ringleader—it will be void and prosecution may follow.[4]

As this suggests, there is a strong link between the civil leniency programme, and the leniency programme operated in relation to the cartel offence. Express provision is made in the Act for the leniency programme at s 190(4) which is as follows:

> Where, for the purpose of the investigation or prosecution of offences under section 188, the OFT gives a person written notice under this subsection, no proceedings for an offence under section 188 that falls within a description specified in the notice may be brought against that person in England and Wales or Northern Ireland except in the circumstances specified in the notice.

The OFT has issued guidance, *The Cartel Offence: Guidance on the issue of no-action letters for individuals* which sets out the terms of its approach to leniency. At the outset it should be noted that the position of no-action letters is a little dif-

[4] Standing Committee B, col 173.

ferent in Scotland than is the case in the remainder of the UK. The OFT cannot bind the Lord Advocate, whose prosecutorial discretion is absolute. However, it was pointed out in Committee that a similar procedure under which Customs and Excise employs a leniency programme has given rise to no substantial problems, and that concerns will be allayed by the good working relationship between the OFT, the SFO and the Scottish authorities.

Because the cartel offence requires 'dishonesty' on the part of any person committing a breach, it is not the case that all employees of an undertaking participating in a cartel would be subject to potential prosecution and therefore would need to seek the benefit of a no-action letter (see below).[5] Clearly an employee or director who was neither involved in the cartel, nor knew of its existence, would be incapable of committing a cartel offence. Those who either knew of, or participated in, any cartel might be capable of being found by a jury to have acted dishonestly, and might thus seek to benefit from the leniency programme.

NO–ACTION LETTERS

The grant of no-action letters

The leniency programme operated in relation to the cartel offence finds its expression in the instrument of 'no-action letters'. These are explained in the following terms in the relevant guidance:

> In the context of the cartel offence, immunity from prosecution will be granted in the form of a 'no-action letter', issued by the OFT under section 190(4) of the Enterprise Act. A no-action letter will prevent a prosecution being brought against an individual in England and Wales or Northern Ireland for the cartel offence except in circumstances specified in the letter. Whilst guarantees of immunity from prosecution cannot be given in relation to Scotland, cooperation by an individual will be reported to the Lord Advocate who will take such cooperation into account.[6]

There are five main conditions that must be met in order for a no-action letter to be issued by the OFT. These are that the individual must: (1) admit participation in a criminal offence; (2) provide the OFT with all available information regarding the cartel; (3) cooperate completely and continuously throughout the investigation; (4) not have coerced another to participate in the cartel; and (5) cease participation in the cartel, unless instructed to continue by the OFT or other investigating authority. It is thus clear that the OFT contemplates that there may be occasions on which it has an informant operating under supervision inside a cartel, passing back all relevant information to the OFT or SFO. Co-operation during the course of the investigation includes:

[5] The OFT's consultation document, *The Cartel Offence: No-action letters for individuals*, July 2002, drew distinctions between certain categories of persons in an undertaking engaged in a cartel. This material was omitted from the published version of its guidance.

[6] *The Cartel Offence: Guidance on the issue of no-action letters for individuals* at para 3.2.

i) voluntarily and without prompting, providing the OFT with all Information that becomes known to him/her or available to him/her relating to the Reported Offence and the Cartel Agreement, in addition to any such Information already provided
ii) providing promptly, and without the OFT using its powers under any section of the Act, all Information available to him/her wherever located, requested by the OFT in relation to the Reported Offence and the Cartel Agreement, to the extent that it has not already been provided.[7]

While satisfaction of these conditions is necessary for the issuance of a no-action letter, it is not sufficient. Where the OFT already has sufficient information to bring a successful prosecution against the applicant individual, or is in the process of gathering that information, it will not grant a no-action letter.[8] The effect of this policy must be to encourage early applications where an investigation is under way. What is not clear from the guidance is the extent to which the OFT may be prepared to issue multiple no-action letters in the course of a single investigation. It would be unlikely, in the case for example of a two-firm cartel controlled by the undertakings' respective sales directors, that the OFT would be prepared to issue no-action letters in favour of both of those directors. The evidence given by the first to come forward would presumably provide the necessary material to contemplate a successful prosecution against the other, so precluding the latter from the application of such a letter. On the other hand, in the case of a cartel with a larger number of members it might well be the case that evidence provided by more than one firm or individual would be necessary to ensure the successful prosecution of other members. In this case the OFT might be prepared to issue no-action letters in favour of a number of individuals from a number of undertakings.

In order to benefit from a no-action letter the approach must come from the individual, or a lawyer representing that person to the OFT. It appears from the OFT guidance that the OFT will not itself initiate the process. Any such approach made by a lawyer may be made at the first instance on an anonymous basis. Approaches may also be made on behalf of a named individual, or a group of named individuals by an undertaking or by a lawyer representing that undertaking in the course of an investigation into breaches of either the Chapter I Prohibition of the CA 98 or article 81 EC in accordance with the terms of the relevant leniency notices (discussed below).[9] In the latter cases the relevant notices apply to undertakings, but where an undertaking qualifies for full immunity from penalties it is anticipated that named individuals within that undertaking, or ex-employees or directors of that undertaking, will be granted the benefit of a no-action letter.

In the event that any such approach is made the Director of Cartel Investigations[10] will give 'an indication' as to whether the OFT might be prepared

[7] Draft letter attached to OFT guidance.

[8] Para 3.4.

[9] For the CA 98 see the OFT's *Guidance as to the appropriate amount of a Penalty* (OFT 423, [2000] UKCLR 431), and for the EC policy see the Commission notice on immunity from fines and reduction of fines in cartel cases (2002) OJ C45/3, [2002] 4 CMLR 26.

[10] As of January 2004, Simon Williams.

to issue a no-action letter. If the OFT is prepared to issue a no-action letter any individual who hopes to benefit from one will be interviewed (a process which may take several sessions), although information given in these interviews will not subsequently be used against them in criminal proceedings. There are two exceptions to this principal. First, where the OFT decides not to issue a no-action letter and the person being interviewed has 'knowingly or recklessly provided information that is false or misleading in a material particular'.[11] Second, where a no-action letter is issued, but is subsequently revoked (see below). At the end of the interview process three results are possible. The first of these is that in fact the OFT concludes that the applicant is not at risk of criminal prosecution. In this case the OFT will not issue a no-action letter, but will instead confirm in writing its conclusion. While the exact legal status of such a communication is unclear, it will at the least raise a legitimate expectation on behalf of the recipient that no criminal action will follow. There does remain the possibility, however, that the OFT may obtain further information subsequently which might influence it to reassess the position. In such a case it would be reasonable to believe that the OFT would reconsider the application, and would be minded to do so favourably.

The second possible result is that the OFT determines that without a no-action letter there would be a possibility of criminal prosecution, but that the applicant confirms that they will meet the criteria for the grant of a no-action letter the grant will be made. Where the prosecution would be brought in Scotland the cooperation will be reported to the Lord Advocate with a request that an early decision be made as to whether the individual remains liable for prosecution. A third possibility is that the OFT determines that a prosecution is a possibility, and that the individual does not meet, or would not in the future meet, the criteria to be issued a no-action letter. In this case, as we have seen, the interview may not be used against the individual. This would imply that there is little to be lost in making an application. In practice however there may be some concerns that while the OFT may not use the information given at the interview, it may be encouraged to pursue lines of inquiry as a result of the interview that it might otherwise have overlooked.

The revocation of no-action letters

No-action letters may be revoked in two circumstances. The first of these arises where the recipient of the letter ceases to satisfy the conditions for the grant of a letter discussed above. The second arises where the recipient has 'knowingly or recklessly provided information that is false or misleading in a material particular'.[12] If any no-action letter is revoked any immunity conferred by the letter will cease to exist as if it had never been granted. A particular consequence of this is

[11] OFT Guidance, para 3.7.
[12] Para 3.11.

that any information given at the initial interview may be used in the course of any subsequent prosecution. Before revoking a no-action letter the OFT will give the recipient notice of the decision in writing, and will give the recipient a reasonable opportunity to make representations. The OFT may, but is not required to, give the applicant the opportunity to remedy any breach of the compliance conditions within a reasonable time after an explanation as to the breach of the conditions has been given.

LENIENCY UNDER EC LAW AND UNDER THE COMPETITION ACT 1998

As has been seen there is a link between the civil leniency programmes operated in respect of breaches of article 81 EC and the Chapter I Prohibition of the CA 98, and the issue of no-action letters in respect of the cartel offence. It is for this reason that the civil programmes are outlined here.

The programme operating in respect of the CA 98 is set out in Part 2 of the OFT's *Guidance as to the Appropriate Amount of a Penalty.*[13] In respect of the first member of a cartel coming forward with information and satisfying certain requirements the OFT will offer total immunity from financial penalties. Any undertaking which is not the first to come forward, or which does not satisfy all the requirements spelt out in the policy may nevertheless benefit from some reduction in the penalty that would otherwise have been imposed. The first set of conditions, set out in para 9.3.2, are those which apply in the event of an undertaking coming forward *before* an investigation has commenced, and are very similar to those applying to the issue of no-action letters. These are that the undertaking must (a) provide the OFT with all the information and evidence available to it regarding the existence and activities of the cartel; (b) maintain continuous and complete co-operation during the investigation; (c) not have compelled any other undertaking to play a part in the cartel, not to have acted as the instigator in the cartel, nor to have played a lead role in the cartel; and (d) refrain from future participation in the cartel. In the case of condition (b) the full extent of the obligations involved are spelt out in a draft letter for leniency published on the OFT website:[14]

> This will include but is not limited to:
> (i) providing the [OFT] with all the facts known to [ ] and all the information, documents and evidence available to it relating to the reported possible infringement in addition to any such information already provided;
> (ii) providing promptly, and without the [OFT] using [its powers under the Act], all the information, documents, evidence or other items in its possession, custody or control, wherever located within the United Kingdom, requested by the [OFT], to the extent that they have not already been produced;

[13] OFT 423, [2000] UKCLR 431. Note that the *Guidance* is being revised in the light of the modernisation programme.

[14] See also [2000] UKCLR 525.

(iii) using its best efforts to secure the complete and truthful cooperation of its current and former[15] directors, officers and employees and encouraging such persons voluntarily to provide the [OFT] with any information relevant to the purported possible infringement of section 2 of the Act in [ ] industry in the United Kingdom;
(iv) facilitating the ability of current and former directors, officers and employees to appear for such interviews as the [OFT] may reasonably require at the times and places reasonably designated by the [OFT];
(v) using its best efforts to ensure that current and former directors, officers and employees who provide information to the [OFT] to respond completely and truthfully to all questions asked in interviews;
(vi) using its best efforts to ensure that current and former directors, officers and employees who provide information to the [OFT] make no attempt either falsely to protect or falsely to implicate any undertaking in any infringement of the Act.

In the case of an undertaking coming forward *after* the OFT has begun an investigation into a cartel (para 9.3.4) the same criteria must be fulfilled, and the undertaking must be the first to provide the OFT with evidence (ie, there is no other undertaking benefiting from total immunity under para 9.3.2 in relation to that cartel). It is expressly provided in the guideline that the immunity granted under para 9.3.4 is *discretionary*:

> The grant of immunity . . . in these circumstances is, however, discretionary. In order for the [OFT] to exercise [its] discretion to grant immunity to the undertaking [it] must be satisfied that the undertaking should benefit from immunity, taking into account the stage at which the undertaking comes forward and whether or not at that stage the [OFT] has sufficient evidence to make a decision that the Chapter I Prohibition has been infringed.

It would appear from the wording of the guideline that there is no discretion at all in respect of an undertaking coming forward under para 9.3.2, ie that the first undertaking to come forward and to meet the relevant conditions is assured of total immunity.

Where the same undertakings are engaged in cartelisation in respect of different markets it would presumably be possible for different undertakings to claim the benefit of immunity from penalties in respect of the different cartels. For example, were the OFT to conduct an investigation into a cartel in respect of product A, undertaking X might claim immunity under para 9.3.4 by being the first to come forward. In respect of the investigation and procedure into this cartel no other undertaking would be able to claim total immunity, but each might, subject to the usual conditions, be able to claim some reduction of penalty for cooperation with the OFT during the course of the investigation. However, were undertaking Y, implicated in the cartel, to come forward with information in respect of an as yet

[15] While it is the undertaking which is being investigated the relevant authorities have the power under s 26, CA 98 to require 'any person' to provide information. This is not limited to present employees, officers and directors of the undertaking. However, the limits on the ability of an undertaking to require its previous personnel to respond to OFT investigations will presumably be recognised in the implementation of the leniency policy.

undiscovered cartel in respect of product B it would be entitled to full immunity from penalties, and so on. While this may seem to be a far-fetched proposition, it is clear from the evidence of the lysine cartel that once undertakings engage in an apparently successful cartel in one market they may be tempted to expand the cartel activity into other markets. In these cases the EC practice at least has been to treat the arrangements in respect of each separate market as a separate cartel, in need of a separate investigative procedure and a separate infringement decision or decisions.

Further reductions in penalties of up to 50 per cent are available to undertakings meeting the same conditions in cases where they are not the first to come forward, 'before written notice of a proposed infringement decision is given' (para 9.4).

The leniency policy of the EC was revised in 2002 when it published its notice on immunity from fines and reduction of fines in cartel cases.[16] Following criticism of the earlier notice, which was imprecise in its terms, the new policy was designed substantially to reduce the uncertainty involved. The Commission (and relevant national authorities investigating cartels) will grant an undertaking total immunity from any fine which might have been imposed on it where either: (a) the undertaking submits evidence which permits the Commission to adopt a decision allowing it to carry out a formal investigation (para 8(a)); or (b) the undertaking submits evidence which may enable the Commission to adopt a decision finding an infringement of article 81 EC (para 8(b)). In the first case the immunity will apply only where the Commission did not at the time the information was given have enough information in its possession otherwise to adopt such a decision. In the second case immunity will be granted where first, no undertaking is benefiting from immunity under para 8(a), and second where the Commission did not at the time have sufficient information to make an infringement decision under article 81. In each case a further set of conditions, similar to those of the OFT policy apply. These are that: (a) the undertaking cooperates fully on a continuous basis with the Commission throughout the investigation; (b) the undertaking ends its involvement in the cartel; and (c) the undertaking took no steps to coerce other undertakings to participate in the infringement. Undertakings that do not meet these criteria may nevertheless benefit from some reduction in penalties where they provide the Commission 'with evidence of the suspected infringement which represents significant added value with respect to the evidence already in the Commission's possession' and which terminate their involvement at that time (para 21).

The revised EC programme may be considered to be a success based on the numbers of applications from those undertakings seeking to avail themselves of its provisions, although it must be recognised that it is difficult to compare like with like in view of the increased priority given by the EC Commission to the detection and punishment of cartel conduct. In the first year of the operation of the Notice over 20 applications for immunity were received in separate cases. This contrasts

[16] (2002) OJ C45/3, [2002] 4 CMLR 26.

with a figure of 16 notifications during the six years of operation of the previous notice.[17] Perhaps more tellingly,

> under the 1996 Notice most leniency applications were made following Commission inspections, with the objective of receiving a reduction in the fines to be imposed, whereas under the 2002 Notice, most applications are immunity applications, made before the Commission has taken any investigative steps.[18]

In almost all of these cases the Commission was quick to grant the full immunity requested.

Information gathered in the course of immunity applications made to the EC Commission may be passed onto national authorities but there are limits in the way in which this information may be used against natural persons. These limits are set in article 12 of Regulation 1/2003,[19] which is in part in the following terms:

> 12(3) Information exchanged pursuant to para (1) can only be used in evidence to impose sanctions on natural persons where:
> —the law of the transmitting authority foresees actions of a similar kind in relation ot an infringement of article 81 or article 82 of the Treaty or, in the absence thereof,
> —the information has been collected in a way which respects the same level of protection of the rights of defence of natural persons as provided for under the national rules of the receiving authority. However, in this case, the information exchanged cannot be used by the receiving authority to impose custodial sanctions.

There are thus two objections to the use of any such information in the course of a cartel offence investigation or prosecution. The first is that undoubtedly the protections available during the course of an approach to the EC Commission by an applicant seeking leniency do not conform to those which would be available to a party subject to investigation under the cartel offence. Even if the protections were of the same standard, the use of any material generated in this way would restrict the penalties that would be available. There remains however a risk that some undertakings, or individuals within them, will be reticent to seek the benefit of a civil leniency programme where there maybe a concern that this could trigger a criminal prosecution. This is recognised by Bertus, although the way forward is clearly uncertain:

> . . . the Commission must ensure that its leniency policy is not undermined by the risk of criminal sanctions being imposed in member states on employees of companies that have received immunity from the Commission. As neither the Commission nor member states can possibly benefit from a faltering leniency policy, they will have to resolve this issue in close cooperation before Regulation 1/2003 enters into force in May 2004.[20]

[17] See V B Bertus, 'The European Commission's 2002 Leniency Notice after one year of operation', *Competition Policy Newsletter*, Summer 2003, 16.

[18] *Ibid.*

[19] Council Regulation 1/2003 on the Implementation of the Rules of Competition laid down in Articles 81 and 82 EC, (2003) OJ L1/1.

[20] Note 17, above, p 22.

That there remains the possibility of tensions in this area is certain. The fact that Regulation 1/2003 makes a specific reference to the powers of member states to impose criminal sanctions on individuals is evidence of the fact that the legality of this policy needed to be spelt out on the face of the core legislation. Were there a demonstrable deleterious effect on the efficacy of the leniency programme through the application of national criminal law it might be argued that article 10 of the Treaty should preclude this. More likely however is the fact that, as Bertus recognises, it is in no-one's interests to damage the EC leniency programme, and that the OFT would be slow to prosecute in cases where it was felt that such an effect might follow. While this will likely be true of individual cases, the overall impact of the mere existence of such sanctions on civil leniency programmes is a matter at the present time of conjecture.

It will be noted that in the case of both the OFT and EC programmes undertakings may benefit from either total, or partial, immunity. It will be noted that in respect of the cartel offence no-action letters will be issued only where the relevant named persons were employees, officers, or directors of those undertakings benefiting from *total* immunity under the respective programmes.

NO-ACTION LETTERS AND COMPETITION DISQUALIFICATION ORDERS

Section 204 of the EA 02 amends the Company Directors Disqualification Act 1986 (CDDA 1986), inserting new ss 9A–9E. Section 9A provides that an appropriate court must make a competition disqualification order (CDO) against any director following an application by the OFT or other appropriate regulator where the conditions are met. The primary condition is that an undertaking of which the person is a director breaches a relevant competition law. The relevant competition laws are articles 81 and 82 EC and the Chapter I and II Prohibitions of the CA 98. Because the reference is to breaches by undertakings, the cartel offence is excluded from these provisions. However, the OFT has indicated that it will not seek CDOs against individuals who benefit from no-action letters in cases where an infringement of article 81 EC or the Chapter I Prohibition is also established.

5

Prosecution, Penalties, and the Consequences of Breach[1]

THE PROSECUTING AUTHORITIES

IN ENGLAND, WALES and Northern Ireland, proceedings in respect of an offence under s 188 may be brought by the Director of the Serious Fraud Office (SFO) or the OFT.[2] If the offence is committed wholly or partially within the jurisdiction of the Scottish courts, the case will be referred by the Lord Advocate to the Head of the International and Financial Crime Unit in the Crown Office who will decide either to investigate or to refer the case to the OFT.[3] In order to prevent vexatious prosecutions, third parties may only bring a prosecution with the consent of the OFT. The initial investigation into anti-competitive agreements is to be undertaken by officers from the OFT's Cartel Investigation Branch (CIB). In appropriate circumstances, the OFT can conduct parallel investigations using both its criminal powers provided by the Act, and the civil powers provided by the CA 98. The OFT investigators will work closely with the SFO who have access to similar investigative powers under the CJA 87. It is anticipated that the SFO will take the lead role and make use of their experience in investigating and prosecuting serious or complex fraud. The OFT will report to the Director of the SFO who decides whether the case merits prosecution. The decision to grant leniency or no-action letters is taken by the OFT who must consult with the SFO where this action could impact upon an existing SFO led cartel investigation. Some concern has been expressed that the OFT might be seen by companies as an arm of the SFO and that commercial relationships could be jeopardised if companies became the subject of a criminal investigation initiated by the OFT. Although it is expected that initially criminal prosecutions will be reserved for the most flagrant cases of price-fixing, it is likely to be difficult to predict with any certainty whether an investigation will result in a criminal prosecution.

[1] While detailed consideration of Scottish law and practice is beyond the scope of this book, where appropriate we identify some of the fundamental principles relevant to Scots law.

[2] The EA 02 s 190(2).

[3] The investigation and prosecution of all criminal offences in Scotland is the responsibility of the Lord Advocate, who is normally represented at local level by the procurators fiscal. The Criminal Law (Consolidation) (Scotland) Act 1995 makes provision for the Lord Advocate to appoint a nominee to exercise investigative powers in respect to serious or complex fraud. This legislation also makes provision for search warrants to be obtained. The responsibility for conducting both the investigation and prosecution of serious fraud rests with International and Financial Crime Unit of the Crown Office.

Co-operation between the OFT and the SFO

Where an OFT investigation indicates that the case may involve serious or complex fraud, the case is to be referred to the Director of the SFO who decides whether to accept the matter for investigation. The SFO acceptance criteria for serious or complex fraud involves consideration of whether

> . . . the sum at risk is estimated to be at least £1 million, cases that are likely to give rise to national publicity and widespread public concern (for example, those involving public bodies) and cases where legal, accountancy and investigative skills need to be brought together[4].

The Director can require the OFT to make further enquires which usually involves using the investigative powers provided by the Act. Where the SFO and the OFT are exercising their formal powers to obtain information, it will be made clear in writing to the person concerned which specific power is being used.[5] In an attempt to limit confusion, a Memorandum of Understanding was signed in October 2003 which establishes the basis of collaboration between the SFO and the OFT.[6] If an OFT investigation under the CA 98 discloses cartel activity, initial criminal enquires will be undertaken by the CIB. The SFO will also refer information relating to potential cartel activity to the CIB. Where a case is referred to the Director of the SFO, he or she will normally decide within 28 days whether to accept the case for investigation or order further enquiries. If the Director considers that the OFT should continue with their investigation, the SFO and the OFT will 'discuss and agree the nature and scope of such enquiries'.[7] Following the completion of the initial enquiry, the Director will review the decision to accept the case. If an OFT referral is accepted, a criminal case team comprising both OFT and SFO officers is set up under the leadership of an SFO case controller who direct the investigation and is the arbiter of any dispute between team members. OFT officers have 'access to all case-related documentation including records of decisions, advices and submission papers'.[8] If a criminal cartel investigation is undertaken by the SFO, the presumption will be that they will use the powers provided by the Criminal Justice Act 1987. However, the criminal case team is at liberty to use the investigative powers available under the EA 02. On occasion, the OFT will proceed with an investigation using its civil powers under the CA 98 while the SFO continues with the criminal investigation. Care will be taken to ensure that the CA 98 investigation does not prejudice parallel criminal investigations. If the OFT becomes aware that an EC Competition authority investigation could involve both a serious or complex fraud and a cartel offence in the UK, it will inform the SFO.

[4] OFT Guidance Note *Powers for investigating criminal cartels*, para 3.18.

[5] *Ibid*, para 3.23.

[6] See appendix 6

[7] Memorandum of Understanding between the Office of Fair Trading and the Director of the Serious Fraud Office October 2003 OFT 547 para 5.

[8] *Ibid* para 7.

If a decision is made to prosecute, the OFT will co-ordinate the progress of both investigations. While decisions whether to grant leniency remains with the OFT, if a leniency decision impacts upon an existing SFO led cartel investigation or prosecution, the OFT will consult with the SFO. The decision whether cease an investigation, or whether to charge and prosecute rests with the SFO, in consultation with the OFT.

Co-operation between the OFT and the IFCU

The basis of the co-operative arrangements between the OFT and the International and Financial Crime Unit in Scotland have been recorded in a Memorandum of Understanding which was signed in October 2003.[9] This document is drafted in similar terms to the agreement between the SFO and the OFT. Thus, where OFT officers suspect that a cartel investigation could lead to cross-jurisdictional issues in Scotland, the case will be referred to the Head of the IFCU who decides whether to accept the case for investigation or whether to ask the OFT to make further enquiries.[10] The nature and scope of these enquires will be agreed by the OFT and the IFCU.[11] An investigation undertaken by the OFT will be conducted by the CIB in accordance with the powers provided under the EA 02. Although PACE and the codes of practice have no application in Scotland, the OFT notes that nothing prevents investigators from following these procedures.[12] Where the IFCU suspects that an investigation into serious or complex fraud discloses cartel activity, it will pass the information to the CIB. Where a cartel case involves the OFT, the SFO and the IFCU, the OFT will assume responsibility for liasing between all three the organisations.[13] Once the IFCU accepts responsibility for an investigation into cartel activity, it will normally use the powers provided under the Criminal Law (Consolidation) (Scotland) Act 1995. However, it is possible to use the powers provided under the EA 02. Where parallel criminal and civil investigations are being pursued, both case teams will take care not to jeopardise the criminal investigation. Any decision regarding immunity in respect of a prosecution in Scotland will be brought to the attention of the Lord Advocate who may indicate whether the individual remains liable to be prosecuted.[14] In Scotland, the decision whether to cease the investigation or to prosecute is taken by the Lord Advocate or the Advocate Depute.

[9] This document is available on the OFT website: www.oft.gov.uk.

[10] Memorandum of Understanding between the Office of Fair Trading and the International and Financial Crime Unit, Crown Office, Scotland, October 2003 para 4.

[11] *Ibid* para 5.

[12] See above n 4 para 4.1 fn 27.

[13] See above n 10 para 6.

[14] See above n 10 para 14.

THOSE WHO MAY BE PROSECUTED

It is not a requirement that a person be an employee or a director of an undertaking in order to commit an offence within the terms of s 188. It will be noted that 'an individual' is guilty of an offence if he dishonestly agrees to implement or 'to cause or made to be implemented' the relevant arrangements with one or more other persons relating to at least two undertakings (s 188(1)). This has the consequence that as well as those within an undertaking entering into such arrangements those who facilitate them from outside the undertaking may also be committing an offence. This would cover, for example, the retired business executive with close personal connections to ABB, identified as a facilitator of the pre-insulated pipe cartel,[15] or the accountant who kept separate records to facilitate market-sharing and price fixing in the case of the lysine cartel prosecuted in the United States.

NON BIS IN IDEM

The principle *non bis in idem* (double jeopardy) provides that no-one shall be tried twice for the same offence. It is recognised in article 4 of Protocol 7 to the ECHR, which has not been ratified by the UK, and concern has been expressed that competition law procedures may in some situations be acting in breach of the principle.[16] Article 4 reads (in part) as follows:

> 1. No one shall be liable to be tried or punished again in criminal proceedings under the jurisdiction of the same State for an offence for which he has already been finally acquitted or convicted in accordance with the law and penal procedure of that State.

This principle was restated in article 50 of the Charter of Fundamental Rights of the European Union.[17] It is generally accepted that, for the purposes of the Convention, an infringement decision taken in respect of breaches of the Chapter I Prohibition and an EC Commission decision finding an infringement of article 81 EC may be categorised as a finding of a criminal infringement, notwithstanding the characterisation in national or EC law of such a finding as a civil or administrative infringement. Thus, for example, in the case of *Napp*,[18] an appeal against a finding of an infringement of the Chapter II Prohibition, the CCAT noted that '[b]oth parties accept that proceedings under the prohibitions imposed by the Act which may lead to the imposition of a penalty . . . involve a "criminal charge" or a "criminal offence" for the purposes of Article 6 of the [Convention]'.[19]

[15] Commission Decision 1999/60, *Pre-Insulated Pipe Cartel* (1999) OJ L 24/1, at para 33.

[16] See generally W P J Wils, 'The Principle of *Ne Bis in Idem* in EC Antitrust Enforcement: A Legal and Economic Analysis', (2003) *World Competition* 26(2), 131.

[17] (2000) OJ C364/1.

[18] *Napp Pharmaceutical Holdings Ltd and Subsidiaries v The Director General of Fair Trading* [2002] CompAR 13.

[19] At para 93.

There are a number of circumstances in which the principle of *non bis in idem* might be jeopardised by competition law procedures. One might be where there is first an action brought under the cartel offence, followed by a subsequent proceeding under either article 81 EC or the Chapter I Prohibition. It appears to be accepted that both provisions might be reasonably used in respect of the same conduct. Thus Whish suggests that '[c]riminal proceedings are likely to be brought before the OFT brings any proceedings against undertakings for infringement of the [CA 98]'.[20] A second concern arise where a cartel prosecution in the UK follows an infringement decision taken under article 81 elsewhere in the EC, addressed in part to an undertaking whose engagement in a cartel triggers a prosecution against certain individuals by the OFT in the UK. However, all of these concerns might be addressed by reference to two significant factors. First, the UK, as noted above, has *not* ratified the relevant part of the Convention, and second, in the case of the cartel offence it is not the undertaking implicated in an infringement decision that is being prosecuted, but rather individuals who are not subject to such infringement decisions.

BURDEN AND STANDARD OF PROOF

The cardinal principle in a criminal prosecution is that the obligation of proving the defendant's guilt rests with the prosecution. The tribunal of fact must be directed that in order to establish guilt in respect of the cartel offence, the prosecution must prove all the elements of an offence. The standard of proof to be applied in respect of the cartel offence is the criminal standard, which requires that the tribunal of fact must acquit if there is a realistic or genuine doubt as to the accused's guilt. The 'beyond reasonable doubt' test is sufficient to satisfy the requirement set out in article 6(2) of the European Convention on Human Rights which provides that a person charged with a criminal offence is to be presumed innocent until proven guilty. While there is no particular approved formula, an appropriate direction on both the burden and standard of proof is an essential part of the trial judge's direction to the jury.

THE ADMISSIBILITY OF EVIDENCE

While the EA 02 imposes some specific restrictions on the use as evidence of statements obtained in compulsory interview, the admissibility of evidence gathered during a criminal investigation into cartel activity will be subject to the usual evidentiary rules. The fundamental rule of the law of evidence in England and Wales is that, subject to the exclusionary rules, all relevant evidence is admissible. Thus, the rule against hearsay, which is an exclusionary rule, prohibits the use of

[20] R Whish, *Competition Law* 5th edn (Lexis Nexis, London, 2003) p 393.

out-of-court statements as evidence of any fact stated. However, the Criminal Justice Act 2003 makes fundamental changes to the admissibility of hearsay evidence in criminal proceedings. Section 114 removes the old common law exclusionary rule and, subject to certain safeguards, renders hearsay evidence *prima facie* admissible. Consequently, a witness's out-of-court statement will now be admissible provided it comes within any provision of Chapter 2 of the CJA 2003,[21] any other statutory provision,[22] a common law exception preserved by the CJA 2003,[23] or the parties agree to its admission.[24] The court also has a discretionary power to admit hearsay if 'it would not be contrary to the interests of justice for it to be admissible'.[25] This broad *inclusionary* power, which in appropriate circumstances extends to multiple hearsay, gives the court the power to admit cogent, reliable hearsay evidence that falls outside one of the other three categories.[26] However, when exercising this discretion the court is required to take account of a number of factors including the circumstances in which the statement was made, the probative value of the statement and the significance of the statement in the context of the case as a whole. The CJA 2003 also clarifies the rule with regard to the evidential value of previous inconsistent statements and other previous statements made by a witness called to give evidence in criminal proceedings. These statements may be tendered as evidence of relevant facts.[27] Thus statements made in response to questions asked by the OFT using its compulsory powers under the Act, which can be used as evidence if the person is prosecuted for some other offence and introduces evidence that is inconsistent with the statement, will now be evidence of fact rather than merely evidence of credibility.

Improperly obtained evidence

Criminal investigations into suspected cartel activity should be conducted in accordance with the requirements of PACE and its codes of practice.[28] Similarly, the use of intrusive surveillance techniques during an investigation should accord with the provisions of the RIPA and its codes of practice.[29] Failure to abide by these procedures might affect the admissibility of evidence in subsequent criminal

[21] A statement is defined in the CJA 2003 s 115 as 'any representation of fact or opinion made by a person by whatever means'.

[22] CJA 2003 s 114(1)(a).

[23] Ibid s 114(1)(b).

[24] Ibid s 114(1)(c).

[25] Ibid s 114(1)(d).

[26] It is noteworthy the difference in emphasis in the Law Commission Report which recommended that judicial discretion to admit hearsay evidence should be limited to where the justice of the case required its admission. See Law Com Report No 245 paras 6.48–6.53.

[27] CJA 2003 ss 119 and 120.

[28] For further discussion see Chapter 3.

[29] The RIPA code of practice 1.8 provides that 'the proper authorisation of surveillance should ensure the admissibility of such evidence under the common law, section 78 of the Police and Criminal Evidence Act 1984 and the Human Rights Act 1998'.

proceedings. Generally, the rules governing the gathering of evidence during any criminal investigation impose restrictions on the activities of law enforcement agencies. In creating these restrictions, the legislature has 'staked out the boundaries for lawful access to evidence and has indicated that beyond these limits it is willing to forego evidence of crime in defence of individual freedom'.[30] While compliance with the rules regulating the questioning of individuals and the search of premises may on occasion result in the authorities being denied access to reliable evidence, failure to comply with regulatory procedures may render the process unlawful, and any evidence seized will have been obtained irregularly. However, any unfairness or impropriety in obtaining evidence will not necessarily affect its admissibility. In Scotland, the question whether evidence is admissible will depend upon the nature of the irregularity and the circumstances under which it was committed.[31] Whether any given irregularity renders evidence inadmissible depends to a large extent upon the discretionary principle of fairness.[32] Similarly, in English law there is no absolute rule that irregularly obtained evidence must be excluded at trial, determination of admissibility is generally left to the discretion of the court.[33] Illegally or improperly obtained prosecution evidence, which is otherwise admissible, may be excluded by the court under its common law powers or under its statutory powers if it is in the interests of justice to do so.[34] Section 78(1) of PACE provides that

> In any proceedings the court may refuse to allow evidence on which the prosecution proposes to rely to be given if it appears to the court that, having regard to all the circumstances, including the circumstances in which the evidence was obtained, the admission

[30] A Zuckerman, 'Illegally Obtained Evidence: Discretion as a Guardian of Legitimacy' (1987) 40 *Current Legal Problems* 55 at 57.

[31] *Lawrie v Muir* 1949 SLT 37; 1950 JC 19.

[32] The rules for determining whether the evidence was obtained in accordance with the law are distinct from the rules governing the admissibility of irregularly obtained evidence. The court considers firstly the legality of the manner in which the evidence was obtained and secondly, if there was an irregularity whether that irregularity ought or ought not to be excused. However, on many occasions the court will reserve the question whether the evidence was obtained irregularly, preferring instead to move directly to the issue of admissibility. Accordingly, the manner in which evidence is obtained is an important consideration for the court when addressing questions of admissibility. Failure by the authorities to observe the formalities during the investigation stage of criminal proceedings can result in exclusion of evidence at trial. The court is required to excuse any irregularity before the evidence can be admitted and the question whether any particular irregularity will be excused depends upon the circumstances.

[33] This rule is subject to a number of exceptions. The most import exception in the context of the cartel offence relates to confessions. Hence section 76 of PACE provides that a confession will be inadmissible unless the prosecution proves that it was not obtained by oppression or as a result of anything said or done that was likely in the circumstances to render any confession unreliable. However, not all irregularly obtained confessions will be excluded under this provision. See generally P Mirfield, *Silence, Confessions and Improperly Obtained Evidence* (Oxford, OUP, 1997).

[34] The common law rule is preserved by s 83(3) of PACE. The court also has the power at common law to stay criminal proceedings as an abuse of process on the ground of improper prosecutorial conduct during the pre-trial stage of proceedings. For further discussion see A Choo, 'Halting Criminal Prosecutions: The Abuse of Process Doctrine Revisited' [1995] *Criminal Law Review* 864; C Gane, and S Nash, 'Illegal Extradition: The Irregular Return of fugitive Offenders' (1996) 1 *Scottish Law and Practice Quarterly* 277.

> of the evidence would have such an adverse effect on the fairness of the proceedings that the court ought not to admit it.

Thus the critical question for the trial judge is whether the use of the impugned evidence at trial would be unfair.[35] An exclusionary discretion creates a 'persistent tension' for judges who need to apply formal evidentiary rules but remain reluctant to exclude seemingly relevant, reliable evidence on the grounds that it was improperly obtained.[36]

Both before and after the enforcement of the Human Rights Act 1998, the appellate courts in England and Wales have tended to exclude evidence only if its reliability has been compromised by the manner in which it has been obtained.[37] While it is acknowledged that the reliability of confession evidence is notoriously sensitive to the manner in which it was obtained, the quality of real evidence is generally unaffected by the manner or circumstances of its acquisition. Consequently, material obtained during a search of premises which fails to comply with PACE and the codes of practice is unlikely to be excluded at trial. In *R* v *Chalkley*,[38] the trial judge permitted the prosecution to adduce evidence of covertly obtained tape recordings of highly incriminating conversations between the defendants. Finding that the trial judge had exercised his discretion appropriately in refusing to exclude evidence, the Court of Appeal observed that

> there was no dispute as to its authenticity, content or effect; it was relevant, highly probative of the appellants' involvement in the conspiracy and otherwise admissible; it did not result from incitement, entrapment or inducement or any other conduct of that sort; and none of the unlawful conduct of the police or other of their conduct of which complaint is made affects the quality of the evidence.[39]

Moreover, the court considered that s 78(1) should not be used to exclude evidence as a mark of disapproval of the way in which it had been obtained.[40] The decision in *Chalkley* indicated that evidence obtained as a result of an irregular search was highly unlikely to be excluded on the ground that it was improperly obtained. Similarly, in *Sanghera*,[41] a search of premises was conducted without the defendant's consent, which is in breach of Code B, para 1.3 of PACE. Dismissing the appeal, the court considered it important to note that there was no issue as to the reliability of the evidence and there was no suggestion that the police were

[35] See generally, C Allen, 'Discretion and Security: Excluding Evidence under Section 78(1) of the Police and Criminal Evidence Act 1984' [1990] *Cambridge Law Journal* 80; A Ashworth, 'Excluding Evidence as Protecting Rights' [1977] *Criminal Law Review* 723; I Dennis, 'Reconstructing the Law of Criminal Evidence' (1989) 42 *Current Legal Problems* 21

[36] I H Dennis, *The Law of Evidence* 2nd edn (London; Sweet & Maxwell, 2003) at p 70.

[37] See generally A Choo and S Nash, 'What's the Matter with Section 78?' [1999] *Criminal Law Review* 929; and N Taylor 'Human Rights and the Discretionary Exclusion of Evidence' (2001) 65 *Journal of Criminal Law* 349.

[38] [1998] 2 All ER 155.

[39] *Ibid*, 180.

[40] The Scottish courts have tended to adopt a different approach to this problem. See for example *HM Advocate v Turnbull* 1951 JC 96.

[41] [2001] 1 Cr App R 299, 304–5.

acting other than bona fide. However, there are examples where trial courts have used excluded evidence in a wider range of circumstances than might appear to be sanctioned by appellate decisions.[42]

This narrow approach to excluding improperly obtained evidence has found favour in Strasbourg. Applying principles established in the case of *Schenk v Switzerland*[43], the European Court of Human Rights considers that its task under the Convention is not to give a ruling on whether evidence is properly admitted but to determine whether the proceedings as a whole are fair. Providing defence rights have been respected, questions of admissibility are for national courts. Thus in appropriate circumstances improperly obtained evidence, including evidence that has been obtained in breach of a right guaranteed by the Convention, may be adduced at trial without violating article 6. In *Khan v UK*,[44] the majority of the Court held that the use of evidence in criminal proceedings obtained in breach of the right to private life did not render the trial unfair. The police in this case had installed an aural surveillance device on the exterior of property, without the knowledge or consent of the owner or occupier. While finding that the applicant's rights under article 8 had been infringed, on the issue of the exclusion of evidence the Court observed that:

> With specific reference to the admission of the contested tape recording, the Court notes that . . . the applicant had ample opportunity to challenge both the authenticity and the use of the recording. He did not challenge its authenticity, but challenged its use at the 'voire dire' and again before the Court of Appeal and the House of Lords. The Court notes that at each level of jurisdiction the domestic courts assessed the effect of admission of the evidence on the fairness of the trial by reference to section 78 of PACE . . .[45]

Hence the Court was satisfied that the appropriate use of the discretionary power to exclude improperly obtained evidence fulfilled the fair trial guarantees provided by article 6. However, in a powerful dissenting opinion, Judge Loucaides considered that the UK court had an obligation 'not to admit or rely on evidence in judicial proceedings which was obtained contrary to the Convention'.

Eavesdropping on conversations in police cells has proved to be a fruitful source of reliable prosecution evidence.[46] However, in *Allan v UK*[47] the Court refused to sanction the use as evidence of a cell conversation obtained in a manner that effectively nullified the applicant's decision to remain silent. The disputed

[42] In *R v Veneroso* [2002] *Criminal Law Review* 306, for example, the trial judge excluded evidence of the finding of drugs on the basis that the police officers, although acting in good faith, had not acted lawfully under section 17(1)(e) of PACE because there was no evidence that they needed to enter the premises to save life or limb or prevent serious damage to property. This, the Court considered, constituted a clear breach of article 8, and as the public interest in bringing the defendant to trial did not outweigh the need to protect his rights under article 8 the evidence should be excluded under section 78.

[43] (1988) 13 EHRR 242.

[44] (2000) 31 EHRR 1016.

[45] *Ibid*, para 38.

[46] *Maqsud Ali* [1966] 1 QB; *R v Bailey & Smith* [1993] 97 Cr App R 365; *R v Khan* [1996] 3 All ER 289; *R v Chalkley* [1998] 2 All ER 155; *Khan v United Kingdom* (2001) 31 EHRR 45 *PG & JH v United Kingdom* [2001] HRCD 707.

[47] (2002) 36 EHRR 143.

evidence comprised of the oral testimony of an informer, H. Distinguishing *Khan*, the Court was satisfied that:

> the admissions allegedly made by the applicant to H, and which formed the main or decisive evidence against him at trial, were not spontaneous and unprompted statements volunteered by the applicant, but were induced by the persistent questioning of H., who at the instance of the police, channelled their conversations into discussions of the murder in circumstances which can be regarded as the functional equivalent of interrogation, without any of the safeguards which would attach to a formal police interview, including the attendance of a solicitor and the issuing of the usual caution.'[48]

Finding for the applicant, the Court was satisfied that the conversations with H had been obtained without sufficient regard to fair trial guarantees. However, it is relevant that the alleged admission had not been recorded and thus the reliability of H's testimony relating to Allan's admission could not be independently verified.

The appellate courts have taken the view that unfairness problems arising from a breach of article 8 can be dealt with by appropriate use of s 78 of PACE. In *R v P*,[49] for example, the House of Lords considered that

> The direct operation of articles 8 and 6 does not . . . alter the vital role of section 78 as the means by which questions of the use of evidence obtained in breach of article 8 are to be resolved at a criminal trial. The criterion to be applied is the criterion of fairness in article 6 which is likewise the criterion to be applied by the judge under section 78.[50]

Similarly, the Court of Appeal in *Loveridge*,[51] found that while covertly filming defendants held in cells in a magistrates' court is contrary to article 8,

> . . . so far as the outcome of this appeal is concerned, the breach of Article 8 is only relevant if it interferes with the right of the applicants to a fair hearing. Giving full weight to the breach of the Convention, we are satisfied that the contravention of article 8 did not interfere with the fairness of the hearing. The judge was entitled to rule as he did. The position is the same so far as section 78 of the Police and Criminal Evidence Act 1984 is concerned.

Following the enforcement of the RIPA and the codes of practice, the proper authorisation of surveillance measures is anticipated to ensure the admissibility of evidence in criminal proceedings, and to meet with the requirements of article 8 and article 6. However, the decision whether to exclude evidence obtained in breach of these procedures remains subject to the trial judge's discretion.

In the context of civil proceedings, the Court of Appeal considers that it is generally in the public interest to admit relevant, reliable evidence obtained in breach of article 8. In *Jones v University of Warwick*[52] the claimant sought damages from

[48] *Ibid*, para 52.

[49] [2001] 2 WLR 463.

[50] See also *R v Sargent* [2001] UKHL 54; [2001] 3 WLR 992; *R* v *Mason* [2002] EWCA Crim 385. For further discussion see A Choo and S Nash, 'Evidence law in England and Wales: The impact of the Human Rights Act 1998' (2003) 7 *International Journal of Evidence and Proof* 31–61.

[51] [2001] EWCA Crim 973; [2001] 2 Cr App R 591, para 33.

[52] [2003] EWCA Civ 151, [2003] 1 WLR 954.

her employer for injuries caused during her employment. While the defendant was prepared to admit liability, he questioned whether the claimant continued to suffer a disability. An inquiry agent gained access by subterfuge to the claimant's home and surreptitiously videotaped her. Having viewed the film, a medical expert considered that the claimant's hand was functioning entirely satisfactorily. The claimant submitted that the videotape should not be admitted as evidence on the ground that her right to private life had been violated. The Court of Appeal considered that in both civil and criminal cases it was appropriate to take a more flexible approach to take account of conflicting public interests. Noting that the weight to be attached to these interests varies according to circumstances, the court observed that:

> The significance of the evidence will differ as will the gravity of the breach of article 8, according to the facts of the particular case. The decision will depend on all the circumstances. Here, the court cannot ignore the reality of the situation. This is not a case where the conduct of the defendant's insurers is so outrageous that the defence should be struck out. The case, therefore, has to be tried. It would be artificial and undesirable for the actual evidence, which is relevant and admissible, not to be placed before the judge who has the task of trying the case.... to exclude the use of the evidence would create a wholly undesirable situation. Fresh medical experts would have to be instructed on both sides. Evidence which is relevant would have to be concealed from them, perhaps resulting in a misdiagnosis; and it would not be possible to cross-examine the claimant appropriately. For these reasons we do not consider it would be right to interfere with the judge's decision not to exclude the evidence.[53]

Accordingly, unless the conduct of a criminal investigation into cartel activity is outrageously unfair and is clearly in breach of fundamental procedural protections, relevant reliable evidence gathered in breach of the evidence gathering rules is likely to be adduced at trial without jeopardising the fair trial guarantees provided by article 6.

[53] Ibid, para 28. Adopting a slightly different approach to a similar problem, the Scottish Court of Session in *Martin* v *McGuiness*, considered that provided the surveillance measures were considered reasonable and proportionate, admitting evidence gathered by subterfuge was not incompatible with article 8. In this case the pursuer brought an action in respect of a road accident. While liability was admitted there remained the issue of the assessment of damages, with the defender contending that the pursuer exaggerated the effects of the accident. The defender sought to rely upon evidence obtained by private investigators through inquiries and surveillance carried out at the pursuer's home. Lord Bonomy held that 'In striking a fair balance between the interest of the pursuer in the security and integrity of his home as part of his right to respect for his private and family life and the competing interest of the defender in protecting his assets and the interests of the wider community in protecting theirs, I have had particular regard to the degree of intrusion into the pursuer's privacy (subterfuge in a conversation with the pursuer's wife at the door of her home and long-range video recording of the activities of the pursuer in the open area within the curtilage of his property capable of being viewed by a passer-by) on the one hand, and the requirement in an adversarial system of litigation that the defender should himself investigate the case against him with a view to defending himself and his assets from a false claim together with the general threat to the assets of the wider community from the impact of successful fraudulent claims on insurance premiums on the other hand.'

The use of silence as evidence

Notwithstanding that failing to answer questions in compulsory interview can amount to an offence under s 201, a refusal to answer questions can also have evidential significance. Section 34 of the Criminal Justice and Public Order Act 1994 provides that in appropriate circumstances inferences can be drawn from the defendant's failure to mention in interview a fact which is later relied upon at trial. Drawing inferences from 'no-comment' interviews remains a controversial issue, particularly where the defendant's decision to remain silent is based upon legal advice.[54] In the landmark decision of *Condron v UK*,[55] the European Court of Human Rights was satisfied that provided appropriate safeguards are in place, silence in interview can be taken into account in assessing the persuasiveness of the prosecution case without violating article 6. However, in the absence of a mechanism to assess the evidential weight attached to silence, the Strasbourg Court has held that it is of paramount importance that the jury be properly directed. The judge's direction must make it clear that adverse inferences may only be drawn where the jury is satisfied that the silence in interview could only sensibly be attributed to their having no answer or none that would stand up to cross-examination. In *Beckles v United Kingdom*[56] the Court noted that the trial judge had undermined the value of the applicant's explanation for his silence by omitting to mention that the applicant had been willing to give his version of the incident to the police before he spoke to his solicitor. The Court observed that the judge had also 'invited the jury to reflect on whether the applicant's reason for his silence was "a good one" without emphasising that it must be consistent only with guilt'.[57]

In order to avoid problems arising from no comment interviews, a practice has developed whereby the suspect provides the police with a prepared statement. In *Knight*,[58] a prepared statement was read out to the police at the beginning of the interview by the appellant's solicitor. At trial, the appellant testified to the fact that he had declined to answer any questions in interview, on his solicitor's advice, because he was worried about getting confused and answering police questions incorrectly. The judge directed the jury that they might infer from the defendant's silence that he wished to prevent his account being scrutinised by police questioning because he believed that it would not stand up to such questioning. Allowing the appeal, the court held there could be no adverse inference here as the defendant gave his full account in the statement, mentioning all the facts he later relied on and did not depart from that in the witness box. The fact that he did not mention the facts specifically in response to police questions was immaterial. The

[54] For further discussion see D Birch, 'Suffering in Silence: A Cost-Benefit Analysis of Section 34 of the Criminal Justice and Public Order Act 1994' [1999] *Crim Law Review* 769; I Dennis, 'Silence in the Police Station: The Marginalisation of Section 34' [2002] *Crim Law Review* 25.

[55] (2000) 31 EHRR 1.

[56] (2002) 36 EHRR 162.

[57] *Ibid* para 64.

[58] [2003] EWCA Crim 1977.

judge's direction rendered the conviction unsafe and accordingly the appeal would be allowed and the conviction quashed. However, the Court of Appeal observed that a pre-prepared statement did not of itself give automatic immunity against adverse inferences. In this case, the Court of Appeal came to the conclusion that the primary purpose of section 34 is to obtain early disclosure of the suspect's account and not to provide a means whereby the police can test the suspect's story during interview. Thus, this legislation was intended to obtain facts from the suspect rather than require answers to questions. Although not prepared to suggest that a requirement to submit to police cross-examination on pain of adverse inferences being drawn would infringe article 6, the court considered that drawing inferences in these circumstances would be 'a significantly greater intrusion into a suspect's general right of silence than is a requirement, or encouragement, upon a suspect to disclose his factual defence.'[59]

OFFENCES

The cartel offence

It is an offence for an individual to dishonestly engage in any of the anti-competitive agreements prohibited by s 188 of the Act.[60] Individuals charged with a cartel offence can be tried either on indictment in the Crown court or in the magistrates court. Currently, a person tried on indictment is entitled to trial by jury. However, the introduction of judge only trials for certain fraud cases, which has been on the political agenda for many years, could eventually impact on cartel trials.[61] Despite some Parliamentary objection to judge only trials, recent criminal procedural reform permits the prosecution in serious or complex fraud cases to apply to a Crown Court judge for the trial to be conducted without a jury. Before making an order, the judge must be satisfied that:

> . . . the complexity of the trial or the length of the trial (or both) is likely to make the trial so burdensome to the members of a jury hearing the trial that the interests of justice require that serious consideration should be given to the question of whether the trial should be conducted without a jury.[62]

Consideration must also be given as to what steps could reasonably be taken to reduce the complexity or length of proceedings. Criminal trials in respect to the cartel offence are likely to involve matters of similar complexity to serious fraud cases making the proceedings burdensome for a lay jury. Indeed, the SFO has taken the view that the cartel offence should be classified in a similar manner to serious fraud cases.[63] Notwithstanding that applications for trial without jury in

[59] *Ibid* para 11.
[60] See more specifically Chapter Two, above.
[61] See for example *Report of the Fraud Trials Committee* (London, HMSO, 1986).
[62] Section 43(5) of the Criminal Justice Act 2003.
[63] Background note to the MOU between the OFT and the Director of the SFO, October 2003.

serious fraud cases will be granted only in exceptional circumstances, it would seem likely that this provision might be extended to cover cartel cases. The maximum penalty following a conviction on indictment is five years imprisonment or a fine, or both. The maximum sentence on summary conviction is six months imprisonment or a fine not exceeding the statutory minimum, or both.

Offences related to the powers of investigation

Section 201 of the Act creates a series of offences related to impeding a criminal investigation into cartel activity. Section 201(1) makes it an offence for a person, without reasonable excuse to fail to comply with any requirement to answer questions or provide information. On summary conviction, the maximum sentence is six months imprisonment or a fine of up to level five on the standard scale, or both. This offence may not be tried on indictment. Providing the OFT with false or misleading information during a criminal investigation can also amount to an offence. Section 201(2) provides that

> A person, who, in compliance with a requirement under section 193 or 194—
>
> (a) makes a statement which he knows to be false or misleading in a material manner; or
>
> (b) recklessly makes a statement which is false or misleading in a material particular,
>
> is guilty of an offence.

A person found guilty of this offence is liable on conviction on indictment to be sentenced to two years imprisonment or to an unlimited fine, or to both. On summary conviction, the maximum penalty is six months imprisonment or a fine of up to the statutory maximum, or to both. Similarly, s 201(4) makes it an offence for a person who knows or suspects that a cartel investigation is underway, to falsify, conceal, destroy or dispose of documents that they suspect or know to be relevant to the investigation. It will be a defence to prove that they had no intention to conceal from the investigators the facts disclosed by the documents. The penalty for a conviction on indictment is imprisonment for a term not exceeding five years or an unlimited fine, or both. The maximum penalty on summary conviction is six months imprisonment or a fine up to the statutory maximum or both. Intentionally obstructing officers executing a search warrant issued under s 194 is an offence that carries a maximum penalty of two years imprisonment following conviction on indictment or an unlimited fine, or both, and on summary conviction a fine not exceeding the statutory maximum.

Offences related to the disclosure of specified information

Section 245 introduces a number of offences in respect of the improper disclosure of information which relates to the affairs of an individual or any business or undertaking, or the improper use of information disclosed under the Act. Unless disclosure of specified information is permitted by the Act, it is an offence to disclose this information during the lifetime of the individual or while the undertaking continues to trade.[64] It is an offence to disclose specified information to an overseas public authority if the Secretary of State has directed that it should not be disclosed.[65] Using information disclosed under the Act for a purpose other than that for which it was disclosed is also an offence.[66] A person convicted on indictment for an offence under this provision is liable to a maximum penalty of two years imprisonment or a fine, or both. On summary conviction, the maximum penalty is three months imprisonment or a fine not exceeding the statutory maximum, or both.[67]

COMPANY DIRECTOR DISQUALIFICATION

The EA 02 amended the Company Directors Disqualification Act 1986 (CDDA 1986) in order to permit the OFT to seek the disqualification of company directors implicated in breaches of the civil competition law provisions of either articles 81 and 82 EC, or the CA 98. Such an order will be known as a competition disqualification order (CDO). This was effected by introducing a new s 9A into the CDDA 1986. However, in the case of the cartel offence, no such provision was necessary.

The position in relation to the cartel offence is explained in the relevant OFT guideline at paras 4.25–4.26:

> Any court by or before which an individual is convicted of an indictable offence (whether tried on indictment or summarily) committed in connection with the management of a company may make a disqualification order against that individual [ss 2(1) and 2(2)(b) CDDA 1986].
>
> Where an individual company director has been convicted of the cartel offence under s 188 EA 02, and that offence has been committed in connection with the management of a company, the convicting court has the power to make a disqualification order against the individual director. The OFT and Regulators take the view that the court by or before which the individual director is convicted of the cartel offence is the most appropriate venue for consideration of a disqualification order, so they would not expect to have to use their powers under section 9A [CDDA 1986] in these circumstances.[68]

The relationship between CDOs and the OFT leniency programme ('no-action letters') is considered in further detail in Chapter 4, above.

[64] The EA 02, s 245(1).
[65] *Ibid*, s 245(2).
[66] *Ibid*, s 245(3).
[67] *Ibid*, s 245(4).
[68] OFT, *Competition Disqualification Orders* [2003] UKCLR 745, paras 4.25–4.26.

CIVIL REMEDIES AND DAMAGES

The rights of injured third parties

It is possible that a breach of the EA 02 will give rise to a statutory tort in England and Wales. However, it would not be necessary to follow such a route, as a breach of the cartel offence must inevitably constitute a breach of the Chapter I Prohibition of the CA 98, and remedies certainly flow in this respect. Damages and other appropriate remedies are available to injured claimants under the CA 98 on the basis that they are also available in respect of breaches of the substantive provisions of EC competition law, and that s 60 of the CA 98 requires a similar approach to be adopted in the UK. Section 58 of the CA 98 further provided that findings of the Director relevant to an issue in proceedings is binding on the parties to those proceedings. This is to say that the facts set out in an infringement decision taken by the OFT would be binding on a civil court, and the only issue would become that of causation and quantum. While this presumption could be overturned if the relevant court 'directs otherwise' (CA 98, s 58(1)) it is not likely that this would happen in practice.

The EA 02 made it easier for injured parties to claim damages in respect of breaches of both domestic and EC competition law, inserting new s 58A into the CA 98. This provides that any court is bound by decisions of the OFT or the EC Commission in the event of an infringement decision being made, and either being upheld on appeal, or the time limit for appeal passing. A new s 47A makes express provision for claims for damages to be brought before the CAT. Neither of these provisions automatically apply to breaches of the cartel offence, and it remains to be seen by what route injured third parties may best seek recompense. As of June 2004 no claims had been initiated under s 47A, and there was no reported case of damages being awarded on the basis of a breach of competition law in the UK.[69]

The rights of companies

Although the cartel offence is directed to individuals, and the undertaking itself is not subject to prosecution, the fact remains that the company may be damaged by an action taken against named individuals. For example, the company may face a loss of reputation, leading to a loss of business. Or it may be poorly managed while staff are responding to the immediate threat of criminal prosecution. Under English common law the directors of companies owe duties to the members of the company as a whole, or rather to the shareholders of the company as a whole.

[69] See generally M Furse, *Competition and the Enterprise Act 2002* (Bristol, Jordan Law Publishing, 2003), paras 6.20–6.43.

Under the directors' fiduciary duties they are required to remain within the scope of the powers conferred upon them, and must act in good faith as to what they believe to be the best interests of the company. Although entering into a cartel arrangement may entail making contractual or other arrangements which would lie within the scope of the directors' powers to manage the company (albeit that explicit contracts implementing a cartel would be illegal contracts), they would not, being criminal arrangements, fall within the requirement to act in good faith. The test to be applied here, as with the cartel offence, is that of dishonesty. Thus:

> In most cases compliance with the rule that directors must act honestly and in good faith is tested on common-sense principles, the court asking itself whether it is proved that the directors have not done what they honestly believed to be right, and normally accepting that they have unless satisfied that they have not behaved as honest men of business might be expected to act.[70]

It therefore appears to be axiomatic that a breach of the cartel offence engaged in by a director of a company would also be a breach of the requirement to act in good faith, and as such would be actionable.

[70] P L Davies, *Gower and Davies' Principles of Modern Company Law* 7th edition (London, Sweet and Maxwell, 2003), pp 387–88.

6

Territoriality

INTRODUCTION—THE BASIS OF EXTRA-TERRITORIAL JURISDICTION UNDER THE CARTEL OFFENCE

THE TERRITORIAL ASPECTS of competition law enforcement have exercised the courts, regulators and commentators for many years. Large-scale anti-competitive conduct is very likely to have effects on more than one territory. In the UK however, the traditional approach to claims of extra-territorial jurisdiction in the application of competition law has been one of scepticism extending to hostility.[1] In particular the UK has not accepted the effects doctrine, and in the Competition Act 1998 took steps to prevent this becoming enshrined in UK law through the application of principles of EC law (discussed below).

The territorial scope of the cartel offence is restricted to those agreements to take part in prohibited cartel activities that are implemented in the UK, or to situations where there is evidence of an intention to implement the agreement in the UK.[2] While agreements made within the UK do not need to have been implemented for a prosecution to commence those made extraterritorially must have actually been implemented, thereby limiting somewhat the extraterritorial scope of the offence. Section 190(3) of the Act provides therefore that:

> No proceedings may be brought for an offence under section 188 in respect of an agreement outside the United Kingdom, unless it has been implemented in whole or part in the United Kingdom.

Thus agreements reached overseas may only be prosecuted if some subsequent action is taken within the UK to further the agreement. However, an instruction to others to implement the agreement, delivered into the UK by telephone or electronic mail, might be a sufficient action for this purpose.[3] Although it is not spelt out in the Act, nor expressly referred to in *Hansard*, the use of the word 'implemented' is, as Frazer suggests, 'in a manner in keeping with the approach of the [ECJ] in the *Woodpulp* case.'[4] As such an approach was explicitly taken in respect

[1] The UK, for example, has enacted the Protection of Trade Interests Act 1980 to limit the effect of certain US judgments in the UK. See A V Lowe, 'Blocking Extraterritorial Jurisdiction: The British Protection of Trading Interests Act, 1980' 75 *American Journal of International Law* 257 (1981).

[2] See Chapter Two for specific territorial limitations in relation to the various elements of the offence.

[3] *Explanatory notes*, para 412.

[4] T Frazer, S Hinchcliffe and K George, *Enterprise Act 2002: The new law of mergers, monopolies and cartels* (London, The Law Society, 2003), at para 4.17. The *Woodpulp* case is discussed below.

of the CA 98[5] this may be a reasonable presumption, although it remains to be tested. Further, it should be noted in relation to bid-rigging arrangements as specified in s 188(5) that the offence will only apply where the bid relates to the supply of goods or services, or the production of a product, in the UK.

The evidence of actions already undertaken in the US and the EC is that international cartels do exist, and the cartel offence may well be applied to situations where there are in place cartels whose impact extends to a wider territory than that of the UK. Although there is no provision in the EC Treaty that imposes criminal penalties for cartels, the Sherman Act in the US does criminalise cartels and individuals have been fined and imprisoned. Further, the Sherman Act can be applied extraterritorially to foreign firms and individuals.[6] In this chapter we deal with the question of the extent to which the cartel offence in the UK may be applied to the conduct of foreign firms and the territorial limits of the offence. This raises issues in relation to the use of investigative powers, and the enforcement of the law on those outside the UK's territory, including issues such as extradition and mutual legal assistance.

JURISDICTION OVER SUBJECTS AND SUBJECT MATTER

The basis of jurisdiction in relation to the cartel offence is not that of the nationality of the individuals allegedly committing the offence, but that of the territory where the offence is committed. Common law countries such as the UK and the US demonstrate a reluctance to exercise extra-territorial jurisdiction, whereas states embracing the civil law tradition are generally content to prosecute regardless of whether the offence took place wholly or partially outside their territory. These opposing views are explained by differing state practice with respect to the exercise of jurisdiction.[7] Common law countries generally abide by the principle of territorial jurisdiction, which gives states criminal jurisdiction for offences committed within their territory. States adhering to this principle have 'jurisdiction over all persons and things within its territorial limits and in all causes civil and criminal arising within these limits.'[8] While the territorial theory of criminal competence has the advantage of easy access to evidence and witnesses, problems can arise if some element of the offence takes place outside the territory of the

[5] Section 2(3), CA98, provides that the Chapter I Prohibition applies only where 'the agreement, decision or practice is, or is intended to be, implemented in the UK'. In the passage of the Act Lord Simon explained that by 'copying out the *Wood Pulp* test on the face of the Bill, we are also ensuring that in the event that EC jurisprudence develops and creates a pure effects-based doctrine, the application of the UK prohibitions will not follow suit' (Hansard (HL) 13 November 1997, col 261).

[6] See, for example, A Robertson and M Demetriou, 'But that was in another country: The territorial application of US antitrust laws in the Supreme Court' (1994) *International and Comparative Law Quarterly* 417; J Griffin, 'Foreign Government Reactions to US Assertions of Extraterritorial Jurisdiction' (1998) *European Competition Law Review* 62.

[7] See generally I Shearer *Starke's International Law* 11th edn (London, Butterworths, 1994); I Bantekas and S Nash *International Criminal Law* (London, Cavendish, 2003).

[8] *Compania Naviers Vascongado v SS Cristina* [1938] AC 485 at 496–97, *per* Lord Macmillan.

prosecuting state.[9] In these circumstances common law states either modify the territorial principle or resort to extra-territorial principles of jurisdiction. There are also many crimes where states assert extra-territorial jurisdiction as a result of international conventions. In the UK, for example, the courts have adopted a range of mechanisms to avoid jurisdictional problems and legislation has been introduced to extend extraterritorial jurisdiction.[10] In the US, the Federal Trade Antitrust Improvements Act, which was enacted, *inter alia*, to clarify the extra-territorial reach of the Sherman Act, provides the US regulators with powers to prosecute non-US nationals involved in cartel activity notwithstanding that they are located abroad.[11]

Many civil law states, including the majority of continental EU countries, prefer nationality-based criminal jurisdiction which relies on the active personality principle. Adherence to this principle provides states with criminal jurisdiction over their nationals, and on occasion their residents, whether an offence was committed on their own territory or abroad.[12] The competence of states to prosecute on the basis of nationality is founded on the concept of national allegiance.[13] States basing their criminal jurisdiction on the nationality of the alleged offender frequently reserve the right to prosecute their nationals for offences committed in other countries. As a consequence, and in accordance with their constitutions, these states will refuse to extradite their nationals. This refusal to extradite nationals can compromise the promotion of international co-operation in criminal matters. Undoubtedly, the refusal of most EU states to extradite nationals is a source of anxiety for the US, which gives support to the proposal that a denial of extradition should be conditional on the requested state prosecuting its nationals under the principle *aut dedere aut judicare.* However in the context of extradition, the territorial theory of criminal competence can also be problematic.[14]

[9] G Gilbert 'Crimes *Sans Frontiers* Jurisdictional Problems in English Law' 63 *British Yearbook of International Law* (1992) 415.

[10] See for example, *Treacy v DPP* [1971] AC 537; *DPP v Stonehouse* [1977] 2 All ER 909; *Liangsiriprasert v Government of USA* [1990] 2 All ER 866 and the Criminal Justice Act 1993 and the Terrorism Act 2000

[11] At the time of writing, the case of *Christie's International plc and Sotheby's Holdings Inc, et al v Charlotte Kruman, et al,* (No 02-340) is before the Supreme Court of the US. In part this requires the Court to clarify the scope of extraterritorial antitrust claims in the US.

[12] G Watson 'Offenders Abroad: The Case for Nationality-Based Criminal Jurisdiction' 17 *Yale Journal of International Law* (1992) 41.

[13] Some common law countries such as the UK choose to adopt the active personality principle in respect to specific offences such as treason, murder and manslaughter and some sex offences (see the Offences Against the Persons Act 1861, s 9; and the Sexual Offences (Conspiracy and Incitement) Act 1996).

[14] In *Re Al-Fawwaz* [2002] 1 All ER 545, the US requested the applicant's extradition from the UK alleging that he had conspired with others in an Islamic terrorist organisation to murder US citizens and other internationally protected persons. The applicant argued that while it was accepted that the offence was within the jurisdiction of the US, the offence took place outside the territorial jurisdiction of the English court. It was argued on behalf of the US that in order to be classed as an extraditable crime it was sufficient for the offence to be indictable in the UK, even if on an extra-territorial basis. The Divisional Court held that it was necessary to show that the crime was alleged to have been committed within the actual territory of the US and that it was not sufficient to allege that a crime was

The basis of extra-territorial jurisdiction under EC competition law

The EC courts have not explicitly embraced the effects doctrine, and have instead relied upon two principles, the economic entity doctrine, and the implementation doctrine. The economic entity doctrine was put forward, in the face of resistance by the UK, in the case of *Dyestuffs*.[15] Here the EEC Commission (as it then was) targeted a pan-European cartel, finding that Geigy, Sandoz, ICI, and three non-EEC undertakings had acted so as to fix prices throughout the EC. ICI, a company registered in the UK, lay outside the EEC at the time of the infringement decision and subsequent appeal. The ECJ, on appeal, took the approach that the legally separate constituents of a single undertaking could be treated as one and the same, such that a parent based outside the EC could be targeted through a subsidiary based in the EC.[16] The same approach had been rejected previously by the UK courts in the case of *Re Schweppes Ltd's Agreement*[17] and the UK protested the application of EC competition law to a company incorporated in the UK that was neither resident in, nor carrying on business in, the EEC. The economic entity doctrine has since entered UK competition law, via the application of s 60, CA 98.

The leading case to deal with extra-territorial jurisdiction in the EC is the *Woodpulp* case The EC Commission took action against an alleged cartel of producers of bleached sulphate wood pulp based in countries as diverse as the United States, Canada, Finland and Sweden (prior to the accession of the latter two states to the EC).[18] In all, some 36 undertakings affected by the decision were not based in the EC. In its decision the Commission argued at para 79 that:

> Article [81] of the Treaty applies to restrictive practices which may affect trade between member states even if the undertakings and associations of undertakings which are parties to the restrictive practices are established or have their headquarters outside the Community, and even if the restrictive practices in question also affect markets outside the EEC.

When the case was argued on appeal before the ECJ the Commission submitted that the approach it had taken was 'not in breach of any prohibitive rule of international law . . . in so far as its jurisdiction is based on the effects within the Community of conduct which occurred elsewhere'.[19] The Commission accepted that the application of the effects doctrine was not without controversy, but

committed within the extra-territorial jurisdiction of the US which would in similar circumstances be governed by the extra-territorial jurisdiction of the UK. Dismissing the appeal, the House of Lords held that the extradition agreement did not require that the acts alleged to constitute the extradition crime were committed within the territory of the US. It was sufficient that the offence for which extradition was sought was triable within the US and an equivalent crime would be triable in the UK.

[15] OJ (1969) 24 July.

[16] *ICI Ltd v Commission* [1972] ECR 619, [1972] CMLR 557.

[17] [1965] 1 All ER 195.

[18] *Wood Pulp* Commission Decision 85/202 (1985) OJ L85/1.

[19] *Re Wood Pulp Cartel: A Ahlstrom Oy v Commission* joined cases C–89 etc [1988] 4 CMLR 901, at 915.

argued that the objections came mainly from the UK, and not from other members of the OECD. The UK, as an intervener in the case, requested that the ECJ resolve the issue by reference to the application of territorial jurisdiction, and not by reference to the effects doctrine. The approach taken by the ECJ is set out here as it may have consequences for the application of territorial jurisdiction in relation to the cartel offence.

> [16] It should be observed that an infringement of Article [81], such as the conclusion of an agreement which has had the effect of restricting competition within the Common Market, consists of conduct made up of two elements, the formation of the agreement, decision or concerted practice and the implementation thereof. If the applicability of prohibitions laid down under competition law were made to depend on the place where the agreement, decision or concerted practice was formed, the result would obviously be to give undertakings an easy means of evading those prohibitions. The decisive factor is therefore the place where it is implemented.
>
> [17] The producers in this case implemented their pricing agreement within the Common Market. It is immaterial in that respect whether or not they had recourse to subsidiaries, agents, sub-agents, or branches within the Community in order to make their contacts with purchasers within the Community.
>
> [18] Accordingly the Community's jurisdiction to apply its competition rules to such conduct is covered by the territoriality principle as universally recognised in public international law . . .

To some extent this judgment avoided the more contentious issue of whether the EC would apply the effects doctrine in its pure form. The ECJ did not deal with what the position might have been had the agreement been both formed *and* implemented outside the EC. For example, if there is a difference, and it is argued that there is one, between the effects doctrine and the implementation approach it would lie in the fact that a cartel agreed upon and implemented by producers based exclusively in the US, with no active sales at all into the EC, and no contracts being made in the EC, would be outside the scope of the implementation route of attack. However, in such a case an aggressive application of the effects doctrine would be capable of targeting the conduct, although difficulties might remain with enforcement. The approach set out in the *Woodpulp* case was relied upon by the CFI in a subsequent merger case,[20] and at present represents the limits of the assertion of EC jurisdiction.

EXTRADITION

The Act makes express provision for extradition in respect to the cartel offence. Thus s 191 provides:

> The offences to which an Order in Council under section 2 of the Extradition Act 1870 (c. 52) (arrangements with foreign states) can apply include—

[20] *Gencor Ltd v Commission* case T–102/96 [1999] ECR–II 753, [1999] 4 CMLR 971.

(a) an offence under s 188,
(b) conspiracy to commit such an offence, and
(c) attempt to commit such an offence

Extradition is the formal process whereby a person accused or convicted of a serious offence is returned to the jurisdiction in which the offence was committed in order to stand trial or serve a sentence of imprisonment. The process of extradition, which is founded on the concepts of reciprocity, comity and respect for differences in other jurisdictions, aims to further international co-operation in criminal justice matters and strengthens domestic law enforcement. Arguably the law of extradition is procedural not substantive law, and extradition proceedings are the means by which domestic criminal proceedings can be pursued abroad. However, extradition is not used to secure the return of persons merely suspected of committing an offence for questioning. The law of extradition, which is a branch of international law, is based on the assumption that the requesting state is acting in good faith and that the person will receive a fair trial. There is no general rule of international law that requires state to surrender persons and extradition arrangements proceed on the basis of a formal treaty or a reciprocal agreement between States. While requests for extradition are traditionally made through diplomatic channels, extradition proceedings frequently involve input from both the executive and the judiciary. Although some countries give exclusive control of the process to either the judiciary or the executive, most countries prefer a hybrid system. In Canada and the US, for example, extradition is a two-step process involving a hearing at which a magistrate or judge considers whether the requesting State has complied with the formalities. Provided the court is satisfied that a legal basis for extradition exists, the person will be committed to await surrender to the requesting state. However, under this system the ultimate decision is an act of executive discretion.[21]

The law of extradition in the UK is now governed by the Extradition Act 2003 (the 2003 Act) which received Royal Assent in November 2003 and came into force in January 2004. This legislation fundamentally changes the extradition regime in the UK. It modernises and reduces the complexity of the scheme which operated under the Extradition Act 1989 which was a consolidation of three earlier provisions, the Extradition Act 1870 (as amended) (the 1870 Act), the Criminal Justice Act 1988, and the Fugitive Offenders Act 1967. Traditionally, UK extradition legislation created a framework that provided different schemes for different categories of requesting states and territories.[22] Extradition to countries who were signatories to the European Convention on Extradition 1957, designated Commonwealth countries, British Overseas Territories and Hong Kong was dealt with under Part III of the Extradition Act 1989 Act. However, extradition to countries that had signed a bilateral extradition treaty with the UK prior to 1989,

[21] This decision lies with the Secretary of State in the US and with the Minister of Justice in Canada.
[22] The categories were 'foreign states', 'colonies', now referred to as 'British Overseas Territories' and designated 'Commonwealth countries'.

which included the United States, proceeded according to an earlier scheme established under the 1870 Act. The 2003 Act makes provision for a range of new extradition procedures including a system of placing extradition partners into two categories, the adoption of the European Council Framework Decision on the European Arrest Warrant,[23] the retention with some modification to current arrangements for extradition to non EU countries, the abolition of the *prima facie* requirement in some cases and a simplified appeal process.

The responsibility for designating extradition partners to a specific category lies with the Secretary of State. However, the *Explanatory Notes* to the 2003 Act indicate that it will be possible for extradition partners to move from one category to the other by an Order in Council. Any change in designation will depend upon the extradition procedures negotiated between the UK and other states. The 2003 Act does not indicate any specific criteria to determine which countries will be designated Category 1 territories. However, territories retaining the death penalty as a punishment under the general criminal law of that country may not be designated as a Category 1 territory.[24] Provision is made to address the problem of extradition in cases involving convictions *in absentia* where the person did not deliberately absent themselves from trial and competing extradition requests. Extradition from the UK to Category 1 territories takes place in accordance with Part 1 of the Extradition Act 2003, which also contains provisions to implement the Framework Decision on the European Arrest Warrant; Part 2 governs extradition to Category 2 territories. Initially all Member States of the EU are designated Category 1 territories, whereas all other countries having existing extradition arrangements with the UK have been placed in the second category.

Extradition within the EU: The European Arrest Warrant

While the creation of a two-tiered system for extradition has been subject to some criticism, arguably the most contentious matter is the implementation of the

[23] 2002/584/JHA. The basis for EU Framework Decisions is Article 34(2)(b) of the Treaty of Amsterdam. The Framework Decision of 13 June 2002 is a follow up to the adoption at the Tampere Special European Council 1999 of the principle of mutual recognition of judicial decisions by Member States of the European Union. The Tampere European Council conclusions stated that: 'the formal extradition procedure should be abolished among the Member States as far as persons are concerned who are fleeing from justice after having been finally sentenced, and replaced by a simple transfer of such persons, in compliance with article 6 TEU. Consideration should also be given to fast-track extradition procedures, without prejudice to the principle of fair trial' (item 35). However, the initiatives to reform the surrender mechanisms within Member States were expedited by the events that took place in the United States in September 2001. At an Extraordinary European Council meeting held on 21 September 2001, the heads of state of the EU, the President of the European Parliament and the President of the European Commission called for the creation of a European warrant for arrest and extradition in accordance with the conclusions reached at the Tampere meeting. Consequently, the European Commission presented a Proposal for a Council Framework Decision on the European arrest warrant and the surrender procedures between the Member States. In its report on this proposal, the UK Parliamentary European Scrutiny Committee expressed some concern at the speed with which this initiative was processed through the EU legislative machinery.

[24] The Extradition Act 2003, s 1(3).

European Arrest Warrant, which will replace formal extradition within the EU with a system of surrender on the basis of the principle of mutual recognition of judicial decisions. Under the new surrender mechanism, national judges in Category 1 territories will directly enforce arrest warrants issued in other Category 1 territories without any reference to the executive. Hence the return of defendants from the UK to Category 1 territories will generally commence with the issuing of a Part 1 warrant, which is an arrest warrant issued by a judicial authority in another Category 1 state. European Arrest Warrants can only be issued in respect to the prosecution of offences carrying a sentence of imprisonment of at least 12 months, or for persons already sentenced to a custodial or detention order exceeding four months. At the extradition hearing, the judge will decide whether the offence mentioned in the warrant is an extradition offence and whether there are any bars to extradition. There is also provision for the judge to decide whether extradition is incompatible with the defendant's rights set out in the Human Rights Act 1998. Bars to extradition with respect to Category 1 territories include the rule against double jeopardy, the person's age, the passage of time, hostage-taking considerations, specialty, which requires the requesting territory to provide an undertaking to prosecute only in respect of the extradition offences set out in the warrant, and an earlier extradition to the UK from either another Category 1 territory or a non Category 1 territory. However, the double criminality rule, which requires that the conduct is an offence in both countries, is removed with respect to Category 1 territories if the judge in the requesting state certifies that the offence is included in the European framework list of 32 serious offences. This list includes terrorism, corruption, swindling, participation in a criminal organisation, money laundering, racketeering and extortion. This does not, at present, include the cartel offence, but the possibility exists that it might be extended to do so in the future. Lack of harmonisation within the criminal law of EU states with respect to the definition of these offences is anticipated to create problems. The decision whether or not to execute the warrant and to order the defendant's surrender to another Category 1 territory will be made solely by the judiciary. Although under these new surrender procedures the defendant has the right of appeal to the High Court or to the House of Lords, the Secretary of State ceases to play any role.

Extradition from the UK to non-EU countries

The procedure for extradition from the UK to Category 2 territories is set out in Part 2 of the Extradition Act 2003. While many of the traditional arrangements for extradition to these states have been retained, there are some important modifications that aim to reduce the duplication and complexity of extradition procedures. Thus an extradition request from a Category 2 territory is sent initially to the Secretary of State for certification, and then forwarded to a judge for consideration. Provided the judge is satisfied that the documentation is in order, he or she considers whether the offence specified in the request is an extradition offence and whether any of the bars to extradition set out in Part 2 are applicable. These include the rule against double jeopardy, extraneous considerations, which prohibit extradition if it appears that the request has been issued for the purpose of prosecuting for reasons of race, religion, nationality, gender, sexual orientation or political opinion, the passage of time and hostage-taking considerations. If there are no bars to extradition, the judge will then decide, in the case of persons awaiting trial, whether there is a *prima facie* case. This requirement does not apply for requesting states which have been designated by order of the Secretary of State as territories not required to submit *prima facie* evidence. In cases which require the judge to consider evidence submitted in support of the extradition request, the 2003 Act creates a new statutory exception to the hearsay rule.[25] Having been satisfied that the request complies with the formalities, and that extradition is compatible with the Human Rights Act 1998, the judge will refer the case to the Secretary of State for consideration. Unlike surrender arrangements to Category 1 territories, the executive still retains the power to refuse a request for extradition to Category 2 territories. The factors to be considered are the risk that the death penalty will be imposed, lack of specialty protection and whether the defendant has been extradited to the UK from another country that has not consented to re-extradition. There is a right of appeal to the High Court and the House of Lords against both the judge's decision to refer the case to Secretary of State, and from his or her decision to comply with the extradition request. However, the 2003 Act does not provide for appeal by way of *habeas corpus* and there is an express provision excluding judicial review. Furthermore, in order to speed up the appeals process and avoid duplication, appeals will be heard after the Secretary of State makes a decision.

Part 4 of the 2003 Act makes provision for the police to obtain search and seizure warrants in extradition cases and for the issuing of codes of practice to cover the use of police powers. Thus many of the coercive powers provided by the Police and Criminal Evidence Act 1984 (PACE) in respect of domestic offences have effectively been extended to cover foreign offences provided they are classified as extradition crimes within the meaning of the 2003 Act. A warrant will authorise the police to enter premises and confiscate relevant material provided it is not legally privileged material, excluded or special procedure material.[26] Applications for production orders in extradition cases to gain access to excluded and special procedure material must be made to a circuit judge. The 2003 Act also provides for entry and search without a warrant in order to arrest; the search of

[25] The Extradition Act 2003 s 114.

[26] Excluded material covers three categories of material held on a confidential basis and includes personal records, human tissue or tissue fluid and journalistic material. Special procedure material includes journalistic material that is not categorised as excluded material and material, other than legally privileged material, which is acquired or created in the course of a business, profession or other occupation and which is held subject to an undertaking to hold it in confidence or a statutory requirement to restrict disclosure.

premises where a person was immediately before arrest; to search a person on arrest and to search premises occupied or controlled by the defendant. Additional seizure powers provided by ss 50 and 51 of the Criminal Justice and Police Act 2001 are also available in extradition cases. Where a person is arrested under an extradition arrest power, fingerprints and non-intimate samples[27] can be taken provided the detainee gives written consent or the police obtain appropriate authorisation. In England and Wales, evidence of identity in extradition cases must be established according to the procedures set out in the 2003 Act.

Extradition between the US and the UK

Traditionally, it has been the practice in the UK and the US for extradition treaties to provide a list of specific extradition crimes. However, the 'list' method has many drawbacks. Extradition will only be granted for offences included in the list, thus, treaties require constant updating to keep abreast of new offences. Furthermore, the requested State lacks the jurisdiction to inquire into the substantive criminal law of the requesting State to determine whether the conduct amounts to an extraditable offence. Although an exchange of notes between the UK and the US governments signed in May 2001 deleted provisions that excluded criminal prosecutions in competition cases from the UK/US Mutual Legal Assistance Treaty, this instrument does not cover extradition. Extradition arrangements between the US/UK are now governed by the 2003 UK/US extradition treaty, which introduces some significant changes to the current extradition arrangements between the UK and the US.[28] This treaty, which was signed in March 2003, has been the subject of some severe criticism.[29] Its main provisions include a limited political offence exception, the removal of the requirement for evidence of a *prima facie* case in requests from the US for extradition from the UK; the replacement of the 'list' of extradition crimes with a conduct based test; a change in the exceptions to the speciality protection, and a restriction on extradition to death penalty states unless appropriate assurances are given. Following the enforcement of the Extradition Act 2003 extradition from the UK to the US must accord with the provisions contained in Part 2 of this Act, which retains many of the traditional bars to extradition including the double criminality requirement.

Where states exercise jurisdiction on the basis of territoriality, the double criminality rule can be problematic in respect of extra-territorial offences.[30] Thus

[27] A sample of hair, swabs taken from the body and footprints are currently classed as non-intimate. Public hair, semen and swabs from the vagina, penis and anus are classed as intimate.

[28] Cm 5821.

[29] The Law Society Parliamentary Brief On US/UK Extradition Treaty May 2003 at www.lawsociety.org.uk, Justice Briefing on Extradition to the USA: The UK–US Treaty of March 2003 at www.justice.org.uk; Statewatch News online: New UK–US Extradition Treaty (Special report no 2) at www.statewatch.org/news/2003/jul/25ukus.htm.

[30] G Mullan, 'The Concept of Double Criminality in the Context of Extra-Territorial Crimes' [1997] *Criminal Law Review* 17.

extradition to the US under the 2003 US/UK extradition treaty could be resisted if the conduct on which an extradition request from the US is based is described with insufficient precision to be identified with an offence in English law. There is no obvious equivalent in English law, for example, for US offences known as racketeering, mail fraud and wire fraud. Problems may also arise with respect to extradition requests from the UK to the US for the cartel offence. The US maintains criminal penalties in place in relation to cartel conduct which is in breach of s 1 of the Sherman Act 1890, but it is not immediately certain that extradition will be available to the US, given the differences between the two relevant substantive provisions. It has been recognised that:

> Automatic extradition requires both states to prosecute an offender for an identical criminal offence. There are some differences between the United Kingdom offence created under the [Act], and the United States offence brought under the Sherman Act. The US offence is not based on dishonesty, therefore a request would need to be reviewed by the UK courts to establish whether the request fulfils the criteria of it being a case where the offence applies in nature to both jurisdictions. Such a review by the courts provides an extra safeguard against automatic extradition, which is ultimately a matter for the courts to decide.[31]

Extradition between the US and the EU

The reluctance of many EU states to extradite their nationals has created some antagonism between the EU and the US. Lack of reciprocity has been a disincentive for law enforcement agencies dealing with extraterritorial and transnational crime to abide by formal extradition arrangements.[32] In June 2003 an agreement was signed which establishes a basic framework for extradition arrangements and mutual legal assistance in criminal matters between the EU and the US.[33] Although this development will result in some changes being made to existing bi-lateral treaties, each EU state will continue to negotiate their own bi-lateral extradition agreements with the US. However, the EU/US extradition agreement does not address the issue of evidence and will have no direct effect on the principle of non-extradition of nationals.[34]

[31] *Hansard*, Standing Committee B, cols 188–89.

[32] C Gane and S Nash, 'Illegal Extradition: The Irregular Return of Fugitive Offenders', 1 *Scottish Law & Practice Quarterly* (1996), 277.

[33] 2003/516/EC (2003) OJ L181/25.

[34] Many civil law States prefer to exercise criminal jurisdiction over their nationals whether an offence was committed on their own territory or abroad. The rationale for this exception is linked to sovereignty, and in some states it is considered to be a fundamental right.

CO-OPERATION WITH OVERSEAS AUTHORITIES AND THE EXCHANGE OF INFORMATION

While most forms of mutual legal assistance proceed on the basis of the principle of international comity, increasingly mutual co-operation in criminal matters takes place by way of bilateral or multilateral treaty. The European countries prefer to negotiate multilateral MLAT's, whereas the US has traditionally demonstrated a preference to enter into bilateral arrangements, which allow for greater specificity.[35] Generally, mutual legal assistance treaties (MLATs) require contracting parties to undertake to provide assistance in taking written testimony; conducting searches for and seizing material for use as evidence; serving summonses and tracing witnesses and suspects. Conventionally, mutual assistance arrangements abide by the *locus regit actum* rule, which permits the requested party to execute letters rogatory in accordance with its national law and practice. While some MLATs encourage requesting states to indicate their preferred method of conducting the inquiry, in practice, they exert little control over the manner in which requests are executed. To increase the effectiveness of MLATs and to combat admissibility problems, assistance mechanisms are placing increasing emphasis on compliance with the procedural requirements of the requesting state. Requests for assistance are generally subject to judicial authorisation in the requested state, which can be cumbersome and time consuming. However, judicial input undoubtedly assists in maintaining a balance between competing interests and safeguards against an abuse of the mutual legal assistance process by governments. Thus requests may be refused if evidence would need to be taken under compulsion or from a witness who would be non-compellable in the requested state. States may also refuse requests if the evidence is protected by the rules of privilege. While some MLAT's state that the requesting state shall not, without the consent of the requested state, use information or evidence provided by the requested state for investigations other than those stated in the request, others allow evidence to be used in the prosecution of non-treaty offences. Most mutual assistance provisions have a double criminality requirement in respect of requests for search and seizure of material and insist on precise information of the place to be searched, the material to be seized and the nature of the offence under investigation. While searches and seizures are usually conducted in accordance with local rules, domestic courts are required to be vigilant to prevent police officers exceeding their investigative powers. Despite moves to introduce measures designed to offer the defence some procedural protection, criticism has been

[35] See for example the 1959 European Convention on Mutual Legal Assistance in Criminal Matters and the 1994 Treaty Between the Government of the United Kingdom of Great Britain and Northern Ireland and the Government of the United States of America on Mutual Legal Assistance in Criminal Matters.

directed towards the lack of corresponding mechanisms for the accused needing to seek assistance from foreign authorities.[36]

Mutual Legal Assistance provision within the EU

Following more than four years of negotiations the text of the 2000 Convention on Mutual Assistance in Criminal Matters between Member States of the European Union (MLAC) was finally agreed in May 2000. It embraces both conventional forms of assistance and some controversial cross-border investigation methods. Although some relief was expressed that this EU Convention was finally approved, it has been the subject of much criticism. While MLAC was originally concerned with judicial co-operation, provisions on police co-operation were added later. It imposes an obligation on contracting parties to execute requests for assistance from another EU state as soon as possible.[37] MLAC's primary purpose is to improve co-operation between judicial, police and customs authorities by modernising existing mutual legal assistance provisions. Although the preamble, and the first article indicate that the new arrangements supplement rather than extend the scope of existing conventions, including arrangements under the Benelux Treaty and the 1990 Convention applying the Schengen Agreement, some provisions represent a fundamental shift in traditional arrangements. This instrument, breaking with the Council of Europe's tradition of allowing contracting parties to enter reservations against any provision, stipulates which provisions contain opt-out clauses.[38] Critical comment has been made regarding the failure to include a provision allowing States to refuse to execute a request on the ground that it would present a threat to sovereignty, security and public order. There has also been criticism regarding resistance to include data protection provisions similar to those found in other Third Pillar conventions. While the new powers were introduced primarily as a response to governmental concerns about the growth in cross-border serious and organised crime, this Convention has been drafted to cover any crime. Although the preamble points out that States will act in a manner which is compatible with the European Convention on Human Rights, the body of the Convention does not allow assistance to be refused on the ground that fundamental rights will be compromised. Speed and efficiency may be achieved by

[36] See generally A Ellis, and R Pisani, 'The United States Treaties on Mutual Assistance: A Comparative Analysis', 1985 *The International Lawyer* 189–223; W Gilmore, (ed), *Mutual Assistance in Criminal and Business Regulatory Matters* (Cambridge University Press, 1995); A Jones, *Jones on Extradition and Mutual Legal Assistance* (London, Sweet and Maxwell, 2001); C Murray, and L Harris, *Mutual Assistance in Criminal Matters* (London, Sweet & Maxwell, 2002); E Nadelmann, 'Negotiations in Criminal Law Assistance Treaties', 33 *American Journal of Criminal Law* (1985) 467–504; ENadelmann, *Cops Across Borders: The Internationalisation of US Criminal Law Enforcement* (Pennsylvania State University Press, 1993).

[37] (2000) OJ C197/1.

[38] For example, the UK has opted out of article 6 which provides for the direct transmission of requests for assistance.

reducing to an unacceptable level the procedural guarantees that provide the accused in transnational cases with protection from over-zealous States. This instrument has subsequently been supplemented by a Protocol which extends mutual assistance provision to matters related to money laundering and financial crime.[39]

Mutual Legal Assistance provision in the UK[40]

Until recently provisions in the UK/US Treaty on Mutual Legal Assistance in Criminal Matters[41] specifically prevented the UK from considering US requests for mutual assistance in respect to criminal anti-trust or competition law cases. These provisions, which operated as a barrier to international co-operation in combating the formation of international cartels, have now been removed. An exchange of Notes between the governments of the UK and the US,[42] which entered into force on 1 May 2001, amended the treaty and enabled authorities in the UK to provide their US counterparts with the full range of mutual assistance mechanisms provided for under the Criminal Justice (International Co-operation) Act 1990. This legislation, which was enacted to enable the UK to co-operate with other states in criminal investigations has recently been amended by the Crime (International Co-operation) Act 2003 (CICA), which received Royal Assent on 30 October 2003. This legislative initiative was introduced to implement some of the UK's outstanding EU commitments in respect to police and judicial co-operation. These include MLAC and its 2001 Protocol, the mutual assistance provisions of the Schengen Implementing Convention[43] and the evidence-freezing provisions in the Framework Decision of 22 July 2003 on the execution in the EU of orders freezing property or evidence. CICA is in five parts and contains six schedules. Part 1 of CICA, which addresses mutual legal assistance provision in the UK significantly amends Part 1 of the Criminal Justice (International Co-operation) Act 1990 and widens the scope of cases in which the UK can make requests and offer mutual assistance in criminal matters, and provides for the direct transmission of requests. The new legislation also contains provisions which

[39] (2001) OJ C 326/1.

[40] Requests for mutual assistance in criminal matters in the UK are the responsibility of the Judicial Co-operation Unit. For further information see http://www.homeoffice.Government.uk/at02/mla.htm.

[41] TS No 14 (1997) Cm 3456.

[42] Cm 5375.

[43] The Schengen Convention provides for the abolition of internal border controls between Member States of the EU. This Convention introduced a system of compensatory measures focued on policing and immigration which were designed to tackle the increase in cross-border crime. These measures included the intensification of external border checks, harmonisation of policies on the issuing of visas and residence permits, a common policy on asylum applications and harmonisation of rules relating to illicit drugs and arms. Signatories to the Schengen Convention undertake that national police authorities will assist each other 'for the purpose of preventing and detecting crime' within the limits of their national law. The 1997 Treaty of Amsterdam integrated the Schengen Convention into the EU treaty structure.

amend the Criminal Justice and Police Act 2001 by providing that the additional powers of seizure of evidence in this statute will also apply to overseas offences or investigations. Part 2 implements the Framework Decision of 13 June 2002 on combating terrorism, which requires the UK to take extra-territorial jurisdiction over a range of terrorist offences. Part 3 introduces the mutual recognition of driving disqualifications.[44] Part 4 implements measures set out in the Schengen Convention which address the area of police co-operation, extradition and data protection, contains provisions to implement the Framework Decision of 28 May 2001 on combating fraud and counterfeiting of non-cash payment and implements the 2003 Framework Decision in respect to terrorist property.

Under the terms of the Crime (International Co-operation) Act 2003 assistance may be requested from a foreign authority in order to obtain evidence located outside the UK for use in domestic criminal proceedings or an investigation. However, evidence obtained abroad for use in domestic criminal proceedings can raise difficult admissibility issues for national courts. Undoubtedly, traditional common law admissibility rules exacerbate the problem and create a potential disincentive to international co-operation in the investigation of serious crime. Some of these difficulties have been circumvented by the provisions of the Criminal Justice Act 2003, which relax the traditional rule against hearsay in criminal proceedings.[45] Before a request for assistance under Part 1 of the CICA is issued, there must be reasonable grounds for suspecting an offence has been committed and either criminal proceedings or an investigation is underway.[46] Evidence obtained from a foreign authority may only be used for the purposes for which it was requested, unless the consent of the requested overseas has been obtained, and is subject to the same admissibility rules as evidence obtained from within the jurisdiction.[47] Provision is also made to assist foreign authorities to obtain evidence located in the UK for use in proceedings abroad.[48] In some circumstances, domestic statutory police powers to search for and seize evidence provided by Part 2 of the Police and Criminal Evidence Act 1984 PACE will be extended to cover foreign offences. However, magistrates or judges are obliged not to issue warrants where there is a reasonable doubt that the material sought is subject to legal privilege, or consists of excluded or special procedure material. Provision is made for taking video evidence of witnesses for transmission abroad and to hear the testimony of witnesses located abroad through live television link.[49] Further, a witness in the UK will now be able to give evidence through live television link or by telephone in criminal proceedings before a court in a country outside the UK.[50] The UK will also be able to respond to requests for telephone hearings but will have no power

[44] The Convention on Driving Disqualification of 17 June 1998 was drawn up on the basis of Article K.3 of the Treaty on European Union.

[45] The Criminal Justice Act ss 114–20.

[46] The Crime (International Co-operation) Act 2003, s 7.

[47] *Ibid*, s 9.

[48] *Ibid*, ss 13–19.

[49] *Ibid*, s 29.

[50] *Ibid*, ss 30, 31.

to compel a witness to attend the hearing. The CICA makes specific provision for the disclosure of information by the Serious Fraud Office in the context of criminal proceedings or investigations and provides for the inspection of overseas information systems.[51] Thus the Information Commissioner can inspect personal data stored on the Schengen information system,[52] the Europol information system[53] and the Customs information system.[54]

OVERSEAS DISCLOSURE OF INFORMATION

The provisions of Part 9 of the Enterprise Act 2002 provide for extensive powers of disclosure of information in relation to competition matters by public authorities in the UK.[55] However in order to protect confidentiality with respect to both commercial and personal information, the Act imposes some general restrictions and conditions for the disclosure of specified information held by public authorities. Failure to comply with these restrictions, or the improper use of information disclosed under these provisions will amount to an offence.[56] These new measures will consolidate and codify the OFT's powers to disclose information to overseas public authorities (OPA) for the purposes of both civil and criminal investigations.[57] Earlier legislation restricting disclosure in competition and consumer matters is repealed and replaced by a general restriction on disclosure, which can now be enforced by means of criminal sanctions.[58] The new provisions aim to increase and harmonise the gateways through which information can be disclosed both in the UK and abroad. While these measures will assist to facilitate co-operation between enforcement agencies in the fight against anti-competitive

[51] The Crime (International Co-operation) Act 2003, ss 80–81.

[52] The Schengen Information System (SIS) was established under Title IV of the Convention implementing the Schengen Agreement of 14 June 1985. It came into operation in 1995 and is a series of national databases connected to a central system which holds information on suspected criminals, missing persons unwanted aliens and stolen vehicles and documents.

[53] The Europol information system was established under Title II of the Convention on the Establishment of a European Police Office. It is an extensive computerised database which stores personal data for use in the prevention and investigation of serious crime. It can be accessed by national units and liaison officers. Each Member State is required to establish a national body to liase between Europol and the competent national authorities.

[54] The Customs information system was established under the Convention on the Use of Information Technology for Customs Purposes.

[55] The Enterprise Act 2002 uses the definition of 'public authority' provided by the Human Rights Act 1998, s 6.

[56] *Ibid* s 245.

[57] In the *Explanatory notes* to the Act (para 627) an overseas public authority is defined as

> . . . any organisation involved in the conduct of criminal investigations or proceedings, and also those organisations involved in the conduct of any civil investigations or proceedings related to the enforcement of competition or consumer legislation. In reality, this will probably include police and security forces together with national competition authorities and organisations with powers linked to consumer legislation (these could be public or private bodies).

[58] See for example, the Fair Trading Act 1973, the Consumer Credit Act 1974 and the Competition Act 1998.

practices and cross-border cartels, some concern has been raised with respect to the breadth of the disclosure provisions.[59] Whether these provisions meet with the requirements of Article 8 of the European Convention on Human Rights remains to be seen.

Article 8 provides

> (1) Everyone has the right to respect for his private and family life, his home and his correspondence.
> (2) There shall be no interference by a public authority with the exercise of this right except such as in accordance with the law and is necessary in a democratic society in the interests of national security, public safety or the economic well-being of the country, for the prevention of disorder or crime, for the protection of health or morals or for the protection of the rights and freedoms of others.

The object of this provision is to offer the individual some protection against unnecessary interference by public authorities. Any interference with this right must be subject to adequate and effective safeguards that offer individuals sufficient protection against arbitrary interference. In order to satisfy the 'in accordance with the law' requirement there must be a legal framework, which is formulated with sufficient clarity to provide people with an adequate indication as to the circumstances in which the authorities are empowered to interfere with their rights. Interestingly, the exception that permits an interference with privacy for 'the economic well-being of the country' does not extend to other rights such as the freedom of expression. To be Convention compliant, any interference with an individual's privacy must be considered necessary and proportionate. While states enjoy a margin of appreciation, the final evaluation as to whether any restrictions placed on article 8 rights are compatible with the Convention rests with the European Court of Human Rights.

Section 237 of the Act provides for a general restriction on the disclosure of 'specified information', which is defined in s 238 and refers to any information obtained under the OFT's statutory powers, including information received before the Enterprise Act entered into force. If this information relates to the affairs of an individual or any business of an undertaking, it must not be disclosed during the lifetime of that individual or while any undertaking is in existence, unless disclosure is specifically permitted by the Act. Disclosure of information is also prohibited if it would infringe the Data Protection Act 1998. Other restrictions on disclosure are contained within the disclosure gateways themselves. There are several exceptions to the general restriction on disclosure. Thus, for example, disclosure is permitted if the information is already legitimately in the public domain;[60] or if there are other powers or duties to disclose which exist apart from the Act;[61] or where consent to

[59] Justice Note on the Enterprise Bill 2002 at www.justice.org.uk.

[60] The Enterprise Act, s 237(3).

[61] *Ibid* s 237(6). For example, from May 2004 article 12 of Regulation 1/2003 on the implementation of the rules on competition laid down in article 81 and 82 will provide the Commission and the designated national competition authorities the power to exchange information to apply articles 81 and 82. Thus there will be no need for the authorities to rely on section 243 of the Act.

disclose is obtained from the relevant parties.[62] Furthermore, the Act does not prohibit disclosure of information held by a public authority if the disclosure is required for the purposes of a Community obligation.[63]

Notwithstanding the general prohibition against disclosure, the Act creates specific disclosure gateways. Thus s 242 provides that a public authority can disclose specified information if it is relevant to a criminal investigation or criminal proceedings which are being conducted in any part of the UK. This information can also be disclosed in respect of any decision whether to start or end the investigation or the proceedings. The recipient must not use information received under this gateway for any purpose other than that for which it was disclosed and public authorities must be satisfied that 'the making of the disclosure is proportionate to what is sought to be achieved by it'.[64] Section 243 provides public authorities with the power to disclose to an overseas public authority for the purpose of facilitating

> . . . the exercise by the overseas public authority of any function which it has relating to—
> (a) carrying out investigations in connection with the enforcement of any relevant legislation by means of civil proceedings;
> (b) bringing civil proceedings for the enforcement of such legislation or the conduct of such proceedings;
> (c) the investigation of crime;
> (d) bringing criminal proceedings or the conduct of such proceedings;
> (e) deciding whether to start or bring to an end such investigations and proceedings.

The OFT has indicated that it will only be prepared to disclose information to OPA's exercising functions of a public nature in relation to the matters listed in s 243(2).[65] Disclosure of information is not permitted under the overseas gateway for specific categories of commercially sensitive information including information obtained under merger or market investigation powers.[66] Section 243(4) provides that the Secretary of State can intervene and prohibit disclosure of information to an OPA where it appears more appropriate that the investigation or proceedings for which the information was requested should be conducted either in the UK or in another country. The OFT has indicated that where it considers that a request for information which merits disclosure raises issues of extraterritoriality under s 243(4), it will forward the request to the Secretary of State to make the final decision.[67]

Factors which must be taken into account by the OFT's when deciding to disclose information under the overseas gateway are set out in s 243(6). These include whether the issue is considered to be sufficiently serious to justify making the disclosure,[68] whether the receiving state provides sufficient protection against

[62] The Enterprise Act, s 239.
[63] *Ibid* s 240.
[64] *Ibid* s 242(3).
[65] Consultation paper on Part 9 of the Act—The overseas disclosure of information, para 3.3.
[66] See above n 60 s 243(3).
[67] Consultation paper on Part 9 of the Act—The overseas disclosure of information, para 3.5, fn 9.
[68] See above n 60 s 243(6)(a).

self-incrimination in criminal proceedings,[69] if there are sufficient guarantees with respect to the disclosure and storage of personal data[70] and whether there is mutual assistance provision which provides for a similar restriction on the disclosure of information obtained under statutory powers.[71] Section 243(7) provides that procedural protections provided by OPA's corresponding to those available in the UK are considered appropriate for the purposes of the Act. The OFT takes the view that a protection is 'appropriate'

> . . . if, considered in the round, it provides an equivalent level of protection to that provided in any part of the United Kingdom, even if it is not directly analogous to the rules in the UK.[72]

While the decision whether OPA's satisfy the considerations set out in s 243 will be decided on a case-by-case basis, the OFT has indicated that it considers that the domestic rules in the US and measures taken by the European Commission provide appropriate protection in respect to both the privilege against self-incrimination and data protection.[73] Similarly, all Member States of the Council of Europe should satisfy the privilege against self-incrimination requirement.[74] The OFT takes the view that the prospect of bringing civil and criminal proceedings on matters related to competition law and consumer protection will be regarded as sufficiently serious to trigger disclosure.[75] However, if a request for information appears to be a fishing expedition or that the information sought by the OPA is considered to be disproportionate to the detriment under consideration, disclosure will be declined.

The signing of an MLAT in respect to the disclosure of specific information is likely to indicate that the matters covered by the treaty are sufficiently serious to justify making an overseas disclosure, and can also resolve any doubt as to whether the considerations set out in s 243(6) have been satisfied. The UK has signed and ratified several MLAT's that specifically address arrangements for co-operation in respect to criminal matters. The existence of an MLAT relating to co-operation in criminal matters will not automatically lead the OFT to disclose information to an OPA for a function it had in relation to civil proceedings.[76] In October 2003 the

[69] See above n 60 s 243(6)(b).

[70] See above n 60 s 243(6)(c).

[71] See above n 60 s 243(6)(d).

[72] Consultation paper on Part 9 of the Act—The overseas disclosure of information, para 4.7.

[73] See *Miranda v Arizona* 384 US 436 (1966). The European Commission is bound by a protection equivalent to article 6 of the European Convention on Human Rights (see below) and the Data Protection Directive (Directive 95/46).

[74] Article 6 of the European Convention on Human Rights provides that in the determination of their civil rights and obligations or of any criminal charge against them, everyone shall be entitled to a fair and public hearing, within a reasonable time by an independent and impartial tribunal. Although not expressing mentioned in article 6, the European Court of Human Rights considers that the privilege against self-incrimination is an internationally recognised standard which are implicit in the right to a fair trial. See also *Funke v France* (1993) 16 EHRR 297; *Saunders v United Kingdom* (1996) 23 EHRR 313.

[75] Consultation paper on Part 9 of the Act—The overseas disclosure of information, para 4.3

[76] *Ibid*, para 4.27.

UK entered into two co-operation agreements relating specifically to the application of competition laws; one with Canada,[77] and the other with Australia and New Zealand.[78] In both cases the agreements, which are in very similar terms, relate to the 'coordination of enforcement activities', and include those activities pursued under the Enterprise Act. The agreements do not extend criminal jurisdiction, nor do they, for example, require the exchange of information where that would be incompatible with the interests of the communicating party.[79] Provided the considerations set out in s 243(6) have been met, the OFT has indicated that the absence of a formal mutual legal assistance mechanism will not necessarily result in the refusal of a request for disclosure.[80] When considering a request from an OPA without a formal arrangement the OFT will take account of several factors. These include the past record of the OPA, whether the OPA has complied with any restriction on disclosure imposed either by authorities in the UK or EU bodies such as the European Commission and whether the OPA has made proper use of the information.[81] The OFT retains a general discretion to refuse disclosure notwithstanding that the conditions set out in s 243(6) have been met. Accordingly, the OFT has indicated that statements obtained under powers provided by the CA98 will not be disclosed unless it is satisfied that the OPA will comply with the restrictions placed on the use of this information as evidence in domestic proceedings.[82] Further, information provided as part of a leniency application will only be disclosed to OPA's in limited circumstances.[83] Section 244 provides that a public body must consider whether any disclosure of specified would be contrary to the public interest and whether, and to what extent, disclosure would cause significant harm to the interests of the business or individual to which it relates. Consideration must also be given to the extent to which disclosure is necessary for the purpose for which the authority is permitted to make the disclosure. The OFT considers that s 244 is comparable to s 56 of the CA98, which has been repealed by Schedule 26 of the Act, and anticipates that it will apply a similar approach to the matter of disclosing potentially harmful commercial or personal information.[84]

[77] Cooperation arrangement between the Commissioner of Competition (Canada) and Her Majesty's Secretary of State for Trade and Industry and the Office of Fair Trading in the United Kingdom regarding the application of their competition and consumer laws.

[78] Cooperation arrangement between the Australian Competition and Consumer Commission, the Commerce Commission in New Zealand and Her Majesty's Secretary of State for Trade and Industry and the Office of Fair Trading in the United Kingdom regarding the application of their competition and consumer laws.

[79] See para VI(2) of the Canada Agreement; and VII(2) of the Australia/New Zealand Agreement.

[80] Consultation paper on Part 9 of the Act—The overseas disclosure of information, para 4.20.

[81] Ibid, paras 5.11–15.

[82] For further discussion see Chapter 3.

[83] Consultation paper on Part 9 of the Act—The overseas disclosure of information, para 5.6–5.9.

[84] Consultation paper on Part 9 of the Act—The overseas disclosure of information, para 5.3.

7

Compliance

INTRODUCTION

ALTHOUGH UNDERTAKINGS ARE not themselves subject to prosecution in relation to the cartel offence, it is certainly the case that in every situation in which an individual is successfully prosecuted the undertaking may face civil action under either article 81 EC or the Chapter I Prohibition as appropriate. This would bring with it the resulting consequences of adverse publicity (which would in all likelihood accompany the prosecution of the individual), loss of reputation, and the risks of a requirement to modify conduct, and/or to pay a penalty, as well as the possibility of subsequent actions for damages by those harmed by the illegal conduct. Such considerations should encourage undertakings to consider the adoption of compliance programmes in order to better achieve fulfilment of the obligations imposed by competition law, although this has clearly not always been the case, and the very fact of the existence of the cartel offence is proof of a recognition by the legislature that some breaches of the pre-existing competition laws were deliberate, calculated, and flagrant. This chapter considers the roles of compliance programmes in preventing breaches of the law, and in mitigating against such breaches where they occur. Some guidance is given as to the construction and implementation of a compliance programme, although the guidance given in a work such as this should not act as a substitute for formal, detailed, undertaking-specific, legal advice.

The decision whether to comply with the civil/administrative law of competition as set out in the EC Treaty and the Competition Act 1998 may have been taken, as was occasionally mooted by the relevant authorities, on the basis of a profit-calculation (ie, was the expected cost of infringement more or less than the expected profit of infringement).[1] It was this supposition that in part influenced the policy of the EC Commission and the OFT to recover the profits of the infringement wherever these could be determined.[2] Writing after the entry introduction of the CA 98 (but before its entry into force) Taylor noted that:

[1] In the literature of compliance this may be termed the 'amoral calculator' (see E Bardach and R A Kagan, *Going by the Book: The Problem of Regulatory Unreasonableness* (Philadelphia, Temple University Press, 1982).

[2] Although note that the CCAT was highly critical of the merits of this approach in the case of *Napp Pharmaceutical Holdings Ltd and Subsidiaries v The Director General of Fair Trading* [2002] CompAR 13. Here the CCAT reviewed a penalty imposed by the Director for a breach of the Chapter II Prohibition, which included an element representing an assessment of the profit incurred by the undertaking due to the infringement. The CCAT argued that:

> '. . . that approach presents certain difficulties. In the first place, there is the practical difficulty of assessing, in any given case, what the gain is. . . . Secondly, we accept the Director's submission . . . that

> The reality is that many undertakings still do not appreciate the need for compliance either because they do not take competition law seriously, are unaware of its scope and significance, or are aware of its importance but view the risks of non-compliance as acceptable in view of the administrative inconvenience of achieving compliance.[3]

Although there has not been a large amount of published research in relation to competition law compliance and the dynamics underpinning it in the EC and the UK it has been suggested in the UK context prior to the introduction of the cartel offence that companies were motivated to comply with the law by reference to questions of legitimacy, rather than profit calculation. Thus in a survey carried out by Frazer 47.7 per cent of respondents agreed with the proposition that 'companies should always comply with all competition laws', and 36 per cent agreed strongly. Less than 1 per cent disagreed strongly.[4] While this research is now somewhat out of date, and dealt only with the position where the sanctions and procedures available to the regulators were 'merely' civil in nature, it is interesting to note that the conclusion drawn at the time by Frazer was that the 'reported perceptions support the idea that greater compliance with UK law may be achieved as much through additional investigative resources as by the imposition of fines'.[5]

The fact remains however, that for whatever reason a company implements a compliance programme, the existence of that programme may be taken into account by both the EC Commission, and the OFT when taking enforcement action in the civil arena. To the extent that compliance programmes were in place before the cartel offence was introduced, it is likely that greater emphasis will be placed on such programmes following the introduction of the personally directed criminal offence. In addition to the individual sanctions there will also, of course, be attendant publicity, with ensuing damage to corporate reputations and business relationships. The fact that a compliance programme exists, however, which would result in some reduction of penalties for an undertaking may not serve as a defence in the case where there has been a flagrant, if unsanctioned breach, by an individual within that undertaking. Compliance programmes in existence prior to the introduction of the cartel offence should be reconsidered in the light of the peculiar features of the offence, and in particular stress should be placed on the increased exposure of the *individual* to liability, and on possible tensions between the individual and the organisation as a result.

There is, in this area, a link between the leniency conditions discussed in Chapter 4, above, and the compliance strategies discussed here.

the approach in the Decision which limits the "gain" to the period of the infringement is extremely conservative, since in a case such as the present the consequences of the infringement for competition do not end on the date when the infringement ends. . . . Thirdly, and in our view more significantly, it seems to us that an arithmetical calculation of the "gain" during the period of the infringement, of the kind carried out here, is likely to understate the real commercial gain from the infringing conduct, and thus risk being an ineffective remedy' (at paras 507–9).

[3] P M Taylor, *EC and UK Competition Law and Compliance* (London, Sweet & Maxwell, 1999) 281.

[4] T Frazer, 'Monopoly, Prohibition and Deterrence' (1995) *Modern Law Review* 846 at 853.

[5] *Ibid*, at 854.

In its Competition Act 1998 *Enforcement* guideline the OFT deals with compliance programmes in the following terms:

> When assessing the amount of any penalty the Director General may take into account, as a mitigating circumstance, the existence of a compliance programme. In order for a compliance programme to reduce a penalty as a mitigating circumstance, the parties will need to show that:
> —the programme has been actively implemented;
> —it has the visible and continuing support of, and is observed by, senior management;
> —there are appropriate compliance policies and procedures in place;
> —there is active and ongoing training for employees at all levels who may be involved in activities that are touched by competition law; and
> —the programme is evaluated and formal audits are carried out at regular intervals to ensure that it is delivering its objectives.[6]

It was a matter of some concern to the OFT that in the case of *Market sharing by Arriva plc and FirstGroup plc*[7] that the active participants in this cartel had acted in clear disregard of internal compliance training:

> 18. FirstGroup had arranged training on the Act for its officers and Mr Graham attended a session on 16 February 2000. Mr Davies received similar training and on 29 February 2000, the staff were issued with report forms on which to record any contact with competitors.
>
> 19. A memorandum signed by Mr Wallace and dated 25 January 2000, confirmed that he had received Arriva's training with regard to the Act. Mr Harvey was also aware of the Arriva Competition Compliance Programme under which the meeting on 14 March 2000 should have been reported. None of the staff reported the meetings of 14 and 17 March 2000 under their companies' compliance programmes, although they reported other meetings with competitors on the relevant forms.

In that part of the Decision dealing with the calculation of the penalty the DGFT therefore noted that 'each member of staff involved was at a senior level in their respective undertakings and they had all undergone compliance training'.[8] The fact that FirstGroup took some steps to address the problems identified would have been a mitigating factor in the calculation of penalties, although the company was already benefiting from full leniency. Thus:

> 27. Notwithstanding that leniency had been granted FirstGroup submitted in mitigation that its employees had received compliance training in which market sharing in circumstances similar to those in the infringement had been specified as banned under the Act. FirstGroup took compliance training very seriously and there had been nothing else that it could have done to establish appropriate internal reporting and clearance mechanisms to alert its employees to their responsibilities and obligations under the Act. However, as a result of this case, FirstGroup have reviewed their procedures and improved their monitoring of adherence to compliance.

[6] Para 4.35 of the first version of this guideline [1999] UKCLR 217.
[7] CA98/9/2002, [2002] UKCLR 343.
[8] Para 54.

We have already seen that in proving the necessary element of dishonesty in the prosecution of the offence 'a failure to seek legal advice' would be a factor to be considered.[9]

In *Acquisitions Monthly*'s August 2003 issue a number of leading practitioners were asked whether firms needed to upgrade their compliance programmes in the light of the greater focus of the competition authorities on cartels and criminalisation. It is not surprising that all respondents were emphatic that more steps needed to be taken. As one respondent however pointed out:

> A compliance manual usually explains the legislation and gives examples of prohibited conduct. Since the basic prohibitions are not changing, these behavioural guidelines should not need any radical overhaul. The explanation on cartels may just need tweaking to highlight the four specific activities caught by the criminal cartel offence . . .
>
> In contrast, explanations about the consequences of an infringement should change. Cartel participation by employees may cost directors their jobs, and cartel participation by directors themselves may cost them their liberty.[10]

Another respondent pointed to one of the more significant features of the introduction of the personal element of the penalty. In the new regime the interests of an individual, perhaps with significant knowledge of the operation of a cartel, or engagement in that cartel, may not be the same as the interests either of the firm or of other individuals in the firm.

Most law firms with a competition practice will be able to offer compliance training and compliance programme design. Here some of the more general factors to be considered are set out.

THE DESIGN AND IMPLEMENTATION OF A COMPLIANCE PROGRAMME

Five elements exist, any combination of which may be features of a compliance programme. These are: (1) an audit; (2) risk assessment; (3) conduct modification in response to the combination of the audit and the risk; (4) training; and (5) culture change if necessary.[11] An audit in this context could be undertaken by either internal or external lawyers with a strong knowledge of competition law in order to identify which activities the undertaking is engaged in that might raise matters relevant to competition law. Were an undertaking to wish to separate out criminal law compliance from civil law compliance (in the light of the exceptionally high penalties handed out in civil/administrative infringement decisions this would be an ill-advised policy) such an audit might take a different nature in the former case. Broadly an audit in this context may be defined as 'the examination of the affairs of a business in order to ascertain the extent to which that business complies with relevant competition rules'.[12] In relation to civil compliance an attempt would be made

[9] Standing Committee B, coll 135–36.
[10] Jill Marsal, associate and competition specialist, Pinsents.
[11] See above n 3 p 281.
[12] T Soames, 'Competition Law Compliance', Solicitors' European Group Conference, 1994.

to arrive at a complete picture of the activities of the undertaking, its position in the market, and the impact of those activities in the market. In the case of a compliance programme tailored specifically at the cartel offence there would be no need to consider, for example, the position of the undertaking on the relevant market, or indeed to make an assessment as to what constituted the relevant market, for there is no obligation on the prosecuting authorities to show that competitive harm flows from the arrangements dishonestly entered into, or that the undertaking has market power. An ideal way to carry out an audit is to begin with a questionnaire addressed to all relevant personnel—typically senior management—seeking the appropriate information as to the undertaking's activity and the internal perception of that activity. Some description of the terminology used, and the legal terminology may assist in the collation of this data. As Taylor reports

> . . . anti-competitive practices are often referred to by names which on the surface at least seem innocuous. Advance price-sharing information might be called 'market intelligence' . . . and out and out market-sharing referred to as 'respecting each other's territory'. In one case, a senior manager described various illegal practices as 'orderly marketing'.[13]

Particular focus in this exercise should be placed on the marketing and sales departments of an undertaking, especially in the context of concerns relating to the cartel offence. Such scrutiny should also extend to persons involved, for whatever reason, in exchanging information with other companies. The persons best placed to undertake such an audit are independent lawyers with substantial experience of competition law and procedures, and who are to an extent insulated from internal company pre-conceptions or politics. A key fact for the undertaking to bear in mind is that

> An audit team should never claim the ability to unearth information, it can simply assess what is laid before it. The members of the team are not police, every step must be taken to avoid that impression being given and impart a feeling of mutual confidence between the team members and the management/employees involved. This is particularly important in the interview stage, for otherwise disclosure will be restricted.[14]

Having considered *what* activity might be subject to competition law, a risk assessment may then take place. In the case of civil law, as suggested in the introduction to this chapter, this might be a calculated cost-benefit analysis, where a degree of risk of detection of illegal conduct is accepted if the costs of the abandonment of that conduct are considered to be greater than any possible penalties discounted by the probability of detection. In the case of the application of criminal law it may be difficult to persuade a business manager—a person 'exquisitely sensitive to status deprivation and censure'[15]—that even a minimal risk of detection is worth

[13] See above n 3 p 281.

[14] See above n 12.

[15] G Geis, 'Deterring Corporate Crime', in M D Ermann and R J Lundman, *Corporate and Governmental Deviance: Problems of Organizational Behavior in Contemporary Society* (New York, OUP, 1978) pp 278–79.

facing if the ultimate penalty is personal imprisonment. Again the risks associated with the cartel offence are different from those associated with a civil infringement. The latter gives rise to non-enforceability of contractual terms and obligations, and is therefore cast in wider terms than the former. Where activity that would fall within the cartel offence is identified the options facing the undertaking are simple: the activity can be terminated, or maintained (notification to the relevant authorities in the hope of obtaining an exemption from the application of either article 81 EC or the Chapter I Prohibition no longer being an option after 1 May 2004, and in any event being highly unlikely to succeed even before that date in the case of hard-core conduct falling within the terms of the offence). It is accepted that some undertakings may choose to continue the conduct, and to take steps to conceal it. The penalties associated with breaches of both the substantive provisions of the offence, and with the procedural elements relating to the concealing and destruction of evidence are dealt with in Chapters 3 and 4. In addition, s 43 of the CA98 creates a number of offences relating to the destruction etc of documents required to be disclosed in the course of investigations under that Act. In addition, there is a general obligation imposed by s 450 of the Companies Act 1985. This is, in part, in the following terms:

> (1) An officer of a company who—
> (a) destroys, mutilates or falsifies, or is privy to the destruction, mutilation or falsification of a document affecting or relating to the company's property or affairs, or
> (b) makes, or is privy to the making of, a false entry in such a document,
> is guilty of an offence, unless he proves that he had no intention to conceal the state of affairs of [the company] or to defeat the law.
> (1A) Subsection (1) applies to an officer of an authorised insurance company which is not a body corporate as it applies to an officer of a company.
> (2) Such a person as above mentioned who fraudulently either parts with, alters or makes an omission in any such document or is privy to fraudulent parting with, fraudulent altering or fraudulent making of an omission in, any such document, is guilty of an offence.
> (3) A person guilty of an offence under this section is liable to imprisonment or a fine, or both.

At a minimum any good compliance programme must contain four key features: (a) support of senior management; (b) appropriate policy and procedures; (c) training; (d) evaluation. While this is an area in which the OFT is understandably reluctant to offer full advice, and indeed it has made clear the position that 'undertakings will need to decide for themselves how to approach the education of their employees'.[16] OFT general guidance on compliance published in 1999 gives some indication of what the OFT considers to be the most important principles in the design and implementation of a compliance programme.

[16] OFT, *How Your Business Can Achieve Compliance: A guide to achieving compliance with the Competition Act 1998*, p 7.

Support of senior management

The OFT stance is that 'senior management support for the programme is vital as an indicator of the undertaking's commitment to complying'.[17] Such support may be evidenced through communications from managers and directors to staff involved, or through the incorporation of a commitment to compliance in a general company mission statement or code of ethics. However, it is important that such public comments are an indication of a genuine commitment to compliance, and are not 'mere puffs', the breach of which is privately either countenanced or encouraged. The House of Lords, in *Director General of Fair Trading v Pioneer Concrete (UK) Ltd*,[18] a case arising from non-compliance with the Restrictive Trade Practices Act 1976, held pertinently

> that a company . . . falls to be judged by its actions and not by its language. An employee who acts for the company within the scope of his employment is the company. Directors may give instructions, top management may exhort, middle management may question and workers may listen attentively. But if a worker makes a defective product or a lower manager accepts or rejects an order, he is the company. When Mr Hayter raised the price of ready-mixed concrete supplied by Smiths or procured some superior or inferior employee to raise the price because Mr Hayter had arranged with employees of three other companies that Smiths would do so, he was acting for Smiths. When Mr Hayter rejected an order from Thame because he had arranged with the employees of three other companies that Smiths would not supply a customer in Thame then Mr Hayter was acting for Smiths. When Mr Hayter procured Smiths to implement the arrangement that he had made in breach of his instructions Smiths became a party to the arrangement and Mr Hayter aided and abetted Smiths to commit a breach of the 1976 Act and a breach of the court orders which bound Smiths.[19]

The same would be true of the CA98 were similar circumstances to prevail. Effective support might be demonstrated by, inter alia, making a member of the board or a senior manager responsible for the implementation of the compliance programme.

Appropriate policy and procedures

An effective compliance policy would, according to the OFT, contain at least the following elements: a clear commitment to comply with the law; the placing of a duty on *all* relevant employees and directors to adhere to this commitment backed up by individual written undertakings to that effect; and a real prospect that disciplinary action would be taken against those who intentionally or negligently breach the law. While procedures for implementing any undertaking's policy

[17] *Ibid*, at p 9.
[18] [1995] 1 AC 456, [1995] 1 All ER 135, [1994] 3 WLR 1249.
[19] Per Lord Templeman, [1995] 1 All ER 135, at 142.

should be sensitive to the requirements and structure of the individual undertaking, at the least the procedure should allow employees to seek guidance on the application of the law in any particular circumstance, and to report any activity that is suspected of infringing the law. One way to disseminate a compliance policy is via a dedicated handbook, or to incorporate the terms into a staff manual. In such cases the OFT recommends that the following should be included: (1) a clear statement of the policy, including the consequences for non-observance; (2) details of the relevant legislation, with explanations of the key provisions and procedures, as well as details of the consequences at law for infringements; (3) examples of conduct which might be illegal, and an explanation of areas where caution should be exercised; and (4) clear details of the compliance procedures put in place by the undertaking.

Training

The policy and its dissemination should be backed up by training, which 'forms a crucial part of an effective compliance programme and is essential for all employees who have dealings that might impinge on competition law'.[20] It is suggested that training should include not only the policy, but also the law itself, and that it should be offered automatically on induction to new staff, and be reinforced by back up sessions after that point.

Evaluation

Even if all three of the above elements are all in place, the OFT maintain, a compliance programme is not likely to be successful unless it is regularly evaluated and, as the need arises, revised. An evaluation programme should contain the following elements: (1) testing of the relevant knowledge of the employees; (2) incorporating adherence to the programme into any relevant individual or departmental performance appraisals; (3) formal audits of sales and procurement processes to check for infringements; and (4) reporting mechanisms whereby employees can communicate actual or potential infringements to senior management.

[20] Per Lord Templeman, [1995] 1 All ER 135, at, at 11.

CHECKLIST FOR ESTABLISHING EFFECTIVE COMPETITION COMPLIANCE PROGRAMMES[21]

Objectives and benefits of compliance programme

Compliance with national and EC competition rules:-

—Potential consequences of breach—unenforceability, fines and civil actions.
—Compliance programme to avoid future breaches may be mitigating factor.
—Compliance must be implemented and maintained effectively.

Preparation

Identify risks and potential problems relevant to your company:-

—Markets in which company operates and market position.
—Position and market power of principal competitors, customers and suppliers.
—Agreements and structures: national and international distribution arrangements, intellectual property licences, joint ventures and other cooperative arrangements.
—Personnel likely to be involved.
—Previous EC/national regulatory problems.

Secure key support:-

—Board endorsement.
—Consultation with commercial sales and marketing, strategic planning, PR.
—Personnel and organisational issues.

Implementation

Uncover existing problems:-

—Comprehensive document review, including electronic records, notes of meetings, etc.
—Use of amnesty.
—Handling 'smoking guns'.

[21] Provided by Simmons and Simmons solicitors: www.simmons-simmons.com.

Educate relevant personnel:-

—Written guidance (see checklist at point 5 below).
—Workshops.

Establish procedures to ensure continuing compliance:-

—Vetting/approval of contracts.
—Trade association meetings.
—Access to guidance.
—Handling mistakes and complaints.

Follow up

Need for regular reinforcement of programme:

—Annual reminders/certification.
—Report developments.
—Refresher courses.
—Ensure new employees and Board members are covered.
—Document retention policy.

Checklist on content of written guidance on competition law compliance

Purpose:

—General objectives.
—Specific competition/regulatory risks.

Scope:

—Relations with competitors.
—Prohibited activities (collusion on prices, market or customer sharing, quotas).
—Trade associations and data exchanges.
—Joint ventures and cooperative arrangements.
—Trading links.

Relations with customers:

—Withholding supplies.
—Discrimination.

—Price restrictions.
—Territorial restrictions.

Commercial arrangements and contracts:

—Exclusive supply and purchase.
—Exclusive licensing.
—Restrictions on terms of supply to third parties.
—Variations of standard terms/standard agreements.
—Long-term restrictive agreements.

Appendices

Appendix One

ENTERPRISE ACT, PART 6

CARTEL OFFENCE

188 Cartel offence

(1) An individual is guilty of an offence if he dishonestly agrees with one or more other persons to make or implement, or to cause to be made or implemented, arrangements of the following kind relating to at least two undertakings (A and B).

(2) The arrangements must be ones which, if operating as the parties to the agreement intend, would—

(a) directly or indirectly fix a price for the supply by A in the United Kingdom (otherwise than to B) of a product or service,
(b) limit or prevent supply by A in the United Kingdom of a product or service,
(c) limit or prevent production by A in the United Kingdom of a product,
(d) divide between A and B the supply in the United Kingdom of a product or service to a customer or customers,
(e) divide between A and B customers for the supply in the United Kingdom of a product or service, or
(f) be bid-rigging arrangements.

(3) Unless subsection (2)(d), (e) or (f) applies, the arrangements must also be ones which, if operating as the parties to the agreement intend, would—

(a) directly or indirectly fix a price for the supply by B in the United Kingdom (otherwise than to A) of a product or service,
(b) limit or prevent supply by B in the United Kingdom of a product or service, or
(c) limit or prevent production by B in the United Kingdom of a product.

(4) In subsections (2)(a) to (d) and (3), references to supply or production are to supply or production in the appropriate circumstances (for which see section 189).

(5) 'Bid-rigging arrangements' are arrangements under which, in response to a request for bids for the supply of a product or service in the United Kingdom, or for the production of a product in the United Kingdom—

(a) A but not B may make a bid, or
(b) A and B may each make a bid but, in one case or both, only a bid arrived at in accordance with the arrangements.

(6) But arrangements are not bid-rigging arrangements if, under them, the person requesting bids would be informed of them at or before the time when a bid is made.
(7) 'Undertaking' has the same meaning as in Part 1 of the 1998 Act.

189 Cartel offence: supplementary

(1) For section 188(2)(a), the appropriate circumstances are that A's supply of the product or service would be at a level in the supply chain at which the product or service would at the same time be supplied by B in the United Kingdom.
(2) For section 188(2)(b), the appropriate circumstances are that A's supply of the product or service would be at a level in the supply chain—

(a) at which the product or service would at the same time be supplied by B in the United Kingdom, or
(b) at which supply by B in the United Kingdom of the product or service would be limited or prevented by the arrangements.

(3) For section 188(2)(c), the appropriate circumstances are that A's production of the product would be at a level in the production chain—

(a) at which the product would at the same time be produced by B in the United Kingdom, or
(b) at which production by B in the United Kingdom of the product would be limited or prevented by the arrangements.

(4) For section 188(2)(d), the appropriate circumstances are that A's supply of the product or service would be at the same level in the supply chain as B's.
(5) For section 188(3)(a), the appropriate circumstances are that B's supply of the product or service would be at a level in the supply chain at which the product or service would at the same time be supplied by A in the United Kingdom.
(6) For section 188(3)(b), the appropriate circumstances are that B's supply of the product or service would be at a level in the supply chain—

(a) at which the product or service would at the same time be supplied by A in the United Kingdom, or
(b) at which supply by A in the United Kingdom of the product or service would be limited or prevented by the arrangements.

(7) For section 188(3)(c), the appropriate circumstances are that B's production of the product would be at a level in the production chain—

(a) at which the product would at the same time be produced by A in the United Kingdom, or
(b) at which production by A in the United Kingdom of the product would be limited or prevented by the arrangements.

190 Cartel offence: penalty and prosecution

(1) A person guilty of an offence under section 188 is liable—

(a) on conviction on indictment, to imprisonment for a term not exceeding five years or to a fine, or to both;

(b) on summary conviction, to imprisonment for a term not exceeding six months or to a fine not exceeding the statutory maximum, or to both.

(2) In England and Wales and Northern Ireland, proceedings for an offence under section 188 may be instituted only—

(a) by the Director of the Serious Fraud Office, or

(b) by or with the consent of the OFT.

(3) No proceedings may be brought for an offence under section 188 in respect of an agreement outside the United Kingdom, unless it has been implemented in whole or in part in the United Kingdom.

(4) Where, for the purpose of the investigation or prosecution of offences under section 188, the OFT gives a person written notice under this subsection, no proceedings for an offence under section 188 that falls within a description specified in the notice may be brought against that person in England and Wales or Northern Ireland except in circumstances specified in the notice.

191 Extradition

The offences to which an Order in Council under section 2 of the Extradition Act 1870 (arrangements with foreign states) can apply include—

(a) an offence under section 188,

(b) conspiracy to commit such an offence, and

(c) attempt to commit such an offence.

Criminal investigations by OFT

192 Investigation of offences under section 188

(1) The OFT may conduct an investigation if there are reasonable grounds for suspecting that an offence under section 188 has been committed.

(2) The powers of the OFT under sections 193 and 194 are exercisable, but only for the purposes of an investigation under subsection (1), in any case where it appears to the OFT that there is good reason to exercise them for the purpose of investigating the affairs, or any aspect of the affairs, of any person ('the person under investigation').

193 Powers when conducting an investigation

(1) The OFT may by notice in writing require the person under investigation, or any other person who it has reason to believe has relevant information, to answer questions, or otherwise provide information, with respect to any matter relevant to the investigation at a specified place and either at a specified time or forthwith.
(2) The OFT may by notice in writing require the person under investigation, or any other person, to produce, at a specified place and either at a specified time or forthwith, specified documents, or documents of a specified description, which appear to the OFT to relate to any matter relevant to the investigation.
(3) If any such documents are produced, the OFT may—

(a) take copies or extracts from them;
(b) require the person producing them to provide an explanation of any of them.

(4) If any such documents are not produced, the OFT may require the person who was required to produce them to state, to the best of his knowledge and belief, where they are.
(5) A notice under subsection (1) or (2) must indicate—

(a) the subject matter and purpose of the investigation; and
(b) the nature of the offences created by section 201.

194 Power to enter premises under a warrant

(1) On an application made by the OFT to the High Court, or, in Scotland, by the procurator fiscal to the sheriff, in accordance with rules of court, a judge or the sheriff may issue a warrant if he is satisfied that there are reasonable grounds for believing—

(a) that there are on any premises documents which the OFT has power under section 193 to require to be produced for the purposes of an investigation; and
(b) that—
  (i) a person has failed to comply with a requirement under that section to produce the documents;
  (ii) it is not practicable to serve a notice under that section in relation to them; or
  (iii) the service of such a notice in relation to them might seriously prejudice the investigation.

(2) A warrant under this section shall authorise a named officer of the OFT, and any other officers of the OFT whom the OFT has authorised in writing to accompany the named officer—

(a) to enter the premises, using such force as is reasonably necessary for the purpose;
(b) to search the premises and—
  (i) take possession of any documents appearing to be of the relevant kind, or
  (ii) take, in relation to any documents appearing to be of the relevant kind, any other steps which may appear to be necessary for preserving them or preventing interference with them;

(c) to require any person to provide an explanation of any document appearing to be of the relevant kind or to state, to the best of his knowledge and belief, where it may be found;
(d) to require any information which is stored in any electronic form and is accessible from the premises and which the named officer considers relates to any matter relevant to the investigation, to be produced in a form—
 (i) in which it can be taken away, and
 (ii) in which it is visible and legible or from which it can readily be produced in a visible and legible form.

(3) Documents are of the relevant kind if they are of a kind in respect of which the application under subsection (1) was granted.
(4) A warrant under this section may authorise persons specified in the warrant to accompany the named officer who is executing it.
(5) In Part 1 of Schedule 1 to the Criminal Justice and Police Act 2001 (powers of seizure to which section 50 of that Act applies), after paragraph 73 there is inserted—

'73A Enterprise Act 2002

The power of seizure conferred by section 194(2) of the Enterprise Act 2002 (seizure of documents for the purposes of an investigation under section 192(1) of that Act).'

195 Exercise of powers by authorised person

(1) The OFT may authorise any competent person who is not an officer of the OFT to exercise on its behalf all or any of the powers conferred by section 193 or 194.
(2) No such authority may be granted except for the purpose of investigating the affairs, or any aspect of the affairs, of a person specified in the authority.
(3) No person is bound to comply with any requirement imposed by a person exercising powers by virtue of any authority granted under this section unless he has, if required to do so, produced evidence of his authority.

196 Privileged information etc

(1) A person may not under section 193 or 194 be required to disclose any information or produce any document which he would be entitled to refuse to disclose or produce on grounds of legal professional privilege in proceedings in the High Court, except that a lawyer may be required to provide the name and address of his client.
(2) A person may not under section 193 or 194 be required to disclose any information or produce any document in respect of which he owes an obligation of confidence by virtue of carrying on any banking business unless—

 (a) the person to whom the obligation of confidence is owed consents to the disclosure or production; or
 (b) the OFT has authorised the making of the requirement.

(3) In the application of this section to Scotland, the reference in subsection (1)—
  (a) to proceedings in the High Court is to be read as a reference to legal proceedings generally; and
  (b) to an entitlement on grounds of legal professional privilege is to be read as a reference to an entitlement by virtue of any rule of law whereby—
    (i) communications between a professional legal adviser and his client, or
    (ii) communications made in connection with or in contemplation of legal proceedings and for the purposes of those proceedings,

are in such proceedings protected from disclosure on the ground of confidentiality.

197 Restriction on use of statements in court

(1) A statement by a person in response to a requirement imposed by virtue of section 193 or 194 may only be used in evidence against him—
  (a) on a prosecution for an offence under section 201(2); or
  (b) on a prosecution for some other offence where in giving evidence he makes a statement inconsistent with it.

(2) However, the statement may not be used against that person by virtue of paragraph (b) of subsection (1) unless evidence relating to it is adduced, or a question relating to it is asked, by or on behalf of that person in the proceedings arising out of the prosecution.

198 Use of statements obtained under Competition Act 1998

In the 1998 Act, after section 30 there is inserted—

'30A Use of statements in prosecution

A statement made by a person in response to a requirement imposed by virtue of any of sections 26 to 28 may not be used in evidence against him on a prosecution for an offence under section 188 of the Enterprise Act 2002 unless, in the proceedings—
  (a) in giving evidence, he makes a statement inconsistent with it, and
  (b) evidence relating to it is adduced, or a question relating to it is asked, by him or on his behalf.'

199 Surveillance powers

(1) The Regulation of Investigatory Powers Act 2000 is amended as follows.

(2) In section 32 (authorisation of intrusive surveillance)—

  (a) after subsection (3) there is inserted—
  '(3A) In the case of an authorisation granted by the chairman of the OFT, the authorisation is necessary on grounds falling within subsection (3) only if it is necessary for the purpose of preventing or detecting an offence under section 188 of the Enterprise Act 2002 (cartel offence).';

(b) in subsection (6) after paragraph (m) there is inserted '; and
(n) the chairman of the OFT.'

(3) In section 33 (rules for grant of authorisations) after subsection (4) there is inserted—
'(4A) The chairman of the OFT shall not grant an authorisation for the carrying out of intrusive surveillance except on an application made by an officer of the OFT.'

(4) In subsection (5)(a) of that section, after 'officer' there is inserted 'or the chairman or an officer of the OFT'.

(5) In section 34 (grant of authorisation in the senior officer's absence)—

(a) in subsection (1)(a), after 'or by' there is inserted 'an officer of the OFT or';
(b) in subsection (2)(a), after 'may be,' there is inserted 'as chairman of the OFT or';
(c) in subsection (4), after paragraph (l) there is inserted—
'(m) a person is entitled to act for the chairman of the OFT if he is an officer of the OFT designated by it for the purposes of this paragraph as a person entitled so to act in an urgent case.'

(6) In section 35 (notification of authorisations for intrusive surveillance)—

(a) in subsections (1) and (10), for 'or customs' there is substituted ', customs or OFT';
(b) in subsection (10), after paragraph (b) there is inserted—
'(ba) the chairman of the OFT; or';
(c) in paragraph (c) of that subsection, at the end there is inserted 'or for a person falling within paragraph (ba).'

(7) In section 36 (approval required for authorisations to take effect)—

(a) in subsection (1), after paragraph (d) there is inserted '; or
(e) an officer of the OFT.';
(b) in subsection (6), after paragraph (g) there is inserted '; and
(h) where the authorisation was granted by the chairman of the OFT or a person entitled to act for him by virtue of section 34(4)(m), that chairman.'

(8) In section 37 (quashing of police and customs authorisations etc) in subsection (1), after paragraph (d) there is inserted '; or

(e) an officer of the OFT.'

(9) In section 40 (information to be provided to Surveillance Commissioners) after paragraph (d) there is inserted ', and

(e) every officer of the OFT,'.

(10) In section 46 (restrictions on authorisations extending to Scotland), in subsection (3), after paragraph (d) there is inserted—

'(da) the OFT;'.

(11) In section 48 (interpretation of Part 2), in subsection (1), after the entry relating to 'directed' and 'intrusive' there is inserted—
'"OFT" means the Office of Fair Trading;'.

200 Authorisation of action in respect of property

(1) Part 3 of the Police Act 1997 (authorisation of action in respect of property) is amended as follows.
(2) In section 93 (authorisation to interfere with property etc)—

(a) in subsection (1B), after 'customs officer' there is inserted 'or an officer of the Office of Fair Trading';
(b) after subsection (2A) there is inserted—
'(2AA) Where the authorising officer is the chairman of the Office of Fair Trading, the only purpose falling within subsection (2)(a) is the purpose of preventing or detecting an offence under section 188 of the Enterprise Act 2002.';
(c) in subsection (3), after paragraph (d) there is inserted ', or
(e) if the authorising officer is within subsection (5)(i), by an officer of the Office of Fair Trading.';
(d) in subsection (5), after paragraph (h) there is inserted '; or
(i) the chairman of the Office of Fair Trading.'

(3) In section 94 (authorisation given in absence of authorising officer) in subsection (2), after paragraph (f) there is inserted—

'(g) where the authorising officer is within paragraph (i) of that subsection, by an officer of the Office of Fair Trading designated by it for the purposes of this section.'

201 Offences

(1) Any person who without reasonable excuse fails to comply with a requirement imposed on him under section 193 or 194 is guilty of an offence and liable on summary conviction to imprisonment for a term not exceeding six months or to a fine not exceeding level 5 on the standard scale or to both.
(2) A person who, in purported compliance with a requirement under section 193 or 194—

(a) makes a statement which he knows to be false or misleading in a material particular; or
(b) recklessly makes a statement which is false or misleading in a material particular,

is guilty of an offence.
(3) A person guilty of an offence under subsection (2) is liable—

(a) on conviction on indictment, to imprisonment for a term not exceeding two years or to a fine or to both; and
(b) on summary conviction, to imprisonment for a term not exceeding six months or to a fine not exceeding the statutory maximum, or to both.

(4) Where any person—

(a) knows or suspects that an investigation by the Serious Fraud Office or the OFT into an offence under section 188 is being or is likely to be carried out; and

(b) falsifies, conceals, destroys or otherwise disposes of, or causes or permits the falsification, concealment, destruction or disposal of documents which he knows or suspects are or would be relevant to such an investigation,

he is guilty of an offence unless he proves that he had no intention of concealing the facts disclosed by the documents from the persons carrying out such an investigation.

(5) A person guilty of an offence under subsection (4) is liable—

(a) on conviction on indictment, to imprisonment for a term not exceeding 5 years or to a fine or to both; and
(b) on summary conviction, to imprisonment for a term not exceeding six months or to a fine not exceeding the statutory maximum, or to both.

(6) A person who intentionally obstructs a person in the exercise of his powers under a warrant issued under section 194 is guilty of an offence and liable—

(a) on conviction on indictment, to imprisonment for a term not exceeding 2 years or to a fine or to both; and
(b) on summary conviction, to a fine not exceeding the statutory maximum.

202 Interpretation of sections 192 to 201

In sections 192 to 201—

'documents' includes information recorded in any form and, in relation to information recorded otherwise than in a form in which it is visible and legible, references to its production include references to producing it in a form in which it is visible and legible or from which it can readily be produced in a visible and legible form;
'person under investigation' has the meaning given in section 192(2).

Appendix Two

Explanatory Notes—The Enterprise Act 2002

These explanatory notes relate to the Enterprise Act 2002 which received Royal Assent on 7 November 2002. They have been prepared by the Department of Trade and Industry (DTI) in order to assist the reader in understanding the Act. They do not form part of the Act and have not been endorsed by Parliament.

Cartel offence

401. Sections 188–202 provide for a criminal offence for individuals who dishonestly engage in cartel agreements ('the criminal offence'). The criminal offence will operate alongside the existing regime that imposes civil sanctions on undertakings that breach the competition provisions of CA 1998. The civil regime applies to a much wider range of anti-competitive activities than are targeted by the criminal offence.

402. The proposal to introduce criminal sanctions as a deterrent to individuals engaging in cartel activity was included in the July 2001 White Paper, '*Productivity and Enterprise: A World Class Competition Regime*', and views were invited from consultees on the general concept and on a number of detailed aspects of the proposal.

403. In the light of responses to the consultation and of contacts with the authorities likely to be responsible for the new offence, the Government announced in November 2001 further details of its proposals for the introduction of the criminal offence, as follows:

—the definition of the offence to be based on individuals having dishonestly entered into horizontal agreements (i.e. agreements at the same level in the supply chain) to fix prices, share markets, limit production or rig bids;
—the investigation to be carried out by OFT investigators under a case controller from the Serious Fraud Office ('SFO'); appropriate investigatory powers to be made available to the OFT;
—the OFT to be able to issue 'no-action letters' to protect informants from prosecution;
—for investigations that lead to prosecution, the SFO to be the lead prosecutor; the OFT also to be a named prosecutor;
—the offence to be triable in either the Magistrates' Courts or the Crown Courts; the maximum penalty for the offence to be five years' imprisonment; fines to be available in addition or as an alternative.

404. Sections 188–202 make the necessary legislative provisions to implement the criminal offence.

Section 188: Cartel offence

405. *Subsections (1) to (6)* define the offence. They provide that an individual will be liable to criminal prosecution if he dishonestly agrees with one or more other persons that two or more undertakings will engage in one or more of the prohibited cartel activities. The offence only applies in respect of horizontal agreements (i.e. agreements relating to products or services at the same level in the supply chain). The offence is committed irrespective of whether or not the agreement reached between the individuals is implemented by the undertakings, and irrespective of whether or not they have authority to act on behalf of the undertaking at the time of the agreement.
406. The prohibited activities are: price-fixing; limitation of production; market-sharing; and bid-rigging. These activities comprise the most serious forms of anti-competitive activity and as such are a sub-set of the practices for which undertakings may be pursued under the civil provisions of CA 1998.
407. *Subsection (2)* specifies the four categories of prohibited cartel activity: price-fixing, limitation of production or supply, the sharing of markets, and bid-rigging. Price-fixing is defined so as to include the direct or indirect fixing of prices. Examples of indirect price-fixing would be likely to include, but would not be restricted to, agreements about relative price levels or price ranges, rebates, discounts, price-change indices, transport charges or methods of quotation. Market-sharing is defined in terms of customers so as to include the sharing of an individual customer or customers.
408. *Subsection (3)* requires, in the case of price-fixing or limitation of production or supply, that for the offence to be committed the other party must reciprocally have intended that the agreement, if implemented according to the intentions of the parties, should result in one of these activities. This means that agreements are not criminal where the agreement only requires one party to fix prices or limit production or supply as defined. This further requirement does not apply in the case of market-sharing and bid-rigging where the activities are by definition reciprocal.
409. *Subsections (5) and (6)* provide a definition of the activities that constitute bid-rigging for the purposes of the criminal offence. Bid-rigging is the only one of the prohibited activities where for all practical purposes the carrying out of the activity described in this section will in itself invariably indicate a dishonest intention and amount to the commission of the offence. Arrangements of which the person requesting bids is aware are not subject to the criminal offence.

Section 189: Cartel offence: supplementary

410. This section relates to subsections 1(2)(a)–(d) and 1(3)(a)–(c) of section 183. It provides that, for agreements involving price-fixing, limitation of production and market-sharing, undertakings must be operating at the same level in the chain of supply or production. The criminal offence does not apply to so-called vertical agreements, which relate to intended activity where the two or more parties are operating at different levels in the chain of supply or production (e.g. as producer and distributor or as distributor and retailer).

Section 190: Cartel offence: penalty and prosecution

411. *Subsection (2)* sets out that the OFT and SFO will be the only named prosecutors for the offence in England, Wales and Northern Ireland. A third party could only bring a prosecution with the OFT's consent. This is designed to enable the OFT to prevent vexatious private prosecutions against recipients of leniency (see below). The Lord Advocate will prosecute the criminal offence in Scotland; no legislative provision is required.
412. The scope of the offence generally extends to agreements that are implemented or intended to be implemented in the UK. This means that in general agreements do not need to have been implemented for an offence to have been committed. *Subsection (3)* provides for the exception to this, which is that agreements reached overseas may only be prosecuted if some subsequent action is taken within the UK to further the agreement. An instruction to others to implement the agreement, delivered into the UK by telephone or electronic mail, might be a sufficient action for this purpose.
413. *Subsection (4)* provides for the leniency process. It provides the OFT with the power to issue an applicant for leniency with a written notice that he or she will not be prosecuted for the particular matter under investigation provided certain contractual conditions set out in the notice are met. These conditions would be likely to include that the applicant: makes an admission of guilt; must not be the lead cartel member; must cease all involvement in the cartel (except as directed by the OFT to avoid arousing the suspicions of the other parties); must co-operate fully with the investigation; and must make a full disclosure. The notice is intended to encourage informants to come forward by providing them with sufficient comfort that they will not be prosecuted. In Scotland, the decision to prosecute rests with the Lord Advocate, who will take into account a report from the OFT.

Section 191: Extradition

414. This section provides that the criminal offence, or a conspiracy or an attempt to commit it, shall be an extraditable offence to which Schedule 1 to the Extradition Act 1989 applies. That Schedule preserves the old extradition regime under the Extradition Act 1870. This will allow extradition in respect of the offence from the UK to countries with whom the UK signed bilateral extradition treaties before 1989—this group includes the United States of America. Requests for extradition to other countries with whom the UK has extradition arrangements (including members of the Council of Europe, Commonwealth countries and Hong Kong, and countries with whom the UK signed bilateral treaties since 1989) are considered under the main provisions of the Extradition Act 1989. Extradition from the UK to these countries will apply in respect of the criminal offence without a specific legislative provision. The extradition provisions do not apply retrospectively.
415. Dual-criminality applies (i.e. a request for extradition may only ever be made to a country that has criminal penalties for the same activity). Thus the introduction of criminal penalties in the UK will make it possible for other countries that criminalise the same activity to request the extradition of individuals from the UK. Requests made by the UK for the extradition of individuals from other countries will be governed by the law of those countries.

Criminal investigations by OFT

416. Sections 192–202 make provisions for appropriate powers of investigations in respect of the criminal offence. They provide the OFT with powers modelled broadly on those already available to the SFO under Section 2 of the Criminal Justice Act 1987 ('CJA87'). The OFT will investigate the criminal offence under the powers provided in these sections, working closely with the SFO, who may draw on their CJA87 powers.

Section 192: Investigation of offences under section 188

417. This section provides that the OFT is only to exercise the powers in sections 193 and 194 in relation to the criminal offence. The OFT will continue to conduct investigations in relation to infringement of Chapter I civil prohibitions of CA 1998 by using investigatory powers set out in Part I, Chapter III of CA 1998. The OFT can only exercise the powers if there are reasonable grounds for suspecting an offence under section 188.

Section 193: Powers when conducting an investigation

418. *Subsection (1)* provides powers for the OFT to require in writing the person under investigation, or any other person, to answer questions or provide information that the OFT considers relates to any matter relevant to the investigation.
419. *Subsection (2)* provides that the OFT may require the production of documents that appear to the OFT to relate to the investigation. The documents required must be specified or described in a written notice or must fall within a category specified or described in the notice.

Section 194: Power to enter premises under a warrant

420. This section makes provision for the OFT to make an application to a judge of the High Court, or in Scotland for the procurators fiscal to apply to the sheriff court, for a warrant authorising a named officer of the OFT to enter premises. The warrant may also cover any other person whom the OFT has authorised in writing to accompany the named officer. This section parallels section 28 CA 1998, which requires the OFT to seek a warrant from the High Court or the Court of Session in order to investigate infringements of the civil prohibitions in Chapter I of CA 1998.
421. *Subsection (1)* grants a judge of the High Court or a sheriff the power to issue a warrant if he or she is satisfied that there are reasonable grounds for believing there are documents on any premises that the OFT has the right to require under section 193. The judge or the sheriff must be satisfied that one of the following circumstances applies before he or she may issue a warrant: (i) that a person has failed to comply with a requirement under section 193 to produce documents; (ii) that it is not practicable to serve a notice under section 193; or (iii) that the service of such a notice might seriously prejudice the investigation (i.e. there are reasonable grounds to believe that information might be destroyed or tampered with).

422. *Subsection (4)* allows people who are not employees of the OFT to accompany and assist OFT officers who are exercising powers under this section. It is anticipated that such people will have expertise that is not available within the OFT but is required to exploit fully the terms of the warrant (e.g. IT experts).

423. *Subsection (6)* amends Part I of Schedule 1 of the Criminal Justice and Police Act 2001 ('CJPA 2001') to add to it the powers of seizure conferred by subsection (2). This will have the effect of incorporating the amendments to statutory powers of seizure introduced by section 50 CJPA 2001.

424. These amendments enable an officer to seize material if it is not reasonably practicable to determine on the premises whether the material is seizeable or not, or, in the case of property some of which is seizeable, which items he or she would be entitled to seize. The exercise of the powers is subject to strict safeguards, which include a requirement to give written notice (section 52 CJPA 2001) and a duty to return legally privileged material (section 55).

425. The OFT's existing civil powers of seizure under section 28(2) CA 1998 are already contained in Part I of Schedule 1 of the CJPA 2001.

Section 195: Exercise of powers by authorised person

426. This section grants the OFT the power to authorise any competent investigator who is not an officer of the OFT to exercise the powers conferred on the OFT under sections 193 and 194. However, no person under investigation is bound to comply unless such authorised person produces evidence of his or her authority.

Section 196: Privileged information etc.

427. This section requires legal professional privilege—i.e. the principle that legal advice is confidential to the client to whom it is given—to be respected in the exercise of powers under sections 193 and 194 and reproduces the requirements in respect of banking professional privilege in section 2(10) CJA 1987.

Section 197: Restriction on use of statements in court

428. This section provides that statements made under compulsion in response to powers exercised under sections 193 and 194 may only be used in court in respect of a prosecution of the person who made them: (i) for making false or misleading statements under subsection 201(2); or (ii) for making an inconsistent statement in respect of a prosecution for another offence.

Section 198: Use of statements obtained under Competition Act 1998

429. The Chairman of the OFT ("the Chairman") will continue to have the powers of the former DGFT to require the provision of information by an individual on behalf of an

undertaking under Part I, Chapter III of CA 1998 as part of a civil investigation. This section amends CA 1998 to provide a safeguard with regard to the use of any such oral information obtained under CA 1998 by compulsion, for the purpose of the criminal offence under section 188. This is intended to provide protection against self-incrimination.

Section 199 & Schedule 26: Surveillance powers & repeals and revocations

430. Section 199 and Schedule 26 amend the Regulation of Investigatory Powers Act 2000 ('RIPA 2000') to grant the OFT access to intrusive surveillance powers for the United Kingdom. With these powers the Chairman may issue an authorisation for the planting of surveillance devices in residential premises (including hotel accommodation) and private vehicles. (A designated officer may grant an authorisation in an urgent case if the Chairman is not available.) Acting on information received from an informant, the OFT could, for example, use these powers to record a meeting of cartelists in a hotel room.
431. Under section 32(3)(b) RIPA 2000, one of the criteria for which an authorisation may be granted is for 'the purpose of preventing or detecting serious crime'. All applications for authorisations are subject to the scrutiny and approval of the surveillance commissioners in line with the existing procedural safeguards in RIPA 2000. When an authorisation is granted, the OFT intends to outsource the technical deployment of the intrusive surveillance activity to other public authorities which already have access to these powers and practical experience of exercising them.
432. The OFT has applied separately to the Home Office for an Order to grant authorised officers access to directed surveillance (essentially monitoring the movement of people and vehicles) and covert human intelligence sources (essentially the use of informants) under sections 28 & 29 RIPA 2000. OFT has also applied to the Home Office for an Order to grant authorised officers access to communication data (primarily postal and telephone records) under section 22 RIPA 2000. These powers will be available for both civil and criminal investigations.

Section 200: Authorisation of action in respect of property

433. This section amends Part III of the Police Act 1997 to grant the Chairman and a designated officer the powers to issue authorisations to interfere with private property. Such authorisations are required to gain access to premises in order to undertake intrusive surveillance.

Section 201: Offences

434. This section makes it an offence for a person to fail to comply with any requirement imposed on him or her in an investigation by the OFT under sections 193 and 194. It is an offence for a person knowingly or recklessly to provide false or misleading information to the OFT or for a person to destroy or falsify documents that he or she has been required to produce. It is also an offence for a person to obstruct a person exercising powers under a warrant issued under section 194.

Appendix Three

Powers for Investigating Criminal Cartels Guidance

Enterprise Act 2002

web www.oft.gov.uk/enterpriseact.htm

This booklet explains how the Office of Fair Trading will exercise its powers for investigating the criminal cartel offence introduced by the Enterprise Act 2002, which came into force on 20 June 2003. It is provided for guidance only. It should not be read as a substitute for the relevant provisions of the Enterprise Act, the Police and Criminal Evidence Act 1984 and related Codes of Practice, the Regulation of Investigatory Powers Act 2000 and the Criminal Justice and Police Act 2001, to which reference should be made as to the specific powers and procedures that will be used by the Office of Fair Trading.

Office of Fair Trading,

Fleetbank House,
2–6 Salisbury Square,
London EC4Y 8JX
Telephone 020 7211 8000
Fax 020 7211 8800
Enterprise Act enquiries 020 7211 8181 or
email enterpriseact.enquiries@oft.gsi.gov.uk

1 Introduction Powers for investigating criminal cartels

1.1 The Enterprise Act 2002 (the Enterprise Act) makes it a criminal offence for an individual to dishonestly agree with one or more other persons that two or more undertakings will engage in certain prohibited cartel arrangements, including those that involve price-fixing, market-sharing, limitation of production or supply and bid-rigging. The offence applies in respect of dishonest agreements both to make or implement such arrangements and also to cause such arrangements to be made or implemented. The criminal offence will be committed irrespective of whether the agreement reached is actually implemented by the undertakings.[1]

[1] Enterprise Act sections 188–89

1.2 The criminal cartel offence will operate alongside the existing regime that imposes civil sanctions on undertakings that breach the Chapter I prohibition on anti-competitive agreements in the Competition Act 1998 (CA98)[2] and Article 81 of the EC Treaty.

1.3 The criminal cartel offence only applies to a dishonest agreement in respect of arrangements between undertakings operating at the same level of the supply chain, known as horizontal agreements. Vertical agreements which are intended to operate between undertakings at different levels in the supply chain, for example between a manufacturer and a distributor, or between a distributor and a retailer, are not covered by the offence.

1.4 The Enterprise Act gives the Office of Fair Trading (the OFT) powers to investigate individuals suspected of having committed the criminal cartel offence.[3] These powers are described in part 3 of this guidance. They are concerned with investigating the criminal offence and they differ to some extent from the powers of investigation available to the OFT in a civil investigation of undertakings under the CA98.[4] The way that the OFT intends to use its powers of investigation in parallel criminal and civil investigations is described in part 4 of this guidance.

1.5 The Enterprise Act also gives the OFT the power of intrusive surveillance[5] along with the related power to interfere with property[6] and these are described in part 5 of the guidance.

1.6 The limitations on the use of the OFT's powers of investigation under the Enterprise Act are described in part 6 and the offences committed by a person who fails to comply when these powers are exercised are described in part 7.

2 Trigger for the use of the powers of investigation

2.1 The OFT can conduct a formal investigation under the Enterprise Act if there are **reasonable grounds for suspecting** that a criminal cartel offence has been committed.[7]

2.2 Whether there are reasonable grounds for suspecting is an objective test and will depend upon the information available to the OFT. Examples of sources of information that may lead to reasonable grounds for suspecting that the criminal offence has been committed include statements provided by employees or ex-employees or former members of a cartel, correspondence evidencing the existence of a secret cartel agreement or information provided in an application made by an undertaking or an individual under the OFT's leniency programmes.[8]

2.3 The OFT may obtain information about individuals, undertakings, agreements and markets at any time through informal enquiries. Such enquiries, which may be made at a meeting, by correspondence, in a telephone conversation or during the course of a voluntary interview may be made in addition to, or instead of, using the formal investigation powers set out in the Enterprise Act. The OFT will make it clear to individuals and

[2] Further information on the CA98 prohibition can be found in the guidance 'The Chapter I Prohibition', OFT 401, published in March 1999

[3] Enterprise Act sections 192–196

[4] Further information on the CA98 powers of investigation can be found in the guidance 'Powers of Investigation', OFT 404, published in March 1999

[5] Enterprise Act section 199

[6] Enterprise Act section 200

[7] Enterprise Act section 192(1)

[8] OFT's CA98 Guidance as to the 'Appropriate Amount of a Penalty' and the Enterprise Act Guidance 'The cartel offence: no-action letters for individuals'

undertakings that they are not compelled to respond to an informal enquiry. Undertakings and individuals are however encouraged to co-operate with the OFT enquiries.

3 Powers of investigation

3.1 The Enterprise Act gives the OFT the power:

—to require persons to answer questions, provide information or produce documents[9]
—to enter and search premises under a warrant.[10]

These powers of investigation are only exerciseable for the purposes of an investigation where it appears to the OFT that there is good reason to exercise them for the purpose of investigating the affairs, or any aspect of the affairs, of any person.[11]

Powers to require information and documents

3.2 For the purposes of an investigation, the OFT has the power to require a person under investigation or any other person who it has reason to believe has relevant information to answer questions, or provide information, and to produce specified documents which appear to the OFT to relate to any matter relevant to the investigation. This power must be exercised by serving a written notice. The notice must indicate the subject matter and purpose of the investigation and the nature of the offences which may be committed by failing to co-operate with an investigation, which are set out in paragraph 7.1 below. The notice will state the time and place at which information or documents must be produced. The notice may also require a person to attend an interview to answer questions with respect to any matter relevant to the investigation. This is referred to as a compulsory interview (paragraph 4.3).

3.3 Where documents are produced, the OFT may take copies or extracts from them and require the person producing the documents to provide an explanation of any of them. Where documents are not produced, the OFT may require the person who was required to produce them to state, to the best of his knowledge and belief, where they are.

3.4 The powers to require information to be provided and specified documents to be produced may be used at any time during the investigation of a suspected criminal offence, including during the execution of a search warrant. A person may also receive more than one notice during the course of an investigation. The OFT is not limited to using the powers against persons under investigation. In setting an appropriate time limit for complying with a written notice, the OFT will consider the amount and complexity of the information required. However, the OFT can require information and documents to be provided immediately if appropriate.

3.5 The '**specified documents**' which the OFT can require to be produced in a written notice (subject to the limitations outlined in section 6 below) include both specified individual documents, for example a particular agreement, or documents of a specified description,

[9] Enterprise Act section 193
[10] Enterprise Act section 194
[11] Enterprise Act section 192(2)

such as price lists or sales invoices over a certain period. The term '**documents**' includes information recorded in any form and includes information that may be held electronically.[12]

Power to enter premises under a warrant

3.6 For the purposes of a criminal investigation and on specified grounds, the OFT may apply to the High Court or, in Scotland, the procurator fiscal may apply to the sheriff, for a warrant authorising a named officer of the OFT, and any other OFT officers and specified persons authorised to accompany the named officer, to enter and search premises and to take possession of relevant documents, or to take necessary steps for preserving them or preventing interference with them.

3.7 The Enterprise Act sets out the circumstances in which a judge in the High Court or the sheriff may issue a warrant to enter and search premises specified in the warrant. The judge or the sheriff must be satisfied that there are reasonable grounds for believing that there are on the premises documents which the OFT has the power to require to be produced in a written notice (paragraph 3.2) and that:

—a person has failed to comply with the requirement to produce them, or
—it is not practicable to serve a written notice, or
—the service of such a notice might seriously prejudice the investigation (for example, relevant documents are likely to be destroyed or tampered with).

3.8 A warrant issued by a judge in the High Court or by the sheriff shall authorise the named officer and OFT officers authorised in writing to accompany him to:

—enter the premises, using such force as is reasonably necessary for the purpose of gaining entry
—search the premises and take possession of documents appearing to be of the kind in respect of which the warrant was granted (subject to the limitations outlined in section 6 below). **Original documents will be taken**, as is the usual practice under search warrants issued in respect of suspected criminal offences although the person who had custody or control of a document before it was taken by the OFT will, on request, be provided with a copy as soon as is reasonably practicable after the execution of the warrant
—require any person to provide an explanation of any document appearing to be of a kind in respect of which the warrant was granted or to state to the best of his knowledge and belief where it may be found
—require information which is held electronically and is accessible from the premises and which the named officer considers relates to any matter relevant to the investigation to be produced in a visible and legible form (or in a form from which it can be readily produced in a visible and legible form) and taken away.

3.9 A warrant can authorise persons who are not employees of the OFT to accompany and assist the named officer in the search. Such persons may be needed, for example, to provide expertise which is not available within the OFT but is necessary to utilise fully the terms of the warrant. For example, an IT expert who could assist OFT officers to retrieve information from computers located on premises for which the warrant was issued.

[12] Enterprise Act section 202

3.10 A warrant will indicate the subject matter and purpose of the investigation and the nature of the offences which may be committed by failing to co-operate with an investigation, which are set out in paragraph 7.1 below. Upon entry to the premises the named officer will produce the warrant and all officers will also produce evidence of their identity. If the occupier is present, a copy of the warrant shall, if practicable, be given to the occupier before the search begins along with a copy of a notice that summarises the extent of the powers being used and explains the rights of the occupier unless the named officer believes this would frustrate the object of the search or endanger officers or other people.[13] Where possible, the person in charge at the premises should designate an appropriate person to be a point of contact for the officer during his investigation.

3.11 The named officer shall first attempt to communicate with the occupier, or any other person entitled to grant access to the premises, explain the authority under which entry is sought to the premises and ask the occupier to allow entry unless:

—the premises to be searched are unoccupied, or
—the occupier and any other person entitled to grant access are absent, or
—there are reasonable grounds for believing that alerting the occupier or any other person entitled to grant access would frustrate the object of the search or endanger officers or other people.[14]

3.12 If any of the above circumstances apply, reasonable and proportionate force may be used if necessary to enter premises if the named officer is satisfied that the premises are those specified in the warrant. Reasonable and proportionate force may also be used where the occupier or any other person entitled to grant access has refused entry to the premises or it is impossible to communicate with the occupier or any other person entitled to grant access.[15] If the occupier is not present, a copy of the warrant and of the notice of powers and rights shall be left in a prominent place on the premises and endorsed with the date and time of the search and the name of the named officer.[16] On leaving premises which have been entered by force, the named officer must make sure that they are secure either by arranging for the occupier or the occupier's representative to be present or by any other appropriate means.[17] If the occupier is informed, he, or one of his representatives, must be given a reasonable opportunity to be present when the warrant is executed.

3.13 In addition, OFT officers also have the power to seize material where it is not reasonably practicable, while on the premises, to determine the extent to which it may be seized, if at all, or for the seizable material to be separated from the non-seizable material in which it is comprised.[18] This may be the case, for example, where there is a large bulk of material or where special technical equipment is needed to separate out material the OFT would be entitled to take from material which it is not (for example, material held on a computer). The factors that the OFT must take into account in

[13] In accordance with the Police and Criminal Evidence Act ("PACE") Codes of Practice—Code B 6.7 and 6.8—the revised version of PACE Code B came into force on 1 April 2003
[14] In accordance with PACE Codes of Practice—Code B 6.4
[15] In accordance with PACE Codes of Practice—Code B 6.6
[16] In accordance with PACE Codes of Practice—Code B 6.8
[17] In accordance with PACE Codes of Practice—Code B 6.13
[18] Criminal Justice and Police Act 2001 section 50 and Enterprise Act section 194(5)

deciding whether to exercise these seize and sift powers are the length of time and the number of persons required to carry out the determination or separation on the premises; whether the determination or separation would (or would if carried out on the premises) involve damage to property; the need for any special apparatus or equipment to carry out the determination or separation; and whether the separation (either in itself or if carried out on the premises by the only practicable means) would be likely to prejudice the use of some or all of the material to be taken.[19] OFT officers must always give careful consideration to whether removing copies or images of relevant material or data would be a satisfactory alternative to removing the originals.

3.14 The exercise of seize and sift powers is subject to strict safeguards and the OFT will fully comply with Home Office guidance on operating these powers and the revised version of PACE Code B.[20]

Access to legal advice during criminal investigations

3.15 When executing a warrant obtained under the Enterprise Act in respect of a suspected criminal offence the OFT officers will not wait for an individual's or undertaking's legal advisers to arrive before commencing the search. However, a friend, neighbour or other person will be allowed to witness the search unless the named officer in charge of the search has reasonable grounds for believing that the presence of the person asked for would seriously hinder the investigation or endanger officers or other people. A search need not be unreasonably delayed for this purpose. A record of the action taken, including the grounds for refusing a request from the occupier, should be made on the premises search record.[21] During the course of a search under a warrant, the OFT officers may be prepared to wait a reasonable amount of time for an undertaking's or an individual's legal advisers to arrive if it is the OFT's intention to remove material from the premises where it is not reasonably practicable to examine it properly on the premises (paragraphs 3.13 and 3.14 above), although the rest of the search will proceed without delay.

3.16 A person suspected of having committed a criminal cartel offence will be advised that he is free to seek legal advice before being interviewed under caution (paragraph 4.2 below). A person being interviewed under the powers of investigation in the Enterprise Act (paragraph 3.2 above) will also be entitled to seek legal advice. OFT officers will not generally conduct interviews under caution or using the compulsory powers of investigation in the Enterprise Act during the course of a search under warrant. An interview under caution may be conducted during the course of a search under warrant if a person voluntarily decides to provide information to OFT officers in which case he will be cautioned and advised that he is free to seek legal advice. A person is not required to be cautioned prior to being asked questions that are solely necessary for the purpose of furthering the proper and effective conduct of a search, such as to obtain computer passwords or safe combinations.[22]

[19] Criminal Justice and Police Act 2001 section 50(3)
[20] Home Office Circular 19/2003 issued 1 April 2003 and Code B 7.7–7.17
[21] In accordance with PACE Codes of Practice—Code B 6.11
[22] In accordance with PACE Codes of Practice—Code B 6.12

3.17 PACE does not apply in Scotland nor do PACE Codes of Practice. Accordingly, the procedures set out in paragraphs 3.10 to 3.12 inclusive and 3.14 to 3.16 inclusive insofar as these relate to PACE Codes of Practice, do not constitute legal requirements for the execution of search warrants in Scotland. Nevertheless, the OFT officers may follow these procedures in Scotland, if appropriate.

Role of the Director of the Serious Fraud Office in criminal investigations

3.18 The OFT will exercise its powers under the Enterprise Act to investigate individuals suspected of having committed the criminal cartel offence in close co-operation with the Director of the Serious Fraud Office ('the SFO'). The SFO is the intended prosecutor for this criminal offence[23] in England, Wales and Northern Ireland where serious or complex fraud is involved. The OFT has agreed a **Memorandum of Understanding**[24] with the SFO which records the basis on which they will co-operate to investigate and/or prosecute individuals in respect of the cartel offence where serious or complex fraud is suspected. The factors that the SFO take into account in defining a serious or complex fraud include cases where the sum at risk is estimated to be at least £1 million, cases that are likely to give rise to national publicity and widespread public concern (for example, those involving public bodies) and cases where legal, accountancy and investigative skills need to be brought together.

3.19 Where a case is identified by the OFT as one that may involve a criminal offence and which is likely to fall within the SFO's definition of a serious or complex fraud, the OFT will inform the SFO who will decide whether the case may be one that is acceptable for investigation. Where further enquiries need to be carried out to determine the extent of a suspected criminal offence, the OFT and SFO will agree the scope of and responsibilities for the further enquiries. The enquiries made at this time are likely to involve the use by the OFT of the powers of investigation in the Enterprise Act. Once these enquiries have been completed, the SFO will decide, following consultation with the OFT, whether the case is one that should be taken forward for criminal prosecution.

3.20 Following the acceptance of a case by the SFO, the SFO may decide to carry out additional enquiries using its powers under section 2 of the Criminal Justice Act 1987 (the 'CJA 1987'). These powers are broadly the same as the OFT's powers of investigation under the Enterprise Act.

3.21 Under section 2 of the CJA 1987, the SFO has powers to require a person to answer questions, provide information or produce documents for the purposes of an investigation. Written notice is given when the SFO exercises these powers. In appropriate cases the SFO may require immediate compliance with a notice. The majority of section 2 notices are issued to third parties that may, in the ordinary course of their business, have information or hold documents relevant to a suspected offence. Anyone issued with a section 2 notice is obliged to provide the information and documents required except that there is no obligation to disclose documents subject to legal professional privilege (although a lawyer may be required to furnish the name and address of his client). In addition, the disclosure of confidential banking material is

[23] EA Section 190
[24] Published on the OFT website at www.oft.gov.uk

also subject to certain safeguards.[25] The Enterprise Act contains similar provisions to the CJA 1987 in respect of the disclosure of documents subject to legal professional privilege and confidential banking information (paragraphs 6.1and 6.2 below). A person who refuses to answer questions or provide information or documents in response to a section 2 notice without a reasonable excuse commits an offence.

3.22 Section 2 of the CJA 1987 also permits the SFO, on specified grounds, to obtain search warrants from a justice of the peace in respect of an investigation which the SFO is conducting. The SFO would not seek a search warrant from a justice of the peace if the OFT had already been refused a search warrant by the High Court in respect of the same premises unless new evidence had come to light during the course of the investigation that would justify the application for such a warrant.

3.23 Where the SFO and the OFT are exercising their formal powers of investigation under either the CJA 1987 or the Enterprise Act to compel documents and/or information, the SFO or the OFT will make it clear in writing to the persons concerned the specific power that is being used.

3.24 In **Scotland**, the Lord Advocate is responsible for all prosecutions and exercises the same powers as the SFO, under the Criminal Law (Consolidation) (Scotland) Act 1995, through the International and Financial Crime Unit in Crown Office. The OFT has also agreed a **Memorandum of Understanding**[26] with the Head of the International and Financial Crime Unit that records the basis on which they will co-operate to investigate and/or prosecute individuals in respect of the cartel offence, where such offences may have been committed within the jurisdiction of the Scottish courts.

4 Parallel OFT criminal and civil investigations

4.1 When the OFT first receives information about alleged cartel activity, it will often not be in a position to know whether to investigate using its formal powers under the Enterprise Act or the CA98. In making its enquiries, however, the possibility that the criminal cartel offence may have been committed will be borne in mind by the OFT. This means that, where appropriate, OFT officers will act in accordance with PACE, all the relevant Codes of Practice and the Criminal Procedure and Investigations Act 1996, or in Scotland, the applicable Scottish criminal law and procedure.[27]

4.2 During their enquiries, if OFT officers suspect that an individual may have committed the criminal offence, that person will be given the standard criminal caution[28] before being questioned about his involvement or suspected involvement in the offence if his answers or failure or refusal to answer may be given in evidence to a court in a

[25] CJA 1987 section 2(10)(a)&(b)

[26] Published on the OFT website at www.oft.gov.uk

[27] PACE has no legal status in Scotland although there is no prohibition to the OFT following its Codes of Practice when conducting its investigations in Scotland

[28] PACE Codes of Practice—Code C paragraph 10.5 (note: a different caution must be given in Scotland)

prosecution.[29] The OFT officers will also remind the person that the interview is voluntary and that he is not under arrest and that he is free to leave at any time. The person will further be advised that he is free to seek legal advice and, if he decides to seek legal advice, the interview will not take place until his legal adviser is present. The person will be told that his answers during the interview may be used in a CA98 investigation against undertakings.

4.3 The OFT officers may also decide to conduct a follow-up compulsory interview with the suspect using its powers under the Enterprise Act (paragraph 3.2 above). The difference between a voluntary interview and a compulsory interview will be explained to the person by the OFT officers: the difference being that in a compulsory interview the person will be required to answer all the questions whereas in a voluntary interview the person may refuse to answer any of the questions. It will also be explained that the information obtained under a compulsory interview cannot be used as evidence against that person in a criminal prosecution except in certain limited circumstances (paragraph 6.3 below) and that it will not be used as evidence in a CA98 investigation against any undertaking which employs him.

4.4 Following the execution of a search warrant obtained under the Enterprise Act (paragraph 3.6 above), the OFT will take possession of original documents found during the search which are relevant to the investigation. The OFT may make use of these documents during its administrative procedures under the CA98 against undertakings. The possibility of instituting an administrative procedure under the CA98 against the undertakings engaged in a cartel will be considered at the same time as individuals are being investigated for their involvement in the same cartel under the Enterprise Act.

4.5 Any documents obtained by the SFO using its powers under the CJA 1987 in respect of a suspected criminal offence (paragraphs 3.19 to 3.21 above) can also be disclosed to the OFT for the purpose of its administrative procedures under the CA98.[30]

4.6 If the OFT decides to institute an administrative procedure under the CA98 against undertakings engaged in a cartel where criminal proceedings are also being considered against individuals in respect of the same cartel, the OFT and the SFO will consult on timing. The OFT will not institute its administrative procedure without prior consultation with the SFO. At any stage of the investigation of a suspected criminal offence, it may be decided to abandon the criminal investigation and to proceed only with the CA98 investigation. All the individuals who are the subject of a criminal investigation will be informed of any decision not to proceed against them.

4.7 In cases where the OFT begins a cartel investigation using its formal powers under the CA98, but the information obtained gives reasonable grounds for suspecting that the criminal offence has been committed, the OFT will consult with the SFO as to the merits of commencing a criminal investigation. In certain cases, the OFT will progress an investigation using its CA98 powers (which may or may not have commenced prior to any SFO involvement), while an SFO led criminal investigation is being progressed. Suitable procedures will be adopted to ensure that the two investigation teams maintain an on-going dialogue and to ensure that the CA98 investigation does not prejudice the parallel criminal investigation.

[29] In certain limited circumstances a person need not be cautioned before being interviewed—Code C 10.1 (a)–(e)

[30] CJA 1987 section 3(5)(a)

4.8 Any **statement** obtained from an individual by the OFT using its compulsory powers of investigation under the CA98 cannot be used in a criminal prosecution against that person except in certain limited circumstances (paragraph 6.4 below). Where an individual has made a voluntary statement to the OFT pursuant to a CA98 investigation without a caution first having been administered, the OFT may repeat the interview under caution to allow the statement to be used as evidence in court (paragraph 4.2 above).

4.9 Any **documents** obtained by the OFT using its powers of investigation under the CA98 may be admissible in any subsequent criminal prosecution of the cartel offence under the Enterprise Act. The OFT intends that when conducting its CA98 investigations in relation to horizontal cartels its procedures in relation to exhibit and property handling, and the storage, management and control of documents conform to the standards of a criminal investigation. The OFT may also use its formal criminal powers of investigation under the Enterprise Act to obtain original versions of documents obtained under a CA98 investigation.

4.10 In cases where a European Commission cartel investigation involves a potential criminal cartel offence in the UK under the Enterprise Act, the OFT and the European Commission will cooperate to coordinate the progress of their investigations.

5 Intrusive surveillance and action in respect of property

5.1 The Enterprise Act introduces new powers of intrusive surveillance for the OFT for the sole purpose of investigating the criminal cartel offence. The Enterprise Act amends the Regulation of Investigatory Powers Act 2000 ('RIPA')[31] and the Police Act 1997[32] to grant the OFT the power of intrusive surveillance and the related power of property interference.[33]

5.2 **Intrusive Surveillance** is defined as covert surveillance carried out in relation to anything taking place on any residential premises (including hotel accommodation) or in any private vehicle[34] and involves the presence of an individual on the premises or in a vehicle or by means of a surveillance device(s) to either hear or see what is happening within the premises or vehicle. **Property Interference** allows for the covert installation of such a device(s) in property which would otherwise involve some element of trespass.

5.3 These forms of surveillance, which will only be used by the OFT in its investigations under the Enterprise Act, require the personal authority of the Chairman of the OFT and the prior approval of the Office of Surveillance Commissioners before deployment can take place. In cases of urgency, which are likely to be rare, if prior approval from a Surveillance Commissioner cannot be sought and granted in time, the Chairman of the OFT (or a designated officer of the OFT) will authorise the deployment of intrusive surveillance and give notice to a Surveillance Commissioner as soon as is reasonably practicable, explaining why it was necessary to use the urgency provisions. If the Surveillance Commissioner is at any time satisfied that there were no

[31] RIPA section 32ff
[32] Police Act 1997 section 93–94
[33] Enterprise Act sections 199–200
[34] Subject to RIPA sections 26(4) and (6)

reasonable grounds for believing the case was urgent, he may quash the authorisation and the surveillance must cease immediately. The use of intrusive surveillance must be necessary to prevent or detect the cartel offence and must be proportionate to what is sought to be achieved by carrying it out.

5.4 Beyond the scope of the Enterprise Act, the OFT has been added to the list of public authorities which can authorise the use of other methods of surveillance in accordance with RIPA.[35] The OFT is allowed to authorise **directed surveillance**[36] (for example, watching a person's office) and **covert human intelligence sources**[37] (i.e. informants) in its cartel investigations under both the Enterprise Act and the CA98.

5.5 The OFT is also authorised to obtain **access to communications data**[38] (for example, obtaining records of telephone numbers called). The OFT can only use the facility to access communications data in its investigations under the Enterprise Act.

5.6 The OFT intends to publish Codes of Practice in relation to its procedures for exercising the various powers outlined in paragraphs 5.2 to 5.5 above in its investigations.[39]

6 Limitations on the use of the powers of investigation

Privileged communications

6.1 The power of the OFT to obtain documents under the Enterprise Act, whether by written notice or during the execution of a search warrant, does not extend to communications benefiting from legal professional privilege ("LPP").[40] A person may not be required to produce or disclose any information or document which he would be entitled to refuse to produce or disclose on grounds of LPP in proceedings in the High Court or in Scottish Courts on grounds of confidentiality of communications. However, a lawyer may be obliged to provide the name and address of his client as part of an investigation being conducted under the powers in the Enterprise Act. LPP does not apply to communications made with the intention of furthering a criminal purpose (whether the lawyer is acting unwittingly or culpably). The OFT will adopt suitable procedures to determine the proper status of disputed LPP material.

6.2 The Enterprise Act also provides a safeguard in respect of confidential banking information, i.e. confidential communication between a bank and its client.[41] A person may not be required under the powers of investigation in the Enterprise Act to disclose any information or produce any document if the information or document is protected by a banking obligation of confidence, unless the person to whom the obligation of confidence is owed consents to the disclosure or the OFT has authorised the disclosure.

[35] SI/2003/3171
[36] RIPA section 28
[37] RIPA section 29
[38] SI/2003/3172
[39] To be published on the OFT website at www.oft.gov.uk
[40] Enterprise Act section196(1)
[41] Enterprise Act section196(2)

Self-incrimination

6.3 The Enterprise Act provides safeguards in relation to the use of information gained by the OFT using its compulsory powers of investigation under the Enterprise Act.[42] Statements made by a person in response to a requirement imposed by the OFT using its powers of investigation under the Enterprise Act, may only be used as evidence in criminal proceedings against that person in two circumstances:

—where that person has knowingly or recklessly made a false or misleading statement in response to that requirement and is then prosecuted for an offence of knowingly or recklessly making a false or misleading statement (part 7 below)
—where that person is being prosecuted for some other offence and he makes a statement that is inconsistent with it and if evidence relating to it is adduced or a question relating to it is asked by him or on his behalf.

6.4 Statements made by a person in response to a requirement imposed by the OFT using its compulsory powers of investigation under the CA98 may only be used as evidence in a cartel prosecution against the person who made it if, in giving evidence during a prosecution of the cartel offence under the Enterprise Act, he makes a statement inconsistent with it and if evidence relating to it is adduced or a question relating to it is asked by him or on his behalf.[43]

6.5 A person's answers to questions required under section 2 of the CJA 1987 (paragraph 3.20 above) may only be used in evidence in criminal proceedings against the person under the same two circumstances outlined in paragraph 6.3 above. Similar restrictions apply to the use in evidence of answers given to questions required under section 28 of the Criminal Law (Consolidation) (Scotland) Act 1995.

Disclosure of confidential information

6.6 The Enterprise Act imposes limits on the disclosure of information that relates to the affairs of any individual or to any business of an undertaking which has been obtained by the OFT as a result of using its powers of investigation under the Enterprise Act.[44] The Enterprise Act requires that such information must not be disclosed during the lifetime of that individual or while the undertaking continues in existence unless consent has been obtained from the person that provided the information (if the information was lawfully obtained by the person and the person's identity is known) and the individual to whose affairs the information relates, or the person carrying on the business to which the information relates.[45]

6.7 There are certain exceptions to this requirement under which the OFT may disclose such information:

—the disclosure is required for the purposes of a Community obligation[46]
—the disclosure is made for the purpose of facilitating the exercise of the disclosing authority's statutory functions. If information disclosed for this purpose is not made

[42] Enterprise Act section197
[43] Enterprise Act section 198
[44] Enterprise Act section 237
[45] Enterprise Act section 239
[46] Enterprise Act section 240

available to the public, there are restrictions on the recipient making further disclosure[47]

—the disclosure is made to any other person for the purpose of facilitating the exercise of the recipient's functions under specified statutes or subordinate legislation. Information disclosed in this way must not be used for any purpose other than a purpose relating to functions mentioned in the specified statutes or subordinate legislation[48]

—the disclosure is made to any person in connection with the investigation of any criminal offence in any part of the United Kingdom; for the purposes of criminal proceedings there, or for the purpose of any decision whether to start or bring to an end such an investigation or proceedings. The recipient must not use the information for any purpose other than that for which it was disclosed.[49] The OFT must not make a disclosure unless it is satisfied that the making of the disclosure is proportionate to what is sought to be achieved by it

—disclosure is made to overseas authorities in certain limited circumstances.[50]

6.8 Before disclosing such information in one of the permitted gateways, the OFT must have regard to the following.[51]

—the need to exclude from disclosure (so far as practicable) any information whose disclosure the OFT thinks is contrary to the public interest

—the need to exclude from disclosure (so far as practicable) commercial information whose disclosure the OFT thinks might significantly harm the legitimate business interests of the undertaking to which it relates or information relating to the private affairs of an individual whose disclosure the OFT thinks might significantly harm the individual's interests

—the extent to which the disclosure of the information is necessary for the purpose for which the OFT is permitted to make the disclosure.

7 Offences relating to the powers of investigation

7.1 The Enterprise Act sets out a number of criminal offences which may be committed where a person fails to co-operate when the investigation powers in the Enterprise Act are exercised.[52] It is an offence for a person:

—to fail to comply with a requirement (as explained in paragraph 3.2 above) to answer questions or provide information or documents without reasonable excuse

—knowingly or recklessly to make a statement which is false or misleading

—to falsify, conceal, destroy or otherwise dispose of or cause or permit the falsification, concealment, destruction or disposal of documents which he knows or suspects to be relevant to an investigation

—intentionally to obstruct a person in the exercise of his powers under a warrant.

[47] Enterprise Act section 241(1) and (2)
[48] Enterprise Act section 241(3) and (4)
[49] Enterprise Act section 242
[50] Enterprise Act section 243. Further information on the disclosure of information can be found in the OFT guidance 'Controls on overseas disclosure of information'
[51] Enterprise Act section 244
[52] Enterprise Act section 201

7.2 A person who falsifies, conceals, destroys or disposes of documents (or causes or permits this) has a defence if he can prove that he had no intention of concealing from the investigators the facts disclosed by the documents.

7.3 Offences will be tried either summarily in the Magistrates' Court or, in the case of more serious offences, on indictment in the Crown Court. In Scotland, offences may be tried summarily in the Sheriff Court, on indictment before a Sheriff and Jury or, in the most serious cases, on indictment in the High Court of Justiciary.

7.4 The sanctions that may be imposed by the courts on a person found guilty of each offence described in paragraph 7.1 are set out in table 7.1 below. The sanctions that are available for each offence differ according to whether the person is found guilty on summary conviction or on indictment.

Table 7.1 The sanctions that may be imposed by the courts on a person found guilty of a criminal offence committed where a person fails to co-operate when the investigation powers in the Enterprise Act are exercised.

Offence	**Sanction on summary conviction**	**Sanction on conviction on indictment**
Fail to comply with a requirement to answer questions or provide information/documents without reasonable excuse	Fine of up to level five on the standard scale and/or up to six months imprisonment	This offence will not be tried in this way
Intentionally or recklessly make a false or misleading statement	Fine of up to the statutory maximum and/or up to six months imprisonment	Unlimited fine and/or up to two years imprisonment
Intentionally destroy, dispose of, falsify or conceal documents	Fine of up to the statutory maximum and/or up to six months imprisonment	Unlimited fine and/or up to five years' imprisonment
Intentionally obstruct a person carrying out an investigation with a warrant	Fine of up to the statutory maximum	Unlimited fine and/or up to two years' imprisonment

Appendix Four

Office of Fair Trading—The Cartel Offence: Guidance on the issue of no-action letters for individuals

1 Introduction

1.1 The Enterprise Act 2002 introduces the cartel offence—a criminal offence for **individuals** who dishonestly engage in cartel agreements. The cartel offence will operate alongside the existing Competition Act 1998 regime, which provides for the imposition of civil sanctions on undertakings[1] that breach the Chapter I prohibition on anti-competitive agreements. (Further information on the Chapter I prohibition can be found in the Office of Fair Trading Competition Act guideline *The Chapter I Prohibition (OFT 401)*). The cartel offence will deter individuals against engaging in cartel activity and supplement the deterrent provided by the threat of financial penalties under the Competition Act for the undertakings involved.

1.2 The Office of Fair Trading (the 'OFT') wishes to encourage individuals to come forward with information[2] relating to any cartel activities in which they are involved. The OFT therefore sets out (in part 3) guidance on when immunity from prosecution—in the form of 'no-action letters'—will be available to such individuals.

2 The cartel offence

The offence

2.1 Section 188 of the Enterprise Act provides that an individual is guilty of an offence if he or she **dishonestly**[3] agrees with one or more other persons that undertakings will engage in one or more of the prohibited cartel activities. These are:

[1] 'Undertaking' includes any natural or legal person capable of carrying on commercial or economic activities relating to goods or services, irrespective of its legal status. It includes companies, firms, businesses, partnerships, individuals operating as sole traders, agricultural cooperatives, trade associations and non-profit making organisations. A parent company and its subsidiaries will usually be treated as a single undertaking if they operate as a single economic unit, depending on the facts of each case.

[2] In this guidance, 'information' means facts, statements, documents, evidence or any other items unless the context indicates otherwise.

[3] The offence is committed only if the individual acts dishonestly, a concept which is well understood in criminal law. For England and Wales and Northern Ireland, the test for dishonesty is that set out in *R v Ghosh* [1982] QB 1053, 75 Cr. AppR. 154 CA, 2 All ER 689, CA.

—price-fixing
—limitation of supply or production
—market-sharing, and
—bid-rigging.

2.2 The offence only applies in respect of agreements between undertakings at the same level in the supply chain, known as horizontal agreements. Vertical agreements[4] will not fall within the scope of the offence.

2.3 The offence will be committed irrespective of whether or not the agreement reached between the individuals is actually implemented by the undertakings and irrespective of whether or not the individuals have the authority to act on behalf of the undertakings at the time of the agreement.

2.4 If the agreement between the individuals is made outside the United Kingdom, proceedings may only be brought where the agreement has been implemented in whole or in part in the United Kingdom.

Penalty and prosecution

2.5 The cartel offence will be triable either in a magistrates' court (summary trial) or before a jury in the Crown Court (trial on indictment). Before the magistrates, a convicted offender may receive a maximum of six-months imprisonment and/or a fine up to the statutory maximum. On conviction on indictment, an offender may receive a maximum of five years' imprisonment and/or an unlimited fine.

2.6 In England and Wales, and in Northern Ireland, prosecutions will generally be undertaken by the Serious Fraud Office (SFO), although the OFT will also have the power to prosecute. Private prosecutions may be brought only with the consent of the OFT. In Scotland, prosecutions will be brought by the Lord Advocate.

2.7 Where cross-jurisdictional issues arise, the jurisdiction in which a case will be brought will depend on the outcome of discussions between the OFT, the SFO and the Lord Advocate's office, and will follow the well-established principles that govern other criminal prosecutions.

3 Immunity from prosecution for individuals coming forward with information

No-action letters

3.1 The OFT considers that it is in the interest of the economic well-being of the United Kingdom to grant immunity from prosecution to individuals who inform competition authorities of cartels and who then cooperate fully in the circumstances set out below. The secret nature of cartels and their damaging effects justifies such a policy. The interests of customers and end-consumers in ensuring that such practices are detected and brought to an end outweigh the policy objectives of imposing penalties on those individuals who have committed an offence but who cooperate fully with the OFT and, where appropriate, any other competition authorities.

[4] A vertical agreement is an agreement between undertakings, each of which operates, for the purposes of the agreement, at a different level of the production or distribution chain.

3.2 In the context of the cartel offence, immunity from prosecution will be granted in the form of a 'no-action letter', issued by the OFT under section 190(4) of the Enterprise Act. A no-action letter will prevent a prosecution being brought against an individual in England and Wales or Northern Ireland for the cartel offence except in circumstances specified in the letter. Whilst guarantees of immunity from prosecution cannot be given in relation to Scotland, cooperation by an individual will be reported to the Lord Advocate who will take such cooperation into account. In suitable cases this may include an early decision as to whether or not a particular individual remains liable to be prosecuted. A draft no-action letter is annexed to this guidance for information. This letter may be amended to take into account any special circumstances of an application.

Conditions for the issue of a no-action letter 3.3 In order to benefit from a no-action letter, and subject to paragraph 3.4 and 3.9 below, an individual must:

—admit participation in the criminal offence
—provide the OFT with all information available to them regarding the existence and activities of the cartel
—maintain continuous and complete cooperation throughout the investigation and until the conclusion of any criminal proceedings arising as a result of the investigation
—not have taken steps to coerce another undertaking to take part in the cartel, and
—refrain from further participation in the cartel from the time of its disclosure to the OFT (except as may be directed by the investigating authority).

3.4 However, the fact that these conditions are satisfied in any particular case is not in itself sufficient for the issue of a no-action letter. Where the OFT believes that it already has, or is in the course of gathering, sufficient information to bring a successful prosecution of an individual, it will not issue a no-action letter to that individual.

Procedure

3.5 When an individual believes that they may require a no-action letter, or an early determination as to whether they are liable to be prosecuted in Scotland, an approach should be made to the Director of Cartel Investigations at the OFT. The approach may be made:

—directly by the individual
—by a lawyer representing the individual, or
—on behalf of named employees, directors, ex-employees or exdirectors, by an undertaking (or by a lawyer representing such undertaking) seeking leniency from the OFT in accordance with the OFT's *'Guidance as to the Appropriate Amount of a Penalty'* (the OFT's Guidance)[5] or in conjunction with an application for leniency from the European Commission in accordance with the Commission Notice on immunity from fines or reduction of fines in cartel cases (the Commission Notice on Immunity)[6].

Initially, approaches by lawyers may be made on an anonymous basis.

[5] The Office of Fair Trading's *'Guidance as to the Appropriate Amount of a Penalty'* (OFT 423).
[6] Commission Notice on immunity from fines and reduction of fines in cartel cases (at the time of drafting: OJ C45, 19.02.02, p 3).

3.6 When an approach is made, the Director of Cartel Investigations will give an initial indication as to whether the OFT may be prepared to issue a no-action letter. In cases where an undertaking has been granted 100 per cent leniency in accordance with the OFT's Guidance or the Commission Notice on Immunity, the OFT will normally be prepared to issue no-action letters to those named employees, directors, ex-employees or ex-directors on whose behalf an approach is made, subject to the conditions set out at paragraph 3.3 above being met and subject to paragraph 3.9.

3.7 If the OFT is prepared to issue a no-action letter the individual applying for immunity from prosecution will be interviewed. Any information they provide in such interviews will not be used against them in criminal proceedings except in the following circumstances:

—where a no-action letter is not issued, if the individual applying for immunity from prosecution has knowingly or recklessly provided information that is false or misleading in a material particular, or

—where a no-action letter is issued, if it is subsequently revoked (see further paragraphs 3.11 to 3.13 below).

3.8 On completion of the interview (which may extend over several sessions), the OFT will advise the applicant in writing whether it is prepared to issue a no-action letter.

3.9 In cases where the OFT concludes that, on the basis of the information that has been given, the applicant is not at risk of criminal prosecution for the cartel offence, it will not issue a no-action letter for this reason and will confirm this in writing.

3.10 If, following discussions:

—the OFT considers that, without a no-action letter, there is a likelihood of prosecution, and

—the applicant confirms that they will meet the conditions for the issue of a no-action letter

a no-action letter will be issued. Alternatively, in a case where prosecution would be brought in Scotland, the cooperation given by the applicant will be reported to the Lord Advocate with a request for an early decision as to whether the individual remains liable to prosecution.

Revocation

3.11 A no-action letter may be revoked if:

—the recipient of a letter ceases to satisfy in whole or in part any of the relevant conditions (set out at paragraph 3.3 above), or

—the recipient of a letter has knowingly or recklessly provided information that is false or misleading in a material particular.

3.12 On revocation any immunity granted by the no-action letter will cease to exist as if it had never been granted and the OFT may rely on any information given by the applicant in a prosecution against them for the cartel offence.

3.13 If a no-action letter is to be revoked the recipient of the letter will be notified in writing and given a reasonable opportunity to make representations.

Competition Disqualification Orders

3.14 Section 204 of the Enterprise Act empowers the OFT to ask the relevant court to make a Competition Disqualification Order (CDO). This is an order disqualifying a director of a company which commits a breach of competition law[7]. For these purposes, a breach of competition law includes an infringement of the Chapter I prohibition or Article 81 EC Treaty.

3.15 The OFT has issued guidance on CDOs[8], in which it states that it will not seek CDOs against individuals who benefit from no-action letters or who are directors[9] of companies that benefit from leniency from either the OFT in accordance with the OFT's guidance or the European Commission in accordance with the Commission Notice on Immunity. Individuals who apply for no-action letters and undertakings benefiting from leniency will receive individual confirmation of this policy.

Annexe

Draft letter

ENTERPRISE ACT 2002 ('THE ACT')

NOTICE UNDER SECTION 190(4)

1 This letter gives written notice to (the 'Applicant') that he/she will not be prosecuted in England and Wales or Northern Ireland for an offence under section 188 of the Act that falls within the description specified in paragraph 2 of this letter (except in the circumstances specified in paragraph 6).

2 The offence for which immunity from prosecution is granted (the 'Reported Offence') is that [**describe** e.g. 'the Applicant dishonestly agreed with one or more other persons to make or implement, or to cause to be made or implemented, arrangements relating to [Undertaking A] and [Undertaking B] to fix a price for the supply by [Undertaking A] in the United Kingdom (otherwise than to Undertaking B) of [a product or service] ('the Cartel Agreement').

3 This grant of immunity from prosecution is made and remains conditional on the Applicant satisfying and continuing to satisfy each of the conditions set out below.

[7] Before granting a CDO, a court must also be satisfied that the conduct of that individual as a director makes him unfit to be concerned in the management of a company.

[8] See Office guideline *Competition Disqualification Orders (OFT 500).*

[9] For the purposes of CDOs, 'director' includes a de facto director as well as a shadow director.

Conditions

a) The Applicant must admit participation in the Reported Offence described in paragraph 2 of this letter.
b) The Applicant must provide the Office of Fair Trading (the 'OFT') with all facts, statements, documents, evidence or any other items ('Information') available to him/her relating to the Reported Offence and the existence and activities of the Cartel Agreement.
c) The Applicant shall maintain continuous and complete cooperation throughout the investigation of the Reported Offence and until the conclusion of any criminal proceedings arising as a result of the investigation. Such cooperation includes but is not limited to the Applicant:
   i) voluntarily and without prompting, providing the OFT with all Information that becomes known to him/her or available to him/her relating to the Reported Offence and the Cartel Agreement, in addition to any such Information already provided
   ii) providing promptly, and without the OFT using its powers under any section of the Act, all Information available to him/her wherever located, requested by the OFT in relation to the Reported Offence and the Cartel Agreement, to the extent that it has not already been provided.
d) The Applicant must not have taken steps to coerce another undertaking to take part in the Cartel Agreement.
e) The Applicant must have refrained from participation in the Cartel Agreement (except as may have been directed by the investigating authority) from and including [date of disclosure to the OFT].
f) The Applicant must refrain from any further participation in the Cartel Agreement (except as may be directed by the investigating authority).

4 The Applicant confirms that he/she has complied with conditions (a), (b), (d) and (e) above, and undertakes to comply with conditions (c) and (f) above.

5 If, in the view of the OFT, at any time before the conclusion of any criminal proceedings arising as a result of the investigation into the Reported Offence, the conditions which are set out in this letter have not been complied with in full by the Applicant or the Applicant has knowingly or recklessly provided Information that is false or misleading in a material particular, the OFT shall give immediate written notice to the Applicant of the nature of the alleged noncompliance and that the OFT is considering revoking the grant of immunity. The Applicant will be given a reasonable opportunity to explain the alleged non-compliance and, if the OFT considers it appropriate, to remedy the breach within a reasonable period of time from the giving of such explanation.

6 If the OFT then determines that the conditions set out in this letter have not been fully complied with, or that the Applicant knowingly or recklessly provided Information that is false or misleading in a material particular to the OFT, the OFT may revoke the grant of immunity from prosecution. On revocation, the grant of immunity will cease to exist as if it had never been granted and any Information provided by the Applicant may be used against him/her in criminal proceedings.

7 Irrespective of whether, the OFT has revoked the grant of immunity, all Information provided to the OFT by the Applicant shall remain in the possession of the OFT.

8 This letter sets out all of the terms and conditions on which the OFT grants immunity from prosecution to the Applicant for the Reported Offence. It supersedes all prior understandings, if any, whether oral or written, relating to the Reported Offence.

9 The signatories below acknowledge acceptance of the terms and conditions set out above which shall only take effect when both parties have signed this letter in duplicate, one original to be retained by each party.

Signed: Date:
Name:
Position: Director of Cartel Investigations.
For and on behalf of the Office of Fair Trading
Signed: Date:
Name:

April 2003

Appendix Five

The Overseas Disclosure of Information
A Consultation Paper

April 2003

ENTERPRISE ACT

Public consultation on guidance on Part 9 of the Act—overseas disclosure of information

1 INTRODUCTION

About this document

1.1 The Enterprise Act 2002 ('the Act') repeals existing controls on information disclosure in competition and consumer protection legislation such as those in the Fair Trading Act 1973, the Consumer Credit Act 1974, and the Competition Act 1998[1]. It introduces a new, unified system for controlling the disclosure of such information by public authorities in the UK and thus applies to all of the Office of Fair Trading's functions.

1.2 This consultation draft provides guidance on how the Office of Fair Trading ('the OFT') proposes to interpret the new provisions relating to disclosure of information to overseas public authorities. It sets out the approach which the OFT will take in deciding whether to disclose such information to an overseas public authority (an 'OPA'). In particular, it explains how the OFT will have regard to the considerations contained in s.243(6) of the Act.

1.3 It also summarises where relevant the powers and restrictions contained in Part 9 of the Act, which apply to the disclosure of information within the United Kingdom. A flowchart at annexe A provides a guide to the working of Part 9 generally.[2]

[1] See s247 of the Act which is reproduced in annexe B.

[2] Note that this flowchart is only intended to be a guide to the provisions. For the definitive provisions on when disclosure of specified information is permissible, it is necessary to refer to Part 9 of the Act itself, which is reproduced at annexe B for convenience (correct at time of printing). Some other relevant parts of the Act (including Schedules 14 and 15) are not reproduced here, but can be found on the HMSO website: http://www.hmso.gov.uk/acts/acts2002.htm.

Why do these provisions exist?

1.4 The OFT's responsibilities for enforcement actions lie, in the main, within the UK. However, where UK consumers are adversely affected, the OFT also has the authority to act in other jurisdictions in respect of certain consumer protection law. Similarly, comparable authorities to the OFT from other countries within the European Economic Area can act before UK courts under certain parts of the Enterprise Act to protect **their** consumers.

1.5 Further, cross-border trade is becoming an ever more significant part of the modern world. For these reasons, cooperation between enforcement agencies is increasingly necessary: for example to protect consumers from unfair trading practices operated overseas, and to combat cartels which cross international boundaries.

1.6 Such cooperation also has the merit of preventing multiple enforcement actions in respect of the same perceived problem.

1.7 Accordingly the OFT has powers to share information with other overseas public authorities and it also receives information from overseas which assists it with its enforcement work in the UK.

1.8 In disclosing to OPAs, however, the OFT must ensure that confidentiality of commercial and personal information is preserved, and that the scope of the disclosure of information (where permitted) is no wider than is necessary for effective enforcement action. The sections below explain the legal constraints on disclosure and how the OFT would decide in practice when and whether to disclose information.

2 RESTRICTIONS ON DISCLOSURE

General restriction on disclosure

2.1 Part 9 of the Act contains provisions regulating the disclosure of information by a public authority. The general restriction is that 'specified information' which relates to the affairs of an individual or any business of an undertaking must not be disclosed during the lifetime of that individual or undertaking.[3]

2.2 'Specified information' is defined in s.238 of the Act. As applied to the OFT, 'specified information' broadly means any information obtained under its statutory powers, including information received before the passing of the Enterprise Act.

2.3 This restriction on disclosure is enforced by means of criminal penalties. A person may commit one of various offences punishable by imprisonment and/or a fine if he or she discloses or uses information contrary to the provisions of Part 9.[4]

[3] Section 237.
[4] Section 245.

Other restrictions on disclosure

2.4 Nothing in Part 9 of the Act permits disclosure if such disclosure would be contrary to the provisions of the Data Protection Act 1998 ('the DPA').[5]

2.5 The OFT retains a discretion not to disclose information to an OPA even if, having had regard to the considerations listed in s.243(6) and s.244, these considerations would otherwise allow the information to be disclosed.

2.6 There are other constraints on disclosure which are contained in the disclosure gateways themselves. An important example of this is that information obtained under merger or market investigation powers may not be disclosed using the overseas information gateway (see paragraph 3.4 below).

3 POWERS TO DISCLOSE TO AN OVERSEAS PUBLIC AUTHORITY

Overseas disclosure under s.243(1)

3.1 Section 243 provides a gateway to disclose information to overseas public authorities under certain circumstances, despite the general prohibition under s.237.

3.2 A public authority may disclose information to an OPA for the purpose set out in subsection (2) of s.243, that is, facilitating the exercise by the OPA of any function which it has relating to:

—carrying out investigations in connection with the enforcement of any relevant legislation[6] by means of civil proceedings
—bringing civil proceedings for the enforcement of such legislation or the conduct of such proceedings
—the investigation of crime
—bringing criminal proceedings or the conduct of such proceedings
—deciding whether to start or bring to an end such investigations or proceedings.

3.3 Before the OFT discloses any information under this section, it must appear to it that the overseas authority exercises functions of a public nature in relation to any of the matters listed in 3.2 above.[7]

3.4 Section 243 does not grant a power to disclose information if that information falls into any of the categories set out in s.243(3). This includes, but is not limited to, information obtained as part of a merger investigation under Part 3 or in connection with a market investigation reference under Part 4.

6 'Relevant legislation' is defined by section 243(12) of the Act and may include overseas legislation, which appears to the discloser to make provision corresponding to the Enterprise Act or to the other enactments or subordinate legislation described in that section.

[5] Section 237(4). Guidance on the application of the DPA is beyond the scope of this document. Further advice on the DPA can be found on the website of the Information Commissioner at www.dataprotection.gov.uk. A list of which UK authorities (including the OFT) are registered as data controllers can be found on the Data Protection Register website at www.dpr.gov.uk.

[6] No footnote in the original.

[7] Section 243(11).

3.5 A disclosure that is otherwise permitted under section 243 may be prohibited by directions made by the Secretary of State.[8] The Secretary of State may make directions if he thinks that, in connection with any matter in respect of which the disclosure could be made, it is more appropriate that an investigation or proceedings be conducted in the UK or in a third country.[9]

3.6 Before disclosing information under s.243, the OFT must have regard to the considerations in **both** s.243(6) and s.244: see sections 4 and 5 below.

Other powers to disclosure information

3.7 There are some circumstances where s.237 does not apply. In such cases, overseas disclosures can be made without relying on the gateway in s.243. These include:

—disclosure of information legitimately in the public domain: s.237(3)
—disclosure required for the purpose of a Community obligation: s.240
—disclosure made with the consents specified in s.239
—disclosure under powers or duties which exist apart from Part 9 of the Act.[10]

3.8 Additionally, in some instances disclosure to an OPA may be justifiable under the gateways in sections 241 and 242 of the Act which relate to UK law matters. In particular, an OPA may be a Community enforcer to which disclosure may be made under s.241(3) to enable it to exercise a power under Part 8 of the Act in the UK.

3.9 Where a gateway for disclosure of 'specified information' exists other than contained in s.243(1) it will **not** be necessary to have regard to the considerations in s.243(6) described below but it **will** be necessary to have regard to the considerations contained in s.244.

4 OVERSEAS DISCLOSURE

Overseas disclosure considerations under s.243

4.1 In order to disclose under s.243(1), a public authority must have regard to the considerations listed at s.243(6) ('the s.243(6) considerations'):

—whether the matter in respect of which the disclosure is sought is sufficiently serious to justify making the disclosure

[8] Section 243(4).

[9] If the OFT considers that a request for information otherwise merits disclosure but raises issues of extra-territoriality under s.243(4), it will pass the request to the Secretary of State for a final decision with reference to the extra-territorial issues raised.

[10] S.237(6). On 16 December 2002, the Council of the European Union adopted Regulation 1/2003 on the implementation of the rules on competition laid down in Articles 81 and 82 of the Treaty ('modernisation'): Official Journal L 1, 04.01.2003, pages 1–25. This regulation will apply from 1 May 2004. Article 12 of the regulation grants the Commission and designated national competition authorities the power to exchange information to apply articles 81 and 82 (and national law in parallel where it does not lead to a different outcome). Such a power would exist 'apart from Part 9 of the Act', and in such cases therefore it would not be necessary to rely on the s.243 gateway.

—whether the law of the country or territory to whose authority the disclosure would be made provides appropriate protection against self-incrimination in criminal proceedings

—whether the law of that country or territory provides appropriate protection in relation to the storage and disclosure of personal data

—whether there are arrangements in place for the provision of mutual assistance as between the United Kingdom and that country or territory in relation to the disclosure of information of the kind to which section 237 applies.

4.2 The Secretary of State may by order modify, add to or delete from the above list of matters to be taken into consideration.[11]

Consideration (a): Matters which are 'sufficiently serious' proceedings and investigations

4.3 The OFT takes the view that the disclosure of information for the purpose of bringing civil and criminal proceedings on matters relating to competition law and consumer protection will generally be 'sufficiently serious' for the purposes of the Act. Other criminal proceedings covered by bi-lateral or multi-lateral mutual assistance agreements to which the UK is party will also normally be 'sufficiently serious' (see paragraphs 4.22 to 4.25).

4.4 Similarly, the OFT takes the view that the disclosure of information for the purposes of investigations which may lead to the sorts of proceedings described above will generally be 'sufficiently serious' for the purposes of the Act.

4.5 The OFT would not disclose information to the extent that it considered the request constituted a 'fishing expedition' and/or where the OPA sought disproportionate information relative to the detriment under consideration. Where either the OFT or the OPA had a reasonable belief that civil or criminal proceedings might legitimately result from an investigation assisted by the disclosure of the information, the OFT would consider such a request 'sufficiently serious' for the purposes of the Act.

Considerations (b) and (c): Appropriate protection

4.6 Section 243(7) of the Act states that protections are 'appropriate' if the relevant protection corresponds to that provided in any part of the United Kingdom ('the UK'). Clearly, therefore, protections which are directly analogous to those afforded in the UK will satisfy this consideration.

4.7 The OFT also takes the view that a protection is 'appropriate' if, considered in the round, it provides an equivalent level of protection to that provided in any part of the United Kingdom, even if it is not directly analogous to the rules in the UK. Further guidance on this point is set out below.

[11] Section 243(8).

Protection against self-incrimination

4.8 In respect of the protection against self-incrimination in criminal proceedings, the OFT considers the protection afforded by the European Convention for the Protection of Human Rights and Fundamental Freedoms ('ECHR') is appropriate for the purposes of the Act, in particular taking account of the Article 6 right to a fair trial and the associated case law. Accordingly, the law of any signatory of the ECHR would be considered to meet the consideration under s.243(6)(b).

4.9 The European Commission is bound by a protection against self-incrimination directly equivalent to that contained in ECHR case law, and would also be considered to meet the consideration under s.243(6)(b).[12]

4.10 Other OPAs will be assessed on a case-by-case basis. An example is given below at paragraphs 4.17 onwards.

Protection of personal data

4.11 In respect of data protection, the OFT considers the protection afforded by Directive 95/46 on the Protection of Individuals with regard to the Processing of Personal Data ('the Data Protection Directive') is appropriate for the purposes of s.243(6)(c) of the Act. The Data Protection Directive has been implemented in the UK through the Data Protection Act 1998.

4.12 The law of those countries in the European Economic Area ('the EEA') including the UK which have implemented the provisions of the Data Protection Directive would accordingly be considered to give appropriate protection under s.243(6)(c).

4.13 The European Commission affords protection in relation to the storage and disclosure of personal data equivalent to that contained in the Data Protection Directive;[13] moreover officials are also bound by Treaty obligations not to disclose 'information of the kind covered by the obligation of professional secrecy'.[14] Accordingly the European Commission is also considered to give appropriate protection under s.243(6)(c).[15]

4.14 The OFT also takes the view that protection would be appropriate in relation to the storage and disclosure of personal data where legislation in the recipient country or territory reflects in a broad way the objectives set out in the DPA.[16]

[12] The European Commission is not, however, an enforcement body for consumer protection matters.

[13] Regulation (EC) No 45/2001 of the European Parliament and of the Council of 18 December 2000 on the protection of individuals with regard to the processing of personal data by the Community institutions and bodies and on the free movement of such data, Official Journal L008, 12/01/2001: http://europa.eu.int/comm/internal_market/en/dataprot/news/286en.pdf.

[14] Treaty Establishing The European Community, Article 287 (ex Article 214)

[15] Note that, in many cases, disclosure of information to the European Commission would be pursuant to a 'Community obligation' and in such cases, the s.243(6) considerations would not apply: s.240 of the Act. See also footnote 10 above.

[16] The OFT would have regard, for example, to the eight 'principles of data protection' contained in Schedule 1, Part 1 of the DPA. An explanation of these principles can be found on the website of the Information Commissioner at http://www.dataprotection.gov.uk/principl.htm.

4.15 The OFT will also take account of any decision of the European Commission as to the adequacy of the protection of personal data in a third country insofar as it may apply to an OPA.[17]

4.16 In cases where the OFT has doubts about the protection relating to the storage and disclosure of personal data, but the protection was not clearly inadequate and the other considerations in subsections (a) to (c) of s.243(6) above were otherwise met, it may also take into account the previous record of the OPA in dealing with information disclosed to it—see paragraphs 5.12 onwards below.

Protections which are not directly equivalent to those in the UK

4.17 An example of a country which has appropriate protections but which is neither a signatory to the ECHR nor bound by the Data Protection Directive is the United States of America ('the USA').

4.18 The USA affords a privilege against self-incrimination to individuals in criminal proceedings, through the Fifth Amendment to its constitution.[18] The OFT accordingly considers that the level of protection afforded by the USA in relation to self-incrimination is 'appropriate' for the purposes of s.243(6)(b).

4.19 The USA affords a number of statutory protections against the further disclosure of information provided by overseas authorities to the Department of Justice and the Federal Trade Commission for the purposes of consumer or competition enforcement.[19] Accordingly, the OFT considers that the level of protection required by s.243(6)(c) would be met in relation to disclosure covered by such statutes.

Consideration (d): Mutual assistance arrangements

4.20 Having had regard to the considerations set out in subsections (a) to (c) of s.243(6), the OFT may reach the conclusion that the controls against the misuse of disclosed information are clearly satisfactory. In such cases, the OFT considers that the absence of formal mutual assistance arrangements will not generally prevent disclosure. This will particularly be the case where the OFT has taken the past record of the OPA into account (see paragraphs 5.12 onwards).

4.21 Conversely, where there is doubt as to whether a consideration is met under any of subsections (a) to (c), the OFT will particularly take into account the existence of arrangements formally made for the provision of mutual assistance.

4.22 The OFT takes the view that where the UK has entered into bilateral or multilateral arrangements for the provision of mutual assistance in relation to the disclosure of a particular kind of information, and in the absence of evidence to the contrary, this will indicate evidence that:

[17] See http://europa.eu.int/comm/internal_market/en/dataprot/adequacy/index.htm.

[18] 'No person . . . shall be compelled in any criminal case to be a witness against himself . . .': see also Miranda v. Arizona, 384 U.S. 436 (1966). Under certain circumstances witnesses can be granted immunity from criminal prosecution, in which case the Fifth Amendment would not apply.

[19] See, for example, the list of legislation in Annexe A of the Agreement Between The Government Of The United States Of America And The Government Of Australia On Mutual Antitrust Enforcement Assistance: http://www.usdoj.gov/atr/public/international/docs/annexea.htm.

—the matters covered by the arrangements will generally speaking be sufficiently serious to justify making an overseas disclosure
—the laws of the country or territory provide appropriate protection against self-incrimination in criminal proceedings
—the laws of the country or territory provide appropriate protection in relation to the storage and disclosure of personal data with respect to the matters covered by the arrangements.[20]

4.23 This will particularly be the case where the arrangements make reference to the subject of the s.243(6) considerations (e.g. if the arrangements relate to the disclosure of information for the purposes of criminal proceedings, or if additional safeguards or assurances are included in relation to the treatment of personal data).

4.24 In the UK, requests for mutual assistance in criminal matters are the responsibility of the Judicial Cooperation Unit (UK Central Authority Mutual Legal Assistance) of the Home Office. Further information is available on its website.[21]

4.25 Examples of arrangements for mutual assistance currently include:[22]

—European Convention on Mutual Legal Assistance in Criminal Matters (1959),[23] and Additional Protocol
—Treaty on Mutual Assistance in Criminal Matters (UK-Canada, 1988)[24]
—Treaty Between the Government of the United Kingdom of Great Britain and Northern Ireland and the Government of the United States of America on Mutual Legal Assistance in Criminal Matters (1994)[25]
—Agreement between the Government of the United Kingdom of Great Britain and Northern Ireland and the Government of the Hong Kong Special Administrative Region of the People's Republic of China concerning Mutual Legal Assistance in Criminal Matters (1998)[26]
—Memorandum Of Understanding On Mutual Enforcement Assistance In Consumer Protection Matters Between The Federal Trade Commission Of The United States of America And Her Majesty's Secretary of State for Trade And Industry And The Director General Of Fair Trading In The United Kingdom (2000).[27]

4.26 The UK is currently in negotiation with Australia, Canada and New Zealand, with a view to signing memoranda of mutual assistance in respect of competition and consumer protection enforcement.

4.27 As mentioned above, the OFT retains a discretion whether to disclose notwithstanding that the s.243(6) criteria are met. The existence of an agreement relating to mutual assistance in **criminal** matters, for example, would not necessarily mean that OFT took the view that it would be appropriate to disclose information to an OPA for a function it had in relation to relevant **civil** proceedings.

[20] Subsections (a) to (c) of section 243(6).
[21] http://www.homeoffice.gov.uk/atoz/mla.htm.
[22] Dates given are when agreements were signed, not when they came into force. UK domestic law provisions include the Criminal Justice (International Cooperation) Act 1990.
[23] http://conventions.coe.int/treaty/en/Treaties/Html/030.htm.
[24] This was extended to all criminal matters in 1992.
[25] This was extended to cover competition law matters in 2001: see Cm 5375 http://www.hmso.gov.uk/ip/command-papers-numerical.htm.
[26] http://www.justice.gov.hk/table3_e.htm.
[27] http://www.ftc.gov/opa/2000/10/ukimsn.htm.

Applying proportionality

4.28 The OFT considers that the examples provided above demonstrate how it will have regard to the s.243(6) considerations in the majority of cases. However in some circumstances the OFT may balance the considerations differently, having regard to the particular circumstances of the disclosure in question.

4.29 For example, in cases where the purpose of the disclosure is overseas criminal enforcement or the information to be disclosed is particularly sensitive, then the considerations in subsections (b) and (c) respectively of section 243(6) will carry proportionately more weight.

5 OTHER CONSIDERATIONS

Further considerations under s.244

The extent of disclosure

5.1 Section 244 of the Act applies to any disclosure of 'specified information' by a public authority. It requires that the OFT have regard to three considerations, namely:

—the need to exclude from disclosure (so far as practicable) any information whose disclosure the authority thinks is contrary to the public interest
—the need to exclude from disclosure (so far as practicable):
—commercial information whose disclosure the authority thinks might significantly harm the legitimate business interests of the undertaking to which it relates, or
—information relating to the private affairs of an individual whose disclosure the authority thinks might significantly harm the individual's interest.
—the extent to which the disclosure of the information mentioned in the bullet points above is necessary for the purpose for which the authority is permitted to make the disclosure.

5.2 Section 244 of the Act is broadly equivalent to the provisions previously contained in s.56 of the Competition Act 1998 ('the Competition Act'), except that it now applies to a wider class of information than before.

5.3 The OFT expects that in having regard to the considerations under s.244, it will do so in the same way as it has previously had regard to the considerations in s.56 of the Competition Act.[28] This may involve in appropriate cases either the redaction of potentially harmful commercial or personal information[29] or the withholding of certain documents altogether.

[28] Sections 55 and 56 of the Competition Act 1998 are repealed by Schedule 26 of the Enterprise Act 2002.

[29] Collectively referred to as 'confidential information' in the *Competition Act 1998 (Director's Rules) Order 2000* SI 2000/293.

Statements obtained under the Competition Act 1998

5.4 S.30A of the Competition Act 1998 (inserted by s.198 Enterprise Act 2002) provides that a statement made by a person in response to a requirement imposed under sections 26 to 28 of the Competition Act 1998 may not be used in evidence against him on a prosecution for the cartel offence[30] unless the following two conditions are met in the proceedings:

—in giving evidence, he makes a statement inconsistent with it, and
—evidence relating to it is adduced, or a question relating to it is asked, by him or on his behalf.

5.5 The OFT would follow this same rule with respect to overseas disclosure for the prosecution of cartel offences. Such information would not be disclosed if the proposed use of the information covered circumstances wider than the two conditions above. Where the OFT is satisfied that the OPA would not use the evidence against that person except in the circumstances above, it would disclose the information.

Leniency applications

5.6 Due to the secret nature of cartels and their especially damaging effects on consumers and the economy, the OFT has the power to grant leniency to individual applicants in respect of the cartel offence[31] and/or undertakings[32] who come forward to cooperate in proving the existence of cartel agreements. Accordingly, in considering whether to disclose information to OPAs, the OFT will take into consideration the need to protect the providers of such information.

Leniency applications by individuals

5.7 Where an individual has voluntarily provided information as part of a leniency application (whether or not he or she in fact benefitted from the granting of a noaction letter), the OFT would not disclose this information to an OPA for the purpose of a criminal cartel prosecution, unless he or she were to be granted immunity from such a prosecution.

Leniency applications by companies

5.8 Where a company has provided information as part of a leniency application (whether or not it has been granted such leniency), the OFT would not disclose this information to an OPA for the purpose of overseas cartel enforcement against that company, unless the company benefits from a similar leniency arrangement with the overseas authority.

[30] Section 188 Enterprise Act.
[31] [See the Enterprise Act guidance *The Cartel Offence: No-action Letters for Individuals,* OFT503].
[32] See *Competition Act 1998—leniency* on the OFT website at http://www.oft.gov.uk/business/legal+powers/ca98+leniency.htm.

5.9 However, the OFT might disclose information to an OPA for the purposes of overseas enforcement against a company or individual **other** than the provider of the information, subject to the terms of the leniency arrangement agreed between the provider and the OFT.

EC Modernisation

5.10 Further protection for individuals is contained in Council Regulation (EC) 1/2003. Where OFT uses its powers[33] under that Regulation to disclose information to a competition authority in another Member State, this information can only be used in the recipient state as evidence to impose sanctions on individuals (as distinct from companies) where:

—the law of the transmitting authority foresees sanctions of a similar kind in relation to an infringement of Article 81 or Article 82 of the Treaty or, in the absence of such sanctions

—the information has been collected in a way which respects the same level of protection of the rights of defence of natural persons as provided for under the national rules of the receiving authority. However, in this case, the information exchanged cannot be used by the receiving authority to impose custodial sanctions.[34]

Past record of the overseas public authority

5.11 The OFT may also take into account additional considerations although the Act does not require it to do so. One such consideration is the past record of the OPA.

Compliance with disclosure conditions

5.12 Where a country has not made bilateral or multilateral arrangements as described in s.243(6)(d), the OFT will, where relevant, take into account whether the OPA has in relation to previous requests:

—disclosed the purpose for which it requested the information

—not used the information for any other purpose contrary to s.243(10)(b)

—not further disclosed the information contrary to s.243(10)(a), or alternatively has complied with any conditions to oppose, within its domestic law, any further disclosure of the information without the consent of the OFT.

5.13 If applicable, the OFT may where relevant take into account the past record of the OPA in respect of disclosures it has received from other authorities which impose similar controls, such as other UK or EU bodies (e.g. concurrent regulators, the European Commission). This may be especially useful, for example, in cases where

[33] See footnote 10.

[34] Article 12 of Regulation EC 1/2003.

the OFT has not previously disclosed information to the OPA but another organisation has done so.

5.14 The OFT would also take into account the considerations in paragraph 5.12 above if it was in some doubt about the adequacy of protections for the storage and disclosure of personal data[35] but where the considerations in s243(6) were otherwise met.

5.15 In any event, in circumstances where an OPA has failed to comply with all of the additional conditions in paragraph 5.12 above, the OFT would be unlikely to disclose information again to that authority. This would be a powerful sanction to ensure compliance, especially in circumstances where no formal assistance arrangements are currently in place.

Reciprocity

5.16 Another consideration which may be relevant might be if the OPA were to have the power to disclose information to the OFT, but had on previous occasions declined to do so in response to a request.

5.17 The OFT considers this would be unlikely to occur in practice, having regard to the OPAs to which it might expect to disclose information. However, in such a hypothetical situation, the OFT might take into account such failures to 'reciprocate' in deciding whether to make further disclosures to an OPA.[36]

[35] See s243(6)c.

[36] See paragraph 2.5 above.

Appendix Six

Memorandum of Understanding Between the Office of Fair Trading and the Director of the Serious Fraud Office

October 2003 OFT 547

Introduction

1 This MOU records the basis on which the OFT and SFO (the Parties) will cooperate to investigate and/or prosecute individuals in respect of the cartel offence established by the Enterprise Act 2002 (EA02) where serious or complex fraud is suspected.

2 The Parties recognise that this MOU may require amendment in the light of future experience.

Initial enquiries and references to the SFO

3 Where the OFT receives information, through use of Competition Act 1998 (CA98) powers or otherwise, that criminal cartel activity may have occurred, Cartel Investigations Branch (CIB) of OFT will undertake any necessary initial criminal enquiries. Therefore, if the SFO receive information suggestive of criminal cartel activity, prior to any related referral from the OFT, the SFO will, in the first instance, refer that information to CIB.

4 If, after any necessary initial enquiries (and informal discussions with the SFO), the OFT identify a criminal cartel case as being likely to fall within the SFO acceptance criteria, the case will be referred to the Director of the SFO (the Director). The referral will provide such background information as is necessary to enable the Director to make an informed decision as to whether or not the matter should be accepted for investigation or, alternatively, whether the OFT should undertake further enquiries. The Director will endeavour to make such a decision within 28 days of referral unless the complexity of the case requires a longer period.

5 If the Director considers that the OFT should make further enquiries, the Parties will discuss and agree the nature and scope of such enquiries (which are likely to be conducted by CIB under EA02 powers.) Once the further enquiries have been completed, the Director will reconsider his decision in the light of any additional evidence so obtained.

The criminal case team

6 If the SFO accept an OFT referral, a criminal case team will be formed comprising of both SFO and OFT staff working under the leadership and direction of an SFO case controller. Where appropriate, one or more officers from a relevant police force will also work on the criminal case team. A first case conference will be convened as soon as reasonably practicable to discuss preliminary matters.

7 Throughout the case, the presumption will operate that OFT team members and their management will have access to all case-related documentation including records of decisions, advices and submission papers.

Use of powers during a criminal investigation

8 The presumption will operate that once the SFO has accepted a criminal cartel investigation, powers under the Criminal Justice Act 1987 will be used rather than those under the EA02 where the two sets of powers would achieve essentially the same objective. However, depending upon the precise circumstances of the case, a criminal case team may determine that EA02 powers could and should be used to pursue particular objectives.

Costs of the investigation

9 The SFO case controller will set a budget for the case. The SFO will be responsible for all of the costs of the investigation, save that all OFT staff costs on the case, including all case-related travel and subsistence, will be borne by the OFT.

Dispute resolution within the criminal case team

10 The Parties accept that it will be the responsibility of the case controller to direct the investigation and that he or she should ordinarily have the final say on any issues of dispute between SFO and OFT criminal case team members. However, the Parties recognise that it may, on occasion, be necessary for issues in dispute to be resolved at a more senior level.

CA98 investigations and EC cases

11 In certain cases, CIB will progress an investigation using CA98 powers (which may or may not have commenced prior to any SFO referral), while an SFO-led case team will progress a related criminal investigation. Suitable procedures will be adopted to ensure that the two investigation teams maintain an ongoing dialogue. Both case teams will thereby seek to ensure that the CA98 investigation does not prejudice the parallel criminal investigation. Where there are issues in dispute between the two case teams which they cannot resolve, the Parties will attempt to resolve matters at a more senior level.

12 Where the OFT becomes aware of an investigation by the EC competition authority (DG Comp) which might involve a potential cartel offence in the United Kingdom involving serious or complex fraud, it will draw the investigation to the attention of the SFO and, if the SFO accept such a case for investigation, the OFT will seek to co-ordinate the progress of both investigations.

Leniency and no-action letters

13 Decisions about whether to grant leniency or issue no-action letters rest with the OFT. However, if any such decision could have an impact on the outcome of an existing SFO-led cartel investigation or prosecution, the OFT will consult the SFO.

Decisions to cease investigation and whether to prosecute

14 Decisions about whether to cease an SFO-led criminal cartel investigation, or whether to charge or prosecute in such a case, rest with the SFO. However, in all cases, the SFO will consult the OFT.

[Background note excluded]

Printed in the United Kingdom
by Lightning Source UK Ltd.
103377UKS00001B/79-87